Outdoors with **Kids**

Philadelphia

100 FUN PLACES TO EXPLORE IN AND AROUND THE CITY

SUSAN CHARKES

Appalachian Mountain Club Books
Boston, Massachusetts

AMC is a nonprofit organization, and sales of AMC Books fund our mission of protecting the Northeast outdoors. If you appreciate our efforts and would like to become a member or make a donation to AMC, visit outdoors.org, call 800-372-1758, or contact us at Appalachian Mountain Club, 5 Joy Street, Boston, MA 02108.

outdoors.org/publications/books

Library of Congress Cataloging-in-Publication Data
Charkes, Susan.
  Outdoors with Kids Philadelphia : 100 fun places to explore in and around the city / Susan Charkes.
    p. cm.
  Includes index.
  ISBN 978-1-934028-74-2 (alk. paper)
  1. Outdoor recreation--Pennsylvania--Philadelphia Metropolitan Area--Guidebooks. 2. Family recreation--Pennsylvania--Philadelphia Metropolitan Area--Guidebooks. 3. Philadelphia Metropolitan Area (Pa.)--Guidebooks. I. Title.
  GV191.42.P4C543 2013
  796.509748'11--dc23
                    2012039259

The paper used in this publication meets the minimum requirements of the American National Standard for Information Sciences-Permanence of Paper for Printed Library Materials, ANSI Z39.48-1984. ∞

Outdoor recreation activities by their very nature are potentially hazardous. This book is not a substitute for good personal judgment and training in outdoor skills. Due to changes in conditions, use of the information in this book is at the sole risk of the user. The author and the Appalachian Mountain Club assume no liability for accidents happening to, or injuries sustained by, readers who engage in the activities described in this book.

Interior pages contain 30% post-consumer recycled fiber.
Cover contains 10% post-consumer recycled fiber.
Printed in the United States of America,
using vegetable-based inks.

MIX
Paper from
responsible sources
FSC
www.fsc.org
FSC® C005010

10 9 8 7 6 5 4 3 2 1   13 14 15 16 17 18

To my brother and sister.
Together we were *SusEvAl*, and so was our family sailboat.

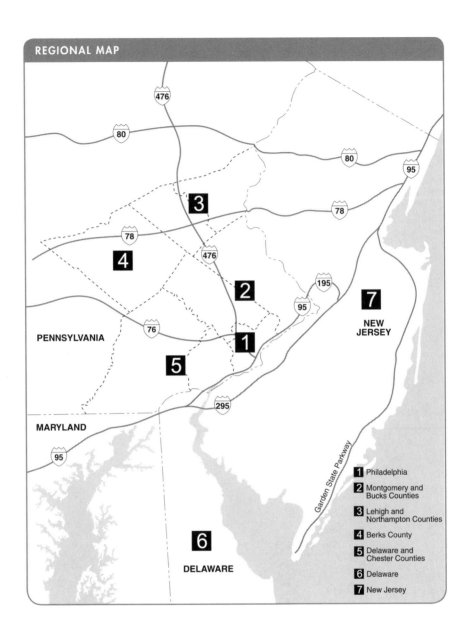

CONTENTS

ESSAYS AND ACTIVITIES

APPENDICES

THE "10 BEST" LISTS

● ●

10 Best for Toddlers

10 Best for Paddling

10 Best for Biking

10 Best for Historical Sites

AT-A-GLANCE TRIP PLANNER

# Trip	Page	Best for Ages	Fee	Public Transit	Dog Friendly	Stroller Friendly
PHILADELPHIA						
1. Bartram's Garden	2	All	$	🚌	🐕	🛺
2. Awbury Arboretum	5	All		🚌	🐕	🛺
3. Cobbs Creek Park	7	All		🚌	🐕	🛺
4. John Heinz National Wildlife Refuge	9	All		🚌	🐕	🛺
5. West Fairmount Park	11	All	$	🚌	🐕	🛺
6. Morris Arboretum	14	All	$	🚌	🐕	🛺
7. Smith Memorial Playground & Playhouse	18	5–8		🚌		
8. Schuylkill Banks & East Fairmount Park	20	All		🚌	🐕	🛺
9. Schuylkill Center for Environmental Education	23	All		🚌		🛺
10. Wissahickon Valley Park	25	All		🚌	🐕	🛺
11. Pennypack Park	28	All		🚌	🐕	🛺
12. FDR Park	30	All		🚌	🐕	🛺
MONTGOMERY AND BUCKS COUNTIES						
13. Lorimer Park	34	9–12			🐕	
14. Green Ribbon Trail	36	All		🚌		🛺
15. Fort Washington State Park	39	All			🐕	🛺
16. Riverbend Environmental Education Center	41	5–8			🐕	
17. Green Lane Park	43	All	$		🐕	🛺
18. Pennypack Preserve	46	9–12			🐕	
19. Curtis Arboretum	48	0–4		🚌	🐕	🛺
20. Briar Bush Nature Center	50	5–8	$	🚌		🛺
21. Schuylkill Canal Park/Lock 60	52	9–12			🐕	🛺
22. Norristown Farm Park	54	All			🐕	🛺
23. Evansburg State Park	56	All			🐕	🛺
24. John James Audubon Center at Mill Grove	58	All	$			

Hike Walk	Bike	Swim Paddle	Play-ground	Camp	Trip Highlights
✓	✓				Interactive activities to learn about nature
✓					Secret Garden and community apiary
✓	✓		✓		Naturalist-led walks through park
✓	✓	✓			A variety of birds to watch for
✓	✓	✓	✓		Butterfly, hummingbird, and sensory gardens
✓			✓		Tree-top-level experience
			✓		1905 Giant Wooden Slide
✓	✓	✓	✓		Fishing locations along bridge and banks
✓					Year-round art and sculpture exhibits
✓	✓				Restored historical village in park's south end
✓	✓		✓		Educational programs at environmental center
✓	✓		✓		Excellent mountain biking
✓	✓		✓		Beautiful cliffside views in picnic area
✓	✓		✓		Stone bridges and ruins along the trail
✓	✓		✓		Great sledding, snowshoeing, and skiing
✓					Visitor center exhibiting live toads, turtles
✓	✓	✓	✓	✓	Challenging trails around reservoir's perimeter
✓	✓				Observation deck by the pond
✓					Leash-free dog park, open lawns
✓			✓		Play area inspired by natural structures
✓		✓	✓		Fishing dock along canal
✓	✓		✓		Good biking route for younger kids
✓			✓		Equestrian-friendly trails
✓	✓				Woods and fields that inspired Audubon's art

#	Trip	Page	Best for Ages	Fee	Public Transit	Dog Friendly	Stroller Friendly
25.	Rolling Hill Park	61	5–8			🐾	
26.	Perkiomen Trail	63	All			🐾	🚼
27.	Valley Forge National Historical Park	65	All			🐾	🚼
28.	Silver Lake Nature Center	67	5–8				🚼
29.	Churchville Nature Center	69	5–8				🚼
30.	Peace Valley Park	71	All	$			🚼
31.	Delaware Canal State Park	73	All			🐾	🚼
32.	Bowman's Hill Wildflower Preserve	75	5–8	$			🚼
33.	Core Creek Park	77	All	$		🐾	
34.	Five Mile Woods Nature Preserve	79	All				
35.	Tyler State Park	81	All			🐾	🚼
36.	Delaware River	83	9–12	$			
37.	Tohickon Valley Park/Ralph Stover State Park (High Rocks)	85	5–8	$		🐾	🚼
38.	Nockamixon State Park	88	All	$		🐾	🚼
39.	Honey Hollow Environmental Education Center	91	All				
40.	Ringing Rocks Park	93	9–12				
41.	Giving Pond Recreation Area	95	All			🐾	

LEHIGH AND NORTHAMPTON COUNTIES

#	Trip	Page	Best for Ages	Fee	Public Transit	Dog Friendly	Stroller Friendly
42.	Mariton Wildlife Sanctuary	98	5–8			🐾	
43.	Lehigh Parkway	100	All	$		🐾	🚼
44.	Pool Wildlife Sanctuary	102	5–8			🐾	
45.	Trexler Nature Preserve	104	All			🐾	
46.	Sand Island Park	107	All			🐾	🚼
47.	Saucon Rail Trail and Lost River Caverns	109	5–8	$		🐾	🚼
48.	Jacobsburg Environmental Education Center	111	All			🐾	🚼

BERKS COUNTY

#	Trip	Page	Best for Ages	Fee	Public Transit	Dog Friendly	Stroller Friendly
49.	Hawk Mountain Sanctuary	114	9–12	$			🚼
50.	Daniel Boone Homestead	117	All	$		🐾	🚼
51.	Blue Marsh Lake	119	All	$		🐾	🚼

Hike/Walk	Bike	Swim/Paddle	Playground	Camp	Trip Highlights
✓			✓		Lovely wildflower/butterfly garden
✓	✓				Varied rural landscape of woods and farmland
✓	✓	✓			Washington's Headquarters exhibit
✓	✓	✓			Sand "fossil pit" in children's play area
✓					Re-created Lenape village
✓	✓	✓	✓		Beautiful views, boating and fishing
✓	✓	✓			Canal boat ride with costumed interpreters
✓					Gentle trails by the creek
✓		✓	✓		Fishing spots along the shore
✓					Mix of flat and rocky geography
✓	✓	✓	✓		Plenty of access to broad, flat creek banks
		✓			Thick forests and quaint towns along banks
✓		✓	✓	✓	Wooded trails along the creek
✓	✓	✓			Waterslides at the swimming pool
✓					Numerous frogs, birds, butterflies, and more
✓					Musical rock, highest waterfall in county
✓		✓			Picnic area overlooking pond
✓					Rock outcrops, views along trails
✓	✓				Fly fishing in the limestone spring creek
✓					Evening stargazing
✓	✓		✓		Bison- and elk- grazing
✓	✓	✓	✓		Urban park, great biking
✓	✓		✓		Playing fields, basketball courts
✓	✓				Centuries-old oak, pine, and hemlock trees
✓					Maginifcent views of the valley below the trails
✓	✓				Colonial farm buildings, barn, blacksmith shop
✓	✓	✓	✓		Sensory trail, orienteering trail, and nature trails

#	Trip	Page	Best for Ages	Fee	Public Transit	Dog Friendly	Stroller Friendly
52. Nolde Forest Environmental Education Center		121	All			🐕	🚼
53. Union Canal Towpath		123	All				

DELAWARE AND CHESTER COUNTIES

#	Trip	Page	Best for Ages	Fee	Public Transit	Dog Friendly	Stroller Friendly
54. Newlin Grist Mill		126	5–8	$		🐕	
55. Haverford College Arboretum		128	0–4		🚌		🚼
56. Taylor Memorial Arboretum		130	5–8			🐕	
57. Ridley Creek State Park		132	All			🐕	🚼
58. Smedley Park		135	5–8		🚌	🐕	
59. Jenkins Arboretum & Gardens		137	0–4				🚼
60. Scott Arboretum and Crum Woods		139	All		🚌	🐕	🚼
61. Marsh Creek State Park		141	All	$		🐕	
62. Struble Trail and Uwchlan Trail		143	All			🐕	🚼
63. Harmony Hill Nature Area		145	All			🐕	🚼
64. French Creek State Park		147	All	$		🐕	
65. Hopewell Furnace National Historic Site		150	All			🐕	
66. Schuylkill River Trail		153	All		🚌	🐕	🚼
67. Hibernia County Park		155	All			🐕	🚼
68. Warwick County Park		157	5–8			🐕	🚼
69. Green Valleys Association at Welkinweir		159	All				
70. Springton Manor Farm		161	All			🐕	🚼
71. Myrick Conservation Center		163	All				
72. Stroud Preserve		165	All			🐕	

DELAWARE

#	Trip	Page	Best for Ages	Fee	Public Transit	Dog Friendly	Stroller Friendly
73. White Clay Creek State Park		168	All	$			🚼
74. Alapocas Run State Park		170	All	$	🚌	🐕	🚼
75. Bellevue State Park		172	All	$		🐕	🚼
76. Brandywine Creek State Park		174	All	$		🐕	🚼
77. DuPont Environmental Education Center		176	All		🚌	🐕	🚼
78. Lums Pond State Park		178	All	$		🐕	🚼

Hike/Walk	Bike	Swim/Paddle	Playground	Camp	Trip Highlights
Hike					Historical Nolde family stone mansion
Hike	Bike				Skatepark, pleasant biking
Hike			Playground		Traditional forging demonstrations
Hike			Playground		Large duck pond with giant snapping turtle
Hike					Giant, twisty-armed musclewood tree
Hike	Bike		Playground		12 miles of paved and dirt trails through woods
Hike			Playground		Garnet-studded rocks
Hike					Climbable sculptural benches
Hike	Bike				Mysterious standing stones of "Crumhenge"
Hike	Bike	Swim, Paddle	Playground		Playing in Brandywine Creek
Hike	Bike	Swim			Ruins along Uwchlan Trail
Hike	Bike	Paddle			Fishing in the creek
Hike	Bike	Swim, Paddle	Playground	Camp	Self-guiding course to learn orienteering
Hike					Picking heirloom apples in fall
Hike	Bike				Seeing eagles, ospreys, and herons
Hike	Bike	Paddle	Playground	Camp	Cottages and ruins from the iron-making era
Hike	Bike		Playground		Observation deck converted from historical truss bridge
Hike					Stepped waterfall near pond
Hike					Butterfly house
Hike					Wildflower meadows full of summer butterflies
Hike					Secluded spots for angling
Hike	Bike		Playground		Mason-Dixon Historic Monument
Hike	Bike		Playground		Rock-climbing wall
Hike	Bike		Playground		Level paths, large fishing pond
Hike	Bike	Paddle			Guided paddles sponsored by the park
Hike	Bike				Interactive exhibits at visitor center
Hike	Bike	Paddle	Playground	Camp	Abundant birds, amphibians, and other wildlife

Hike / Walk	Bike	Swim / Paddle	Play-ground	Camp	Trip Highlights
Walk					3-acre "Enchanted Woods"
Walk					Annual fall Hawk Watch
Walk		Paddle			Observation Tower's spiral staircase and panoramic view
Walk	Bike		Playground		Boat rentals at the beach
Walk					Beautiful view of the house from garden path
Walk					Children's Garden, Butterfly Garden
Walk	Bike	Paddle	Playground	Camp	Unusual plant life, including carnivorous pitcher plants
Walk					Interactive displays
Walk	Bike	Swim / Paddle		Camp	Standing on boulders overlooking the lake
Walk	Bike	Paddle	Playground		Trailside Zoo and merry-go-round
Walk					Apple orchard, beehive, and herb garden
Walk		Swim / Paddle			Annual horseshoe crab migration in May/June
Walk					Colorful peacocks strutting the grounds
Walk	Bike	Swim / Paddle			Horseback riding on the beach (by permit)
Walk	Bike				Solar-powered Great Waterfall at Vista Lake
Walk	Bike	Paddle			River views along D&R Canal
Walk	Bike	Swim / Paddle	Playground		Blacksmith shop and print shop demonstrations
Walk	Bike	Swim / Paddle	Playground		Themed gardens designed to attract wildlife
Walk	Bike	Swim / Paddle	Playground		Displays of native reptiles and fish
Walk	Bike	Paddle	Playground		New Jersey's largest playground
Walk		Swim / Paddle		Camp	Restored historical village
		Swim / Paddle		Camp	Sandy beaches along the banks

PREFACE

. . . .

I've been writing about nature and the outdoors for many years. Whether I'm hiking, biking, paddling, or just cloud-watching, when I go outdoors I'm a kid again, exploring the world and delighting in adventure: curious about my surroundings, stimulating my senses, exercising my body, testing my limits, and inspiring my imagination.

When I was a kid growing up in suburban Philadelphia, I spent a lot of time outdoors, and much of that time, especially when I was very young, was with adults. My parents took me, along with my younger brother and sister, on regular family outdoor expeditions: hiking and biking (and sledding in winter) in local parks; swimming and sailing on lakes and bays.

It wasn't only family who shaped my interests—it was other caring adults who loved sharing their enjoyment of the outdoors with kids. There was Mr. Baldwin, the Ardmore Junior High School science teacher who led my first predawn birding bus trip to the misty, mysterious tidal salt marshes of New Jersey (to what's now the Edwin Forsythe National Wildlife Refuge). He bequeathed to me a lifelong compulsion to seek out and identify birds, those beautiful, elusive creatures (though I've yet to internalize the urge to wake up before sunrise). Equally important was my Girl Scout troop, whose leaders— ordinary suburban moms (including my mother) during the week—turned into intrepid camping organizers in their evening and weekend off-hours. I was introduced to more extended hiking and backpacking in summer camp, and to long-distance bicycle camping on summerlong group bike trips. Young adult counselors led both of these kinds of outdoor activities—people who were old enough to serve as role models, but young enough that I could see myself becoming them.

My son, Nick, raised for most of his life in the Delaware Valley, was a part of our family outdoor activities from an early age—actually, he experienced hiking even before he was born. As he grew up, I took joy in passing on to him the places familiar to me from my childhood, and in discovering places new to both of us. In one of my favorite photos of Nick as a toddler, he's on the beach at Stone Harbor, red-cheeked with hair askew on a windy, chilly day, smiling broadly as he holds up a nubbly orange starfish he's just found. It's an expression of pure delight in the moment, in the sharp sting of the elements, in the wondrous surprise that the outdoors is always giving to us.

Writing this book gave me a wonderful opportunity to be outdoors with kids—many different kids, some of whom I knew and some of whom I came to know. I was constantly surprised that children had so much fun outdoors in ways that I hadn't imagined. Why? Well, for one, because they took such joy in being surprised by simple things outdoors: the way dandelions explode into flight, the way a rock "turns into" a turtle. Because being outdoors let them run and jump and climb and cartwheel, delighted in the sheer pleasure of physical activity. And because the outdoors stimulated their imagination. A hollow tree is a home for fairies, and bridges are where trolls live; falling leaves are tollbooth tickets; a mountaintop is a throne.

It is my hope that this book will enable many kids to experience the joy of the outdoors and that they will grow to love it, respect it, and care for it so that more children will grow up in a world full of wonder.

ACKNOWLEDGMENTS

This is the second project in which I have enjoyed the genuine pleasure of working with the stellar staff at AMC Books, beginning with former publisher Heather Stephenson, whose grasp of both the creative and organizational aspects of book development continues to astound me. Kimberly Duncan-Mooney was everything an author could want in an editor, providing a grateful writer with thoughtful ideas, steady support, and professional guidance. I also received extremely helpful advice on photography from Athena Lakri. Kristen Sykes, along with her husband, Fred Beddall, shared firsthand knowledge of places well known and obscure throughout the region. Pam Hess, AMC director of education programs, and Kevin Breunig, vice president for communications and marketing, added their expertise. Early in the process, Kristen Laine was instrumental in bringing me to the project and providing creative guidance.

Members of the Appalachian Mountain Club's Delaware Valley Chapter helped in identifying places to go and people to go with: Joan Aichele, Jeff Lippincott, Allen and Bette Male, Morgan Masterson, Vicky Bastidas, and Sue Caskey. Mark Zakutansky and John Brunner of the AMC Mid-Atlantic Conservation Office were always available to tell me everything I needed to know about the Pennsylvania Highlands (see page 45).

Numerous families generously devoted time to helping with the project. Special mention must go to Kristyn, Zane, Annika, and Ridge Lederer, who showed me new ways to experience places I'd been to many times before—but never so fast! Their grandparents Geri Huey and Craig Keemer (Yaiyai and Papou) took it in stride. Many thanks for many fun trips to my sister Alice Charkes and niece Olivia Charkes Howe; to Judy Boshoven, Marcelo Tognelli, and Emilio and Luca Tognelli; Kyle, Emma, Addison, and Caroline Fliszer; Thea, David, Jake, and Luke Howey; Caitlinn Henn and Bridget Werner; Kris, Derek, Mila, and Caleb Huey; Claudia, Paul, Peter, and Lucas Gard; Samantha, Francois, Eliza, and Alex Jouin; MaryEllen, Ron, and Zane Kanarr; Jennifer, Paul, Peyton, and Arianna Kovach; Emma and Brian Lear; Gabriella, Jonathan, Isabel, and Alexander Milley; Cary Schockemoehl, Ed Davis, and Benjamin Davis; Claudia Thormer, Thomas Weber, and Felix and Valentin Thormer; John Leslie and Jonathan Maguire; Allen and Bette Male;

and Cheryl, Cameron, and Caden Wine. I'm grateful to Ann Summer, Nancy Charkes, and AMC's Cathy Frankenberg for putting me in touch with families. Grant Clauser provided advice on family camping. Thanks to Stuart Fineman for logistical and artistical support.

Finally, the book could not have been completed without the extraordinary contributions of Gabriella Milley, who enthusiastically explored the New Jersey outdoors with her own family, as well as with a diverse group of friends from all over the world. Gaby brought to the book not only a tremendous commitment of time, but also an attention to detail, an adventurous spirit, and, most important, an eye and ear attuned to what makes a trip fun, safe, and rewarding for kids and their caregivers alike.

INTRODUCTION

Is there a more glorious place to be a kid outdoors than the Philadelphia metropolitan region? Can any place beat its four moderate seasons; its abundance of open space stretching from the city to the suburbs and into the countryside; its ever-growing network of walking and biking trails; and most of all, its incredible diversity—woods and meadows; creeks, ponds, and lakes; mountains and hills; marshes and shores?

Of course, I'm biased. Not only was I a kid here, I raised my own kid here too. I think this region offers more kinds of wonderful places to engage in that most essential childhood activity—playing outside—than any kid could possibly tire of.

And the good news is that it's getting even better. The region is in the midst of a flood of interest in creating opportunities for families to enjoy the outdoors. Communities everywhere are building new walking and biking trails, and connecting them to create intricate networks that stretch across the region.

The city of Philadelphia itself has led the way, with beautiful new parks along the Schuylkill and Delaware rivers. Land trusts and municipalities have preserved open space and created new opportunities for public access. Long-abandoned rail lines are seeing new life as recreational trails. As interest in kayaking and other water sports has risen, so has the number of water trails and outfitters. The region has long been blessed with an extraordinary collection of public gardens and arboretums; many of these have been expanding programs for children and families. They join the still-increasing number of nature centers with unparalleled expertise in engaging children with the outdoors. We've also seen a literal sprouting of new farms dedicated to forging bonds with communities. And there are still numerous parks and myriad streams where you can walk, fish, swim, watch birds, climb trees, and explore. For kids who are differently abled, real efforts are being made to expand accessibility of outdoor activities like fishing (for example, at the John Heinz National Wildlife Refuge, Trip 4, and Ridley Creek State Park, Trip 57), hiking (such as at Hawk Mountain Sanctuary, Trip 49, and Cattus Island Park, Trip 97), and playgrounds (such as Smith Playground, Trip 7, and Alapocas Run State Park, Trip 74).

Hundreds of outdoor destinations are in the Philadelphia area. For this book I've selected 100 locations that offer a variety of things to do outdoors, for kids of all ages and interests. Most are within an hour of the city; other places are worth the longer drive. Most are free, and most of those that are not charge only nominal fees. All the locations are featured because they are great places where kids can be active, in an unstructured outdoor environment.

It wasn't too long ago that outdoors was kids' natural domain. After school, on weekends, and during summer vacations were all times you spent outdoors, no matter where you lived. Kids knew the local fishing spots, trees to climb, and hills to race up and down. Nowadays, with busy structured lives filled with technology and new media—as well as increasing concerns for safety—kids have more of a need to be introduced to the outdoors by the adults in their lives.

Outdoors is where we can all be children, and when we're outdoors with kids, we get to share those feelings like nowhere else in our lives. Full of possibility, wide-open spaces inspire us to be creative, to express ourselves physically, to run and jump, swim like a fish, hop like a frog—to experience the pure joy of being alive. Outdoors is the original source of wonder, the best teacher because it encourages curiosity about the universe, starting with what we can touch, hear, and see. We can expand our comfort zones, trying new activities or exploring new places.

No one knows your kids better than you do. But spending time outdoors with your kids is a great way to get to know them in new ways—and for them to discover new things about themselves.

That's why the book is called *Outdoors* **with** *Kids*, not *Outdoors* **for** *Kids*. The book is designed to help you go places with your kids, nurturing that close bond that comes with enjoying outdoors activities together.

HOW TO USE THIS BOOK

With 100 destinations to choose from, you may wonder how to decide where to go. The regional map at the front of this book and the locator maps at the beginning of each section will help you narrow down the trips by location, and the At-a-Glance Trip Planner that follows the table of contents will provide more information to guide you toward a decision. The four 10 Best lists might also influence your selections.

If your children are old enough, involve them in the selection process. Do they love to fish? Do they want to look for birds? Do they have a yen to try paddling? Try connecting potential trips to what they're studying in school. Are they learning about the winter at Valley Forge? About the creatures that live in ponds? Maybe their friends have been somewhere and they want to go too. When kids have a say in the trip they are taking, they will be more vested in the excursion and everyone will likely have a much better time.

Once you settle on a destination and turn to a trip in this book, you'll find a series of icons that indicate whether the destination is reachable via public transportation; is stroller-friendly; offers hiking, bicycling, swimming, or paddling; has a playground or camping facilities; or charges fees. An icon also indicates the ages for which the activities there are best suited. The recommendations are based on my perceptions; read the full description to see if it sounds appealing for your family.

The **trip overview** (in italic type) summarizes the main activities or points of interest that children will enjoy at the destination. Information on the basics follows: address, hours of operation, fees, contact information, bathrooms, water/snacks, and available maps. Hours, fees, and other details are all subject to change, so be sure to check websites or call the locations before heading out.

The **directions** explain how to reach the destination by car and, for some trips, by public transportation. The Directions section also includes global positioning system (GPS) coordinates. When you enter the coordinates or the street address into your GPS device, it will provide driving directions. Whether or not you own a GPS device, it is always a good idea to have a road map with you. (Note: The directions assume a starting point of Center City Philadelphia; depending on your location, you may need to adjust them or refer to an online resource.)

Where the destinations are easily reached within or from Philadelphia by public transportation (including short walks to the final destination), the directions include suggested routes by bus, subway, or rail, all operated by SEPTA (the Southeastern Pennsylvania Transportation Authority). In the city, there are two main subway lines (the north–south Broad Street Line and the east–west Market-Frankford Line or the "EL"), a Subway-Surface Trolley Line in West Philadelphia, several light-rail lines, and numerous buses. Philly PHLASH is a special bus route that runs in Center City during the summer season, stopping at many of the city's most popular tourist destinations. The Regional Rail lines connect Center City with outlying neighborhoods and suburbs. SEPTA has been expanding the accessibility of its buses to passengers with bicycles. For specific information on schedules and routes, see septa.org. Note that SEPTA buses require exact change in payment of the fare (currently $2; plans for modernizing the fare system are under way).

The **maps** that accompany some of the trips will help you understand the lay of the land at the destination. For those destinations without maps, websites and other information about where to find maps are included in the bolded section at the start of each description.

At the end of each trip overview, the **Remember** section does one of two things. In some cases, it provides insights that can help you sidestep potential glitches on the trip, like rules about keeping your pets leashed. In others, it alerts you to sights or experiences that are worth the extra effort to pursue.

Every trip includes a **Plan B** section, which gives ideas for nearby activities in case the original plan does not work out. Choosing Plan B should never be seen as a failure. Sometimes the weather doesn't cooperate, while other times a long hike or day away from home isn't in the cards for a cranky child. Keep in mind that you're trying to share and foster a love of the outdoors with your kids, not make them go on a march.

Kids—and adults—may need extra food or supplies, like wipes, diapers, or sunblock, while out and about. A **Where to Eat Nearby** section offers tips for finding restaurants, delis, cafés, or shops near the destination, or a recommendation that you pack your own provisions.

All of the trips in this book have some sort of "payoff," from swimming and kayaking to destination playgrounds that have interesting themes and equipment. Some payoffs, such as kayaking on the Delaware River (see Trip 36), are the focus of the trip, while others are a layover on, or the end point of, a longer journey.

There are other payoffs to taking children outdoors, of course: payoffs in family time, in children's growing confidence and skills, and in their increased comfort in the outdoors and connection to the natural world.

STEWARDSHIP AND CONSERVATION

Frequent, unstructured outdoor play can increase children's health, school performance, self-esteem, and feelings of connection to nature. Kids who feel connected to nature today are likely to be tomorrow's conservation leaders. The Appalachian Mountain Club (AMC) is committed to helping kids build strong connections to the outdoor world, and through that connection build an appreciation for the natural world. When you bring young people outdoors, you should teach them to take care of the natural resources around them.

The first step in raising a conservation-conscious child takes place when that child falls in love with a special place. Foster a sense of fun at the outdoor destinations you visit, and then go one step further: Teach your children the Leave No Trace guidelines. Join volunteer groups and participate in park cleanups, or sign up for a naturalist-led walk to explore the plants, animals, rocks, trees, and waterways.

LEAVE NO TRACE

The Appalachian Mountain Club is a national educational partner of Leave No Trace, a nonprofit organization dedicated to promoting and inspiring responsible outdoor recreation through education, research, and partnerships. The Leave No Trace program seeks to develop wildland ethics—ways in which people think and act in the outdoors to minimize their impact on the areas they visit and to protect our natural resources for future enjoyment. Leave No Trace unites four federal land management agencies—the U.S. Forest Service, National Park Service, Bureau of Land Management, and U.S. Fish and Wildlife Service—with manufacturers, outdoor retailers, user groups, educators, organizations such as AMC, and individuals.

The Leave No Trace ethic is guided by these seven principles:

1. **Plan Ahead and Prepare.** Learn all you can about the area regulations before you head out. Be prepared; weather can change quickly and so can the temperature. Know where you are going, know how you are going to get there, and make sure you tell at least one person of your itinerary.

2. **Travel and Camp on Durable Surfaces.** If you are hiking in a park area with hiking trails and established campsites, please use them. The purpose

of designated hiking trails is to minimize the environmental damage to the area from hikers traipsing over the ground and ground cover.

3. **Dispose of Waste Properly.** Pack it in, pack it out. The best and easiest way to take your garbage out with you is to bring along a large Ziploc bag and toss your garbage inside. Deposit solid human waste in catholes dug 6 to 8 inches deep, at least 200 feet from water, camps, and trails. Pack out toilet paper and hygiene products. To wash yourself or your dishes, carry water 200 feet from streams or lakes and use small amounts of biodegradable soap. Scatter strained dishwater.

4. **Leave What You Find.** Sometimes it may be tempting to bring home a souvenir from your hiking trip. If everybody removed a souvenir or two, what would be left for you to see? Digital cameras are great for capturing those memories. Cultural or historical artifacts, as well as natural objects such as plants and rocks, should be left as found.

5. **Minimize Campfire Impacts.** Cook on a stove. Use established fire rings, fire pans, or mound fires. Besides the danger of starting a forest fire, even small campfires can cause permanent damage to the surrounding area.

6. **Respect Wildlife.** Observe wildlife from a distance. Feeding wildlife is hazardous to their health. They need to be able to hunt and find their own food without becoming reliant on hikers for snacks that may or may not be what their natural diet is made up of. Protect wildlife from your food by storing rations and trash securely.

7. **Be Considerate of Other Visitors.** Be courteous, respect the quality of other visitors' experience, and let nature's sounds prevail.

AMC is a national provider of the Leave No Trace Master Educator course. AMC offers this 5-day course, designed especially for outdoor professionals and land managers, as well as the shorter 2-day Leave No Trace Trainer course, at locations throughout the Northeast.

For Leave No Trace information and materials, contact the Leave No Trace Center for Outdoor Ethics, P.O. Box 997, Boulder, CO 80306. Phone: 800-332-4100 or 302-442-8222; fax: 303-442-8217; web: lnt.org. For a schedule of AMC Leave No Trace courses, see outdoors.org/education/lnt.

GETTING STARTED

Creating a lifetime connection to the outdoors starts with sharing fun experiences. Getting your kids outside doesn't need to be difficult—focus on enjoyment and exploration, one hike, day at the beach, bike ride, or winter walk at a time.

GETTING OUTSIDE NEAR HOME
A great way to get started is to get outdoors in your backyard or neighborhood. Whether walking to a local park or climbing trees in your yard, make time to play in nature and reap the benefits. Here are some ideas for projects and activities you can do close to home and in all types of weather.

In Your Neighborhood
- Build Fairy Houses: Construct tiny "homes" from sticks, twigs, leaves, rocks, and other natural materials. (Don't use living plants.)
- Feed the Birds: Set up a bird feeder (you can make a simple one by spreading peanut butter on a pinecone and rolling it in birdseed). See which types of birds come; have the kids draw pictures and keep a log of which birds visit. Keep a simple bird guide near the window to help identify the visitors.
- Plant Something: Start small with a flowerpot or window box. Or plant a vegetable garden, a flower garden, a butterfly garden, an herb garden, or a tree.
- Follow a Map: Devise a local treasure hunt, or try orienteering using a map or GPS (see page 116).
- Take the Inside Outside: Bring out your kids' traditionally indoor toys and set up a play space outside. Getting out of a routine can be entertaining.
- Embrace the Dark: Go on a night walk and gaze at the moon and stars. The world will feel different and bigger.

In a Park
- Enjoy a Picnic: Have your kids help you plan a picnic and enjoy eating together at your favorite park. After eating, they can play.
- Celebrate Outdoors: Plan birthday parties, family visits, or holiday traditions that involve getting outside.

- Volunteer: Many parks have volunteer organizations that plant trees, clean streams, and hold events. If your local park doesn't have such an organization, consider starting your own.
- Join a local family activity run by an organization like AMC. To see a list of AMC activities in the Philadelphia area, visit activities.outdoors.org.
- Register for AMC's free online community at kids.outdoors.org for local expert advice and activity ideas.

Through the Seasons

- During spring, look for signs of life in streams, ponds, puddles, or vernal pools. Local nature centers often make note of the seasonal vernal pools and organize events around salamander crossings.
- When it's raining, head out with umbrellas or put kids in bathing suits and let them run around and splash in puddles.
- During fall, try leafy crafts. Have kids collect leaves they like and iron them between sheets of waxed paper to make a bookmark or window decoration. Or make a leaf sailboat from fallen pinecones, sticks, or pieces of bark. A leaf can be the sail, a stick the mast, and a pinecone or piece of bark the boat body.
- In winter, go sledding, look for animal tracks, build a snow fort, or make snow sculptures

GROWING UP IN THE OUTDOORS

As parents or caregivers, we learn quickly that children have different needs at different ages. That's true of children in the outdoors as well. Remember, your enthusiasm is contagious. If you show excitement for the outdoors, your children will become excited too.

Babies, Toddlers, and Preschoolers (up to age 4)

With very small children, your primary goal is to create a positive association with being outdoors.

- It's surprisingly easy to bring babies on many outdoor excursions. Babies are carried and their needs are relatively simple: Keep them fed, warm, and dry. Nursing moms shouldn't hesitate about getting outside with their babies. No need to pack food for a baby who's nursing!
- Once children begin walking, you may cover less distance than with babies. Small children love repetition and engage with nature on a micro level. Young explorers may count every wildflower or try to jump over every rock on a trail, or want to turn around after half a mile or half an hour. Children at this age respond well to simple games, songs, and storytelling.

- Small children have a limited understanding of time, distance, and danger, and require constant supervision, especially near water and on steep terrain.

Young Children (ages 5 to 8)

Young children want to do everything you do and they'll try hard to keep up. This makes them great company outdoors.

- Children these ages are eager to learn new skills and information. Simple lessons work well.
- Young children are easily distracted or discouraged, but are also readily engaged and are easily motivated by clear goals and imaginative games. Offer encouragement and support for their efforts.
- Children at this stage still need you to set boundaries and safety guidelines. They're old enough, though, that you can share your reasoning with them. You can also start asking children to carry their own backpack.
- Inviting a friend along on an outdoor adventure lets children share the experience with someone their own age—and often makes your job easier.
- Young children may be able to join in child-focused group activities in the outdoors, but may not have long enough attention spans to join mixed-age groups.

Older Children (9 to 12)

Older children can take on more trip responsibilities and may enjoy testing their limits in outdoor activities. They may also focus more on peer relationships.

- Being outdoors offers parents the chance to engage their children with lessons about nature, history, weather, or any number of topics.
- Enlist older children in trip planning and decision-making; reading maps and assisting in navigation; and carrying personal gear.
- Leave electronic devices behind or turn them off. Talking on a phone, texting, or playing an electronic game is distracting and noisy.
- Children at this age often want to bring friends along on outings, but may be more reluctant to try something new in front of their peers or to follow safety guidelines.
- Some preteens will be ready to join organized mixed-age groups (such as trips organized by parks, nature centers, or recreational organizations like AMC) and educational activities.

TRIP PLANNING

When you're heading farther than the local park, you will want to map out your day and activity ahead of time. Just be prepared for changes.

Choose Your Goals

For most outdoor adventures, shorter is better with young children. Consider your child's pace and stamina when selecting destinations and routes.

- Start small and work up to more-difficult routes; children will appreciate the feeling of attaining goals and will gain confidence as they continue to master challenges.
- Think about payoffs: Hike to a waterfall, visit a farm, or bike to a beach with public swimming.
- For cycling, plan trips that are not as hilly or lengthy as adult trips and that minimize traffic and maximize children's safety. Bike paths are often fun for families, but can be busy; when kids are just learning to ride, you may be better off heading to a park or preserve with bike trails.

Before You Go

- Check the weather forecast. Be prepared for changes in the weather conditions.
- For longer hikes or remote routes, leave a trip plan with someone you trust before you head out.
- Check directions, available parking, and facility hours.
- Pack provisions. See page xxxvi for suggestions.

Once You're There

- If you're going to be exploring trails, go over your route with children; show them the map. You might even let them decide on some trail choices when there's an opportunity. Give them trail names when hiking, point out trail blaze colors, and on longer hikes, talk about stopping points and turn-around times. Remind them that the group must stay together.
- Make a contingency plan for if you get separated, and make sure children understand it. Some parents opt to provide their children with emergency cell phones. Just be aware that service is unreliable in rural areas.
- Find the bathroom. Each trip description in this book gives information on where bathrooms are located. On hikes far from bathrooms, teach kids to be able to use the woods away from the trail; bring sanitizing gel or wipes.

Schedules and Routines

- Keep children's schedules and routines in mind. If your daughter eats lunch every day at 11:30 a.m. but you're holding out for the picnic tables at the end of the trail, no one is going to have fun.
- Flexibility is important too. If kids are having a blast climbing on rocks, there's no need to make them stop just because it's lunchtime.

- Always remember a Plan B. If your children are not enjoying the activity you originally planned, switch gears and engage them with something else.

Sharing the Outdoors with Others
- Inviting other children can make a big difference in fun and motivation.
- Having other adults along on a trip can give you extra sets of eyes—and arms. But be careful that socializing does not take your attention away from children. This is especially important with small children.

Fees, Deals, and Discounts
Most of the destinations in this guide are free or have a minimal cost. Some ask for voluntary donations. The following tips can help you save money while getting outdoors.
- Becoming a member of the Appalachian Mountain Club links you to a local chapter that organizes outings and offers discounts on everything from guidebooks and maps to Family Adventure Camps. Visit outdoors.org for more information about deals, discounts, and events.
- Entrance to fee-based public gardens and arboretums is often free to members of any garden in the American Horticultural Society. For a list of participating gardens in the Philadelphia region, see ahs.org. The same goes for zoos; see aza.org/reciprocity.
- Online outdoor parenting communities such as kids.outdoors.org or metrokids.com are good sources for news about discounts, coupons, and reduced-fee programs.

CLOTHING AND GEAR
Good-fitting, well-functioning clothes and equipment—from rain jackets and backpacks to hiking boots—can mean the difference between a good time and a miserable one. But you don't need to spend a lot of money; you can often find well-made snowsuits, synthetic long underwear, and life jackets for children at thrift stores or gear swaps. You also don't need all of the items listed below for every type of outing. For a day in the park, a fleece jacket, sturdy shoes, and long pants may do the trick.

Outdoor Clothing Basics
- Put kids in long-sleeved shirts and long pants for increased sun protection or to keep bugs away from tender skin.
- Lightweight and easily packed, hats offer quick warmth, shade children from sun, and protect from wind.
- Teach kids to wear clothes that are quick-drying and retain warmth even when wet. For light outdoor activity in dry weather, jeans, sweatpants,

and cotton shirts can be fine, but wicking synthetics, fleeces, wools, and quick-drying nylons will keep everyone more comfortable during vigorous activities.

- Dress children in layers. Light wicking layers go under heavier layers, which are under warm outer layers and wind protection. Adding or removing layers keeps kids from being soaked with sweat or rain, and from becoming too hot or too cold.

Footwear

- Choose appropriate footwear. For hiking, wear closed-toe shoes, preferably waterproof, with good ankle support; for exploring creeks and ponds in warmer months, sturdy water shoes work well, and you don't have to worry about wet socks on the trail. For biking, wear closed-toe shoes such as sneakers, not sandals or flip-flops. For paddling, pick closed-toe shoes that can get wet repeatedly and dry quickly. For snowshoeing, choose thick snow boots or hiking boots that hold their shape under snowshoe straps or buckles.
- Synthetic liner socks under wool socks offer the most warmth and blister protection when hiking, skiing, or snowshoeing. If you need smaller sizes that outdoor manufacturers don't make, kids' nylon dress socks work decently as liners.
- Use water shoes for swimming or paddling to protect sensitive feet.

Helmets

- Helmets are a must for bicycling, including riding in trailers and in bike seats. Fit is important for safety; the helmet should sit level on a child's head and fit securely with the strap fastened.
- Babies may not have the neck strength to wear a helmet until after age 1.
- Although it may be tempting to buy a used helmet at a yard sale, you may have trouble assessing its condition and whether it meets current safety standards.

Personal Flotation Devices

- When paddling, children should always wear personal flotation devices (PFDs). Parents should set an example by wearing PFDs as well.
- Ensure the PFD fits your child well. The PFD should fit snugly. Choose based on your child's weight:
  - Infant PFDs are for children 8 pounds to 30 pounds
  - Child PFDs are for children 30 pounds to 50 pounds
  - Youth PFDs are for children 50 pounds to 90 pounds

- To test the fit, secure your child in the PFD, then grasp the shoulders of the PFD and lift your child. The child's ears and chin should not slip through the PFD.
- PFDs come in five types. Most children will use a Type III, which is a flotation aid suitable for various activities. Infants can use Type II PFDs, which are designed for use in calm waters.

Dressing for Summer
- Sun hats protect children from intense sun. Look for lightweight hats with wide brims or visors long enough to shade a child's entire face. "Safari" hats with removable neck protection also work well, as do bandannas.
- Protect children's eyes with sunglasses, especially if you're traveling on water or over open landscapes. Expect to lose a few pairs along the way.
- Always wear sunscreen.
- Bring non-DEET insect repellent and apply to exposed skin and pant cuffs or socks.

Dressing for Winter
- Don't overdress your children for winter. When active, people generate heat quickly. Dress in layers and remove a layer as necessary.
- One-piece snowsuits work best for younger children. Older children should practice the same layering system as adults.
- Balaclavas are great winter hats for kids because they cover both head and neck, leaving just an opening for the face.
- Keep toes warm—invest in a pair of wool or fleece socks.
- Mittens keep hands warmer than gloves, so unless children need to use their fingers, mittens are best in winter. Wool socks can double as mittens.
- Remember sunglasses when out on the snow.
- Attach plastic bags over hands or mittens and over socks or shoes to protect against rain or to add warmth in cold conditions.
- Bring packets of hand warmers and foot warmers for emergencies (like "I forgot my gloves"); they're inexpensive and long-lasting, and they can make all the difference to the success of an outing on a cold day.

Snowshoes and Skis
- Select snowshoes by weight, and look for ones that are easy for children to put on and take off.
- Waxless skis are the best choice for children who are learning the basics of cross-country skiing.

- Many Nordic centers and downhill ski resorts rent snowshoes and cross-country ski equipment for children.

Dressing for Wind or Rain

- Getting wet is often a safety risk, so be sure children have rain gear that is waterproof, not just water resistant. For extended trips, rain pants are a good addition to a rain jacket. Ponchos aren't recommended because they don't cover enough of the body and are useless in wind. If you plan to be out and active in rain for any length of time, breathable rain gear works best.
- Wearing a visored hat under a raincoat helps keep the hood of the raincoat out of a child's eyes.
- Wind protection is especially important when hiking or snowshoeing in the mountains or in exposed areas; paddling on the ocean or open water; bicycling; or cross-country skiing.

Dressing Babies for the Outdoors

- In hot weather, try thin, cotton one-pieces without feet to keep babies from overheating.
- In summer, choose brimmed hats with a strap under the chin so they stay on.
- In cooler weather, babies may need a hat (with a chin strap) or mittens before you do because they're not moving their bodies.
- In winter, babies stay warmer in snowsacks, rather than snowsuits with legs. If you hike, ski, or snowshoe with a child in a back carrier or open sled, remember that the child is not exercising and warming up as you are. Dress a baby in warm layers, minimize exposed skin, and check often to be sure the baby's nose, face, neck, and limbs are warm. Don't go so far that you can't get back to warmth quickly if the baby gets cold.
- Pack twice as many diapers, covers, and clothing changes as you think you'll need. Bring several sturdy plastic bags to carry out soiled diapers and clothing.

PACKING

No single packing list can cover every activity in this book. The basic list below should work well for most day outings. I've also provided specific tips for children's packs and for carriers, trailers, and sleds.

Basic Pack

You'll want to have the following items in your bag or backpack on outings in every season.

- ❏ Food: Crankiness is increased by hunger. Pack high-energy snacks such as nuts, dried fruit, or granola bars. Pack a lunch for longer trips. Bring extra snacks; you won't be sorry. Include children in this task as much as possible.
- ❏ Water: Two quarts per person is usually adequate, depending on the weather and the length of the trip.
- ❏ Outerwear: wind protection, rain protection, warm jackets. Pack for the range of weather you're likely to encounter.
- ❏ Extra clothing: Extra socks, mittens, hats, and sunglasses come in handy and don't take up much room. Bringing extra warm clothes in all but the hottest weather is a good idea. If your activity takes you to a lake, river, stream, or ocean, a change of clothing may be required for everyone.
- ❏ Toilet paper or a pack of tissues
- ❏ First-aid kit: adhesive bandages, athletic or hospital tape, gauze, blister protection, small scissors, children's antihistamines, nonprescription painkillers, and tweezers for removing splinters and ticks
- ❏ Map and compass
- ❏ Whistle
- ❏ Flashlight or headlamp
- ❏ Cell phone: Be sure to have emergency phone numbers on hand, though service is unreliable in rural and remote areas.
- ❏ Wet wipes
- ❏ Plastic bags
- ❏ Sunscreen
- ❏ Insect repellent
- ❏ Extra clothes to leave in the car for the trip home

Optional Items

- ❏ Binoculars
- ❏ Camera
- ❏ Books: guidebooks, nature guides, picture books for young children
- ❏ Journal or loose paper plus pens, pencils, or crayons
- ❏ Bandannas
- ❏ Fishing poles
- ❏ Trekking poles
- ❏ GPS device

Children's Packs

For many reasons—including safety, increasing skills and responsibility, and engaging them in the outdoors experience—children should carry some of their gear as early as possible.

- Food: Carrying their own snacks or lunches lets children replenish their energy on the go and also minimizes arguments among siblings over who has more of a favored food.
- Water: Carrying their own water encourages children to drink on the trail.
- Clothing: When kids have their own jackets, rain gear, or wind protection, they're more likely to put them on and take them off when needed.
- Teach children how to use a whistle for safety.
- Map and compass: Older children can help with route-finding (and learn a valuable skill while they're at it).
- Address and phone number: Put this important information in a waterproof bag and in a place (such as a pack or pocket) where your child knows to find it.
- Fun stuff: sketch pad, magnifying glass, binoculars, ball, coloring books, harmonica. Young children may want to bring a favorite toy or stuffed animal.

Carriers, Trailers, and Pulks

At very young ages, for trips that don't involve a stroller, children can be carried in a front pack, backpack, or sling, in a bike trailer, or on a sled behind skis. As children get older, bike seats and bike extensions may help you enjoy the outdoors together.

- Front packs are a good idea for babies up to about 6 months of age. They get the benefit of your body warmth, and you have a close-up view of them.
- You can move older babies to a child backpack when they're able to hold up their heads unaided.
- Children can ride in bike trailers as soon as they're able to support the weight of a bike helmet, about 1 year old. Be careful on bumpy terrain, however, and remember bike helmets, as with any cycling activity.
- Attached bike seats are appropriate when children can hold their heads upright while wearing a helmet and can comfortably sit upright on their own.
- For a period of a few years in between riding in a bicycle trailer and riding longer distances on a separate bicycle, your child may enjoy riding on a one-wheel child bike extension, complete with pedals, that attaches to the back of your bicycle. This may extend the distance you are able to enjoy riding together, but requires training and good communication.
- When cross-country skiing, it's easier and safer to use a sled built specifically for pulling children, called a pulk, than it is to ski with a baby

in a backpack or front child carrier. You may start using a pulk with a child between the ages of 6 and 12 months. The sled has two poles that are secured to the adult with a padded waist belt. Many cross-country ski areas have pulks available for rent.

Paddling Gear

- When paddling, store gear in specialized dry bags or in double-bagged, heavy-duty plastic bags. Older children can be responsible for their own bags of personal gear.
- If you do a lot of paddling, you may want to invest in sized-down paddles so children can participate.
- Everyone should wear a properly fitted personal flotation device (see page xxxiv).

SAFETY

Being prepared and taking a few precautions can reduce problems on your outings.

Sun and Heat

Children's sweat glands don't fully develop until adolescence, so they have a harder time managing extreme heat than adults.

- Apply sunscreen thoroughly before setting out for activities.
- During very hot weather, seek out shade or water to play in.
- Make sure children drink plenty of liquid to prevent heat exhaustion or heatstroke. Be alert for symptoms, including nausea, headache, dizziness, pale skin, and shallow breathing.
- If a child becomes overheated, move to a cool, shady spot. Apply wet cloths, loosen clothing, and have the child sip water.

Hypothermia

Hypothermia is a life-threatening condition that occurs when the body's core temperature drops. Hypothermia can happen in any season, even summer. Wet, windy conditions can be as dangerous as severe cold. Hypothermia happens very slowly; watch for early signs so you can prevent it from progressing.

- The best treatment for hypothermia is prevention. Cool to cold temperatures combined with moisture and wind cause hypothermia, so stay dry and choose clothing that keeps you warm even when wet, such as wool and fleece. Remember your raincoats. Keep well hydrated and nourished.
- Know the signs: shivering, stumbling, having to go to the bathroom, sleepiness, loss of judgment, trouble speaking (including slurring words), and difficulty with motor skills such as unzipping a coat.

- A child who has become chilled should immediately be removed from the windy and cold conditions and changed into dry, warm clothes. Give the child warm, sweet liquids to drink and food with protein and sugar, if possible.
- To check a baby, feel the neck, torso, and limbs. If limbs feel cool to the touch, a baby may be at risk for hypothermia.

Dehydration

Dehydration happens when your body does not have enough water as a result of heavy sweating, hard exercise, or sickness. It is especially likely to occur if you are hiking in hot weather and direct sunlight, though any time you are exercising and sweating, you risk dehydration. Infants and small children are much more likely to become dehydrated than older children or adults, because they can lose more fluid quickly. Thirst is the first sign of dehydration, along with dark urine. Mild to moderate dehydration can include symptoms such as irritability, lightheadedness, and dry mouth.

- Make sure children drink plenty of water when active outdoors.
- Have a drink of water at each stop—make a game of it. Make sure you do this in hot and cold weather. It may be harder to get kids to drink water when they are cold, but they still need it.
- Bring your own water. Never drink untreated water from outdoor sources.

Insects

- In the Northeast, some mosquitoes carry West Nile virus, a rare but potentially fatal disease that can be transmitted to humans. The threat is generally greatest in the evening hours, when mosquitoes are most active.
- Ticks can carry Lyme disease or other dangerous illnesses. Have children wear long sleeves, and long pants tucked into socks. After every outdoor adventure, don't forget to check for ticks (visit cdc.gov/ticks for tips).
- If any child on your trip is allergic to bee or wasp stings, the child (or a designated adult) should carry an Epi kit.
- Insect repellent containing DEET is not recommended for children. Teach older children to wash their hands after applying repellent, if possible, and to avoid getting it in their eyes or mouths.

Plants and Animals

- Poison ivy is ubiquitous in the Northeast; it can cause a very itchy rash when touched. Teach children to identify its clusters of three leaves that shine in the sun but are dull in the shade, and to try to avoid touching them or the "hairy" vines that climb up trees, or brushing against them with bare skin. If a child comes into contact with poison ivy, wash the affected area with soap as soon as possible.

- Stinging nettle, while less common than poison ivy, is quite common along streams and other wet, open places. It causes a sharp sting when touched; while it lasts only a few minutes, it's not fun. Teach children to identify stinging nettle's paired, loosely toothed leaves with long strands of tiny flowers dangling underneath.
- Train young children not to eat or drink anything they find outside, including berries, plants, mushrooms, and water from lakes, rivers, and streams. Older children can learn how to safely identify common wild edible fruits and berries; local nature centers are a good source of educational programs.
- Teach children to observe, but not feed, wild animals. Explain that they shouldn't get between a mother and her young, such as a mother bear and cubs.

Lightning
- If you're caught in a lightning storm, seek shelter, preferably in a building or car. If neither is nearby, seek shelter among trees that are of equal height. Avoid peaks, towers, and single trees in open areas. Remove packs and anything containing metal. Squat down, if possible on a foam pad, with your heels touching, knees apart, and hands off the ground.
- If you're on water and see a storm approaching, immediately head for shore.
- Count the number of seconds between lightning and thunder to estimate how far you are from the storm. Estimate one mile for every five seconds. If the number of seconds is decreasing, the storm is headed your way.

Water Safety
Children should always be supervised while around water. Remember these swimming safety tips, adapted from the American Red Cross:
- Never leave a young child unattended near water and do not trust a child's life to another child; teach children to always ask permission to go near water.
- Have young children and inexperienced swimmers wear U.S. Coast Guard–approved personal flotation devices (PFDs) around water and in boats, but do not rely on PFDs alone. See page xxxiv for more information.
- The Coast Guard does not recommend taking infants on board recreational boats and cautions that Infant Type II personal flotation devices for babies up to 18 pounds may not always perform as expected.
- Establish rules for your family and enforce them without fail. For example, no swimming unless you can touch bottom.
- Know how to safely operate the type of watercraft you will use. Plan what you will do if a boat capsizes. Enroll in a boating safety class.

Getting Lost

- When hiking, sign in and out at trail registers to leave a record in case of emergency.
- Adults in the group should be able to use a map and guidebook. Keep the group together, with everyone within eyesight. Try a game, such as everyone counting off, to keep track.
- Teach children to stay together, keep to the trail, and wait at every trail junction. Point out landmarks as you go along to help build images of the trail in children's minds.
- Teach children to stay in one place, preferably in the open, if they get lost and to blow their whistles (three short blasts). The best thing adults can do in this situation is to stay calm and to keep the rest of the group together.
- Consider enrolling in a program like AMC's Lost and Alone workshops, which teach children how to stay with a group in the outdoors and also what to do if they become separated from the group.

Hunting

- Many parks and natural areas in the region allow hunting. Some of these sites may close trails on designated hunting days, so call ahead before setting out.
- Other trails remain open to visitors and hunters alike. If you are going to a park that permits hunting, wear bright colors (blaze orange is recommended by state game agencies), stay on designated trails, and keep pets leashed and put bright colors on them too.
- Hunting is not permitted on Sundays in Pennsylvania, Delaware, or New Jersey.

Section 1

Philadelphia

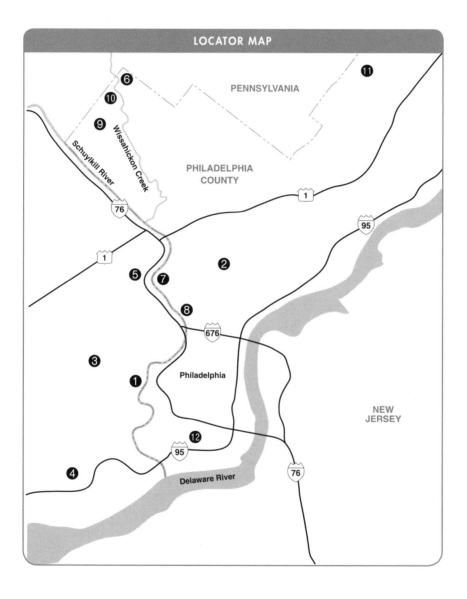

Trip 1

All Ages

Bartram's Garden

Explore meadows, gardens, a farm, and the riverfront at the eighteenth-century estate of John Bartram, the founder of American botany.

Address: 54th Street and Lindbergh Boulevard, Philadelphia, PA
Hours: Grounds open daily, except on city-observed holidays; Welcome Center (including Garden Shop) and Green Room open Thursday through Sunday, with varying hours (see website for details)
Fee: Grounds, free; admission charged for Green Room and guided tours: adults, $12; seniors, students, and children ages 16 and under, $10; members and children ages 2 and under, free
Contact: bartramsgarden.org, 215-729-5281
Bathrooms: In the courtyard; in the Welcome Center and next to the Garden Shop (when open)
Water/Snacks: Snacks and water available in the Garden Shop (when open)
Maps: None
Directions by Car: Take 23rd Street south below Market Street. Merge right onto Gray's Ferry Avenue just beyond South Street, and cross the Schuylkill River. Take the first left onto Paschall Avenue. Turn left at the next light onto 49th Street, and follow the bend onto Gray's Avenue. Follow the trolley tracks and bear left at a fork onto Lindbergh Boulevard. Just beyond the 54th Street sign, immediately after crossing a railroad bridge, make a sharp left turn into Bartram's entrance, which is not visible until after crossing the bridge. Continue on the driveway to the parking area next to the garden entrance. *GPS coordinates:* 39° 56.011′ N, 75° 12.933′ W.
Directions by Public Transit: Take the SEPTA No. 36 Trolley from City Hall to 54th Street. Cross the railroad bridge to Bartram's entrance on the left.

Bartram's Garden is an oasis in the midst of a dense, urban Southwest Philadelphia neighborhood, and a green break in an industrial shoreline along the lower Schuylkill. In 1728, John Bartram purchased 102 acres along the Schuylkill River, where he created gardens that are of enormous importance to the history of American science. Bartram and his son William collected plants from all over North America and planted them in their gardens. Today, parents will enjoy the historical importance; kids will love the green meadow and trail, the river dock, snowy day sledding, and the fun, educational programming.

Look for carnivorous plants (no, they won't bite) tucked off the trail in Bartram's Garden.

Families can walk trails in the gardens, along the river, and through the meadow. Bring bikes to explore the Schuylkill River Trail (SRT) connection between Bartram's Garden and the river; the trail is stroller-accessible too. On the SRT and throughout the site, there are great views of the city skyline and (except in the historical garden) plenty of places to run. Informational signs explain the site's historical significance. A child with a green thumb will love to explore the labeled gardens for ideas to bring home.

Visit the recently created community gardens, orchard, and farm at the southern end of the site. These spaces are dedicated to promoting the value of growing fresh food and improving nutrition in urban areas. Indoors at the Green Room, kids can engage in interactive activities to learn about nature and local history. Visit Bartram's website to find more information about current programming, including Family Discover Days, offered during spring and summer school breaks, and Little Explorers, a monthly garden program for toddlers.

Remember: Except within the 8-acre historical section, pets and picnicking are permitted.

PLAN B: If your kids are interested in science and history, visit the Academy of Natural Sciences or Franklin Institute in Center City.

WHERE TO EAT NEARBY: It's best to bring lunch or snacks. Picnic tables are available on the grounds.

There's nothing like the experience of gathering their own fruit or vegetables to change kids' views of food. Stretching up to pick apples from fruit-heavy trees, plucking ripe, juicy raspberries from drooping canes, and gently coaxing carrots from sun-warmed soil are physical activities that are more fun than going to the supermarket. And the kids will never forget the vibrant taste of just-picked produce.

Just walking around a farm, seeing the rows of crops, and watching the work being done will open young eyes to the connection between food and land, and between land and the people who depend on it. Local food networks support sustainable communities.

The Philadelphia area is home to a burgeoning number of farms that invite the surrounding communities to visit.

Community Supported Agriculture (CSA) farms—typically small and often organic—sell annual memberships to the public. Members get a share of the produce and can often do some work at the farm. Some CSAs invite the public to visit at any time; others may be able to handle visitors only during events like harvest festivals. (Always contact the farm first to find out if visitors are welcome.) CSAs are all over the region, including urban areas. (Yes, there are farms in the city of Philadelphia!) To find a CSA near you, check the websites localharvest. org, buylocalpa.org, slowfoodphilly.org, and slowfoodcentralnj.org.

Pick-Your-Own Farms (PYOs) enable visitors to pick their own berries, apples, pumpkins, and other produce. Often, PYOs are larger commercial operations specially geared to entertain families, not just with fruit and vegetable picking, but with other seasonal activities such as corn mazes, hayrides, or sleigh rides. To find a PYO near you, check pickyourown.org. Here are a few of the well-known PYOs in the Philadelphia area:

Highland Orchards, West Chester, PA; open all year; pick-your-own season May through October; highlandorchards.net

Linvilla Orchards, Media, PA; open all year; pick-your-own season May through October; linvilla.com

Solebury Orchards, New Hope, PA; open from mid-June to early November; soleburyorchards.com

Terhune Orchards, Princeton, NJ; open all year; pick-your-own season May through October; terhuneorchards.com

Trip 2

All
Ages

Awbury Arboretum

Unlock a secret garden, walk between tall rows of growing vegetables, and run after butterflies at this Germantown oasis of green.

Address: 1 Awbury Road, Philadelphia, PA
Hours: Grounds open dawn to dusk daily; office (Francis Cope House) open
  Monday through Friday 9 A.M. to 5 P.M.
Fee: Free
Contact: awbury.org, 215-849-2855
Bathrooms: At the Francis Cope House (when open)
Water/Snacks: Water fountain outside the Francis Cope House
Maps: awbury.org/map_grounds.html
Directions by Car: From City Center, take Kelly Drive west to continue onto
  Lincoln Drive. Take a slight right onto West Harvey Street. After 0.8 mile turn
  left onto Germantown Avenue, and then take the first right onto East High
  Street. After 0.8 mile turn left onto Chew Avenue. The entrance is almost
  immediately on your right. Continue up the drive to the parking area behind
  the Francis Cope House. *GPS coordinates:* 40° 3.046′ N, 75° 10.061′
Directions by Public Transit: Take the SEPTA Regional Rail Chestnut Hill East
  line to the Washington Lane station. Alternatively, take the SEPTA bus 18,
  25, or XH to Chew Avenue and Washington Lane. Entrance is directly across
  Chew Avenue.

Awbury Arboretum's 55 acres provide a breath of fresh air in the midst of the
historical, bustling neighborhood of Germantown. Set on a high hill topped
by the 1862 Francis Cope House (where the arboretum's offices are located),
Awbury's forested, parklike grounds are traversed by winding, easily walkable
trails and some paved drives near the Cope House.

Trails start near the office, where maps may be obtained. In summer, the
meadows are full of butterflies, while the pond is home to turtles and frogs.
Birds are abundant here, and not just urban birds. Soaring hawks and musical
warblers alike are attracted to this green refuge in Northwest Philadelphia.
For kids who love to be near water, take the woodland trail that heads down
to the wetlands, where a pond and creek invite exploration. A short walk
downhill from the Cope House is a Community Apiary with beehives that
educate young visitors about bees' lives and their importance to flowers, trees,

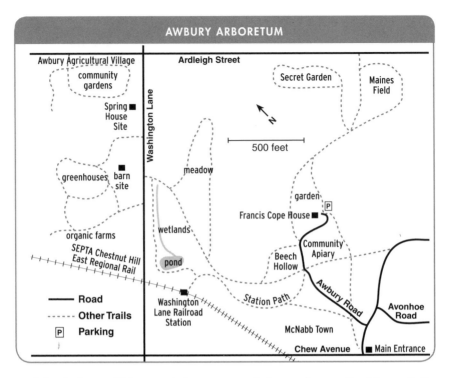

and food plants. Kids can sit in a stump circle to observe the hive activity, and the beekeeper conducts regular children's programs. Near the apiary is a huge basswood tree that looks like a fairy tale monster. Ask the office staff to unlock the Secret Garden, which is northeast of the office; a kid need not be a fan of the classic children's book to get a thrill from a visit. The garden is romantically spooky with its stone walls overgrown with vines.

Across Washington Lane is the arboretum's 16-acre Agricultural Village. Here, the Weaver's Way Co-op runs a 2-acre farm and children's garden that works to educate the community about growing food. Take your kids into the fields, read interpretive signs, and talk to a farmer about what's underground. This is an opportunity for kids to see what carrots look like before they get picked, de-leafed, peeled, and plastic-bagged.

The arboretum has an active calendar of children's programs and summer camps. Visit awbury.org for more information.

Remember: At the Agricultural Village, areas outside the Weaver's Way Co-op are not open to the public. Also, picnics are not permitted.

PLAN B: Wissahickon Valley Park (Trip 10) has hiking and bicycle trails, plus fishing in the creek.

WHERE TO EAT NEARBY: Head over to Germantown Avenue, toward Mount Airy, to find restaurants and shops.

Trip 3

Cobbs Creek Park

Follow wooded biking and hiking trails along the creek in this up-and-coming neighborhood park.

Address: 700 Cobbs Creek Parkway, Philadelphia, PA
Hours: Park grounds 8 A.M. to 1 A.M. daily; Cobbs Creek Community Environmental Education Center (CCCEEC): Monday through Thursday, 10 A.M. to 2 P.M., and during special programs
Fee: Free
Contact: fairmountpark.org, 215-683-0200; cobbscreekcenter.org, 215-685-1900; nlreep.org/cobbs_creek.htm
Bathrooms: At the CCCEEC
Water/Snacks: None
Maps: fairmountparkconservancy.org/downloads/FPMapBrochure.pdf; citymaps.phila.gov/map
Directions by Car: From City Center, take Market Street west to 38th Street. Turn left onto 38th Street, then right onto Walnut Street. Take Walnut Street to South 63d Street (Cobbs Creek Parkway) and turn left. After another 0.6 mile, at Catharine Street turn right into the park and proceed to the parking lot. *GPS coordinates:* 39° 57.119´ N, 75° 15.038´ W.
Directions by Public Transit: Take the Market–Frankford EL to 63rd Street. Walk down 63d Street (which becomes Cobbs Creek Parkway) to the entrance opposite Catharine Street, which leads to the CCCEEC.

Cobbs Creek Park, once a forgotten link in the Fairmount Park system, has benefitted from renewed attention and creative funding. The park now provides opportunities for experiencing the natural beauty of the wooded Cobbs Creek in West and Southwest Philadelphia. The Cobbs Creek Environmental Education Center (CCCEEC), opened in 2001, has become a community resource where kids and young adults can learn about nature and contribute to improving and protecting streams, woods, and trails. (Its hours vary during the year, depending on scheduling of programs.)

The 700-acre, irregularly shaped park follows the meandering path of rocky Cobbs Creek from City Avenue in the Overbrook Park section of the city, southwest to Woodland Avenue in Kingsessing (at the historical Blue Bell Tavern), passing the Mount Moriah Cemetery along the way. The first mill in Philadelphia was built in 1645, along the creek near the tavern.

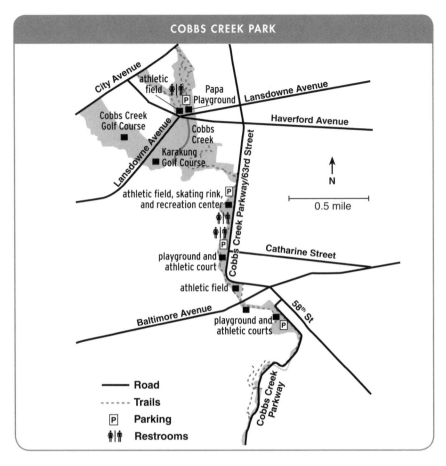

COBBS CREEK PARK

City Avenue · athletic field · Papa Playground · Lansdowne Avenue · Cobbs Creek Golf Course · Cobbs Creek · Lansdowne Avenue · Haverford Avenue · Karakung Golf Course · Cobbs Creek Parkway/63rd Street · athletic field, skating rink, and recreation center · N · 0.5 mile · Catharine Street · playground and athletic court · athletic field · Baltimore Avenue · playground and athletic courts · 58th St · Cobbs Creek Parkway

—— Road
- - - - Trails
P Parking
Restrooms

Seven miles of trails in the park wind through the woods. For families, the easiest way to get acquainted with the park's trail system is to join a naturalist-led walk; check the CCCEEC website or call for a current schedule. A paved 4-mile bike trail runs from 63rd and Market streets, past the bucolic cemetery (whose paths can be explored as well) to 70th Street. Plans are to extend this trail to the John Heinz National Wildlife Refuge (Trip 4). The park is also home to two golf courses, three playgrounds and recreation centers, and an indoor skating rink.

Remember: Dogs must be leashed.

PLAN B: West Fairmount Park (Trip 5) offers walking and biking trails, and the Please Touch Museum.

WHERE TO EAT NEARBY: Numerous small commercial areas are in West Philadelphia. Bring a lunch or snacks to enjoy a picnic in the park.

John Heinz National Wildlife Refuge

Walk or bike, fish or paddle, and follow easy trails surrounded by peaceful tidal marsh.

Address: 8601 Lindbergh Boulevard, Philadelphia, PA
Hours: Grounds open sunrise to sunset daily; visitor center open 8:30 A.M. to 4 P.M.
Fee: Free
Contact: fws.gov/heinz, 215-365-3118
Bathrooms: In visitor center (when open)
Water/Snacks: Water fountain in visitor center (when open)
Maps: fws.gov/heinz (click on About the Refuge)
Directions by Car: Take I-95 South to Exit 14 (Bartram Avenue). At the fifth light, turn right onto 84th Street. Go to the second traffic light and turn left onto Lindbergh Boulevard. Follow this street to the first stop sign. The refuge entrance is on the right. Continue to visitor parking. *GPS coordinates:* 39° 53.495′ N, 75° 15.426′ W.
Directions by Public Transit: Take the SEPTA Regional Rail Airport line to Eastwick station on Bartram Avenue between 84th and 85th streets. Walk up Bartram Avenue to 84th Street and continue as above. Alternatively, take the SEPTA bus 37 or 108 to 84th Street and Lindbergh Boulevard, and continue as above.

The refuge is a great place to walk, bike, or fish. Start at the education center, which features fascinating exhibits, including one on tidal marsh wildlife: a life-size, eye-level cross-section diorama that reveals what's under all that mud and water. The refuge contains 200 acres of freshwater tidal marsh, the largest remaining in Pennsylvania. It is an important habitat for many species of birds, amphibians, fish, and other wildlife.

Trails lead from the visitor center out to the impoundment—a huge freshwater pond. The long pedestrian bridge over the pond provides great views of the pond and the many ducks, herons, and other birds that are attracted to it; there are often expert birders hanging out on the bridge who are only too happy to share with kids the fun of looking at birds through binoculars. You can follow the trail all the way around the pond (about 3 miles), turn back to head into the woods, or go past the observation deck to follow

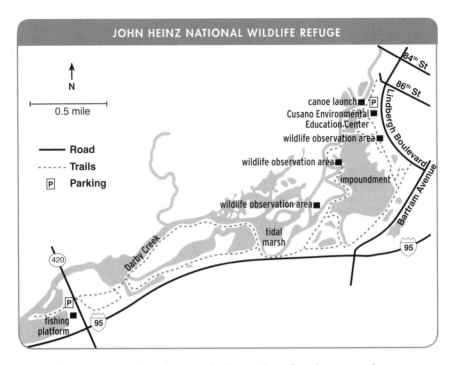

the paths out across the tidal marsh. Ten miles of trails are on the property, and they're all level. Bikes are permitted on most trails. The pedestrian bridge and Impoundment Trail are stroller-friendly, and a 0.6-mile, wheelchair- and stroller-accessible Nature Trail begins at the visitor center and leads to an accessible fishing pier.

Kids can fish in designated areas in the refuge, and a handicap-accessible fishing dock is just across the bridge. Visit fws.gov/heinz/recreate.htm for fishing information and regulations.

Paddling is also permitted in designated areas, including a launch on Darby Creek just north of the visitor center. The creek flows through the marsh. Don't attempt to paddle without checking the tide tables, though. The creek is navigable only within two hours before and after high tide. See the refuge's website for more information.

The refuge sponsors many walks and programs for families, such as wildflower walks and nature story times. Call ahead for details.

Remember: Bikes are not allowed on woodland trails or the boardwalk north of the impoundment. Dogs must be leashed.

PLAN B: Watch the planes take off and land. Or, if you are in a car, head to Ridley Creek State Park (Trip 57) for more hiking, biking, and fishing opportunities, along with a playground and picnicking.

WHERE TO EAT NEARBY: It's best to bring snacks.

Trip 5

West Fairmount Park

Walk or bike around historical buildings, take in Belmont Plateau's skyline views, visit a Japanese house, and discover hidden sculptures.

Address: Belmont Avenue and Montgomery Drive, Philadelphia, PA

Hours: Trails and grounds open 8 A.M. to 1 A.M. daily; Horticulture Center grounds open daily, 8 A.M. to 6 P.M. (closes at 5 P.M. from November through March); Shofuso open weekends in April and October, 11 A.M. to 5 P.M., and Wednesdays through Fridays 10 A.M. to 4 P.M., Saturday and Sunday 11 A.M. to 5 P.M., from May through September; Kelly Pool open 11 A.M. to 7 P.M. in season

Fee: Admission to grounds is free. Admission to Shofuso: adults, $6; children ages 3 to 17, $4

Contact: fairmountpark.org, 215-683-0200; fairmountparkconservancy.org, 215-988-9334; shofuso.com, 215-878-5097; Kelly Pool, 281 North Concourse Drive, 215-685-0174

Bathrooms: None

Water/Snacks: None

Maps: fairmountparkconservancy.org/downloads/FPMapBrochure.pdf; citymaps.phila.gov/

Directions by Car: Take I-76 West (Schuylkill Expressway) to the Montgomery Drive exit. Turn left at the bottom of the ramp, and take Montgomery Drive to Belmont Avenue. Turn left. To enter the Horticulture Center, take the next left. Otherwise continue to the next light and turn left into the park, at the entrance to the Please Touch Museum. Park on the street where permitted. *GPS coordinates:* 39° 59.148′ N, 75° 12.941′ W.

Directions by Public Transit: Take the SEPTA bus 38 or Philly PHLASH to the Please Touch Museum stop.

West Fairmount Park is a huge expanse of green that spreads out along the plateau high above the Schuylkill River. While the Please Touch Museum, in Memorial Hall, is the park's justly celebrated family showpiece, the trails, gardens, and other outdoor features deserve to be as well-known a destination. The park, which is being improved under a long-term plan, is conveniently located and popular.

Memorial Hall dates from the 1876 Centennial Exposition, when 236 acres of Fairmount Park were dotted with numerous pavilions and exhibit halls that

Enjoy some quiet time at the exquisitely serene Shofuso Japanese House and garden in West Fairmount Park.

showcased American scientific and technological accomplishments. "Centennial District" is the official name for this part of the park. Keep an eye out for the numerous sculptures, both old and new, that line the paths and peek out from hidden alcoves.

From the museum, pick up any of the paved paths to walk, stroller, or bike around the park. Several options exist for a route around the area. A marked 5K loop path begins behind the museum. You can make a short, easy loop walk or ride by starting near the museum at the colossal gateway of the Smith Memorial Arch, heading north to the Horticultural Center, and then returning back along Belmont Avenue. To extend the loop, follow signs up to Belmont Plateau, which provides a fabulous skyline view of the city. The 27-acre Horticulture Center and Centennial Arboretum contains several small gardens for kids to explore: a butterfly garden, a hummingbird garden, and a sensory garden, maintained by visually impaired gardeners.

During the warm months, Shofuso Japanese House opens to visitors. The replica seventeenth-century house, with its tatami floors and bark roof, along with the surrounding beautiful Japanese-style courtyard garden and large koi pond, are exotic enough that older kids will enjoy a short tour.

Concourse Lake, currently being restored with plantings, signage, play and picnic areas, and paved paths, is a 7.5-acre lake off of Belmont Avenue, between Avenue of the Republic and South Concourse Street. The restoration project, scheduled for 2013 completion, will make the lake an attractive, stroller-accessible destination for children to discover shoreline wildlife.

Kelly Pool, a free public swimming pool, is next to the Please Touch Museum.

Remember: If visiting Shofuso, you must remove your shoes to enter; socks or stockings are required.

PLAN B: The Philadelphia Zoo is nearby. Across the Schuylkill (take the Spring Garden Street bridge) is the Smith Playground (Trip 7) for young kids, and bike and walking paths along Kelly Drive.

WHERE TO EAT NEARBY: Centennial Café, in the park off Belmont Avenue, is open seasonally. Other than the museum snack bar, food options are scarce. It's best to bring a picnic.

Trip 6

All Ages

Morris Arboretum

Get a squirrel's-eye view of the trees, "Out On A Limb."

Address: 100 East Northwestern Avenue, Philadelphia, PA
Hours: 10 A.M. to 4 P.M. daily and until 5 P.M. weekends, April through October; Thursdays until 8:30 P.M., June through August. Closed New Year's Day, Thanksgiving, Christmas Eve, and Christmas Day.
Fee: Adults, $16; children ages 3–17, student and active military, $7; children under 3, free; seniors (65+), $14; hike, bike, or SEPTA adults, $7, kids, $3; members and PennCard holders, free
Contact: morrisarboretum.org, 215-247-5777
Bathrooms: At the visitor center
Water/Snacks: Water and seasonal café available at the visitor center; picnicking on benches permitted when café is closed
Maps: morrisarboretum.org (click on Plan Your Visit)
Directions by Car: From Center City, take the Ben Franklin Parkway to the Museum of Art. Bear right onto Kelly Drive and follow it to the end onto Lincoln Drive (about 4 miles). Follow Lincoln Drive to its end (3.6 miles) and turn right onto Allens Lane. Allens Lane ends at Germantown Avenue, where you'll turn left. Follow Germantown Avenue through Chestnut Hill. After descending a long hill, turn right onto Northwestern Avenue. The arboretum entrance is 750 yards farther on the right. Continue up the hill to the parking lot. *GPS coordinates:* 40° 5.283′ N, 75° 13.314′ W.
Directions by Public Transit: Take the SEPTA Regional Rail Chestnut Hill East or West line to the Chestnut Hill station. Then take the SEPTA L bus toward Plymouth Meeting Mall. Ask to get off at the Germantown Avenue and Northwestern Avenue stop. Walk down Northwestern Avenue 0.5 mile to the arboretum gate.

Morris Arboretum takes its trees seriously. For families, that means a seriously fun adventure among paths, ponds, wetlands, gardens, plants, and rare trees. Located in Chestnut Hill along the Wissahickon Creek, the 92-acre historical grounds provide plenty of opportunities to play and learn about nature at the same time. Originally a summer home for the local Morris family, the arboretum has been open to the public since 1932, dedicated to promoting an understanding of the relationship among people, plants, and place. Kids can

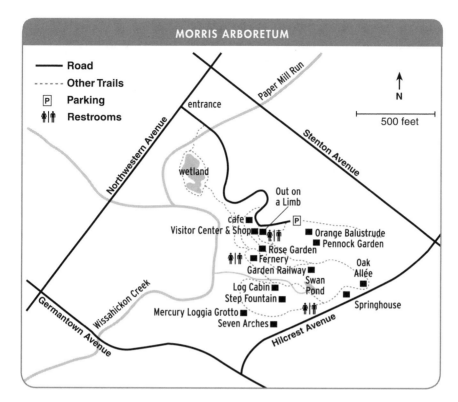

MORRIS ARBORETUM

Road
Other Trails
P Parking
Restrooms

Paper Mill Run

entrance

N

500 feet

Northwestern Avenue

Stenton Avenue

wetland

Out on
a Limb

café
Visitor Center & Shop
P Orange Balustrude
Pennock Garden
Rose Garden
Fernery
Oak
Garden Railway
Allée
Swan
Log Cabin Pond
Step Fountain
Mercury Loggia Grotto
Springhouse
Seven Arches

Germantown Avenue

Wissahickon Creek

Hilcrest Avenue

pick up a "Passport to Tree Adventure" booklet that invites them to do a series of activities all around the arboretum. (See page 17 for a naming-trees activity.)

For children, the centerpiece of the arboretum is "Out On A Limb," a 50-foot-high structure designed to give the experience of living at treetop level. It features a giant bird's nest with child-scale blue robins' eggs, and a "squirrel scramble"—huge rope nets to walk, slide, and bounce across. From the walkways there's a beautiful bird's-eye view of the woods. To find it, follow signs from the visitor center a short distance—or follow the excited kids who have been there before.

Many contemporary sculptures—some interactive, all designed to complement the natural landscape—are scattered throughout, including a giant bell. Stroller-friendly paved walkways wind around the rolling hills, as do gentle woods footpaths, connecting open fields, formal gardens, and shady woods. Among the horticultural highlights are a formal rose garden, an azalea meadow, a Japanese hill and water garden, and a fernery.

During winter, young children delight in the Garden Railway, dozens of model trains that wind in and out of rustic plantings and overhead. Visit the Morris Arboretum website to download winter family fun cards and other activity booklets.

Remember: Don't miss the Swan Pond, the Mercury Temple and (underground) Grotto, and a 1908 log cabin by a stream, which served as the playhouse for young Lydia Morris when her family summered here.

PLAN B: The entrance to Wissahickon Valley Park (Trip 10) is at the bottom of the hill as you continue down Northwestern Avenue. The park offers walking, hiking, biking, and fishing.

WHERE TO EAT NEARBY: Germantown Avenue has a few restaurants, but more places to eat are in Chestnut Hill farther east down the avenue.

During their development, children quickly learn the names of things that are familiar to them, and to distinguish similar-looking objects. Typically, that means naming items they see or play with every day, like cars or video game characters. A century or more ago, their knowledge was more likely to include the names of plants and animals.

Given the chance, kids today will eagerly learn the names of things found in nature too, especially if the activity is easy and fun to do. Trees are a great way to start—they're big, they're everywhere (even in cities), and they can be identified all year round.

An arboretum is the perfect place to teach kids the names of common trees, since the trees are typically labeled there. Once kids learn the name of a tree and what it looks like at eye level, they can deepen their examination. Encourage kids to do more than just look—what they learn from their other senses will be even more memorable:

- Ask them to run their hands over the bark to see how it feels—rough like an oak or smooth like a beech? Is the bark furrowed, like an ash or an oak, or flaky, like a sycamore or a plane tree?
- Have your kids rub a leaf or crush a twig to smell its fragrance. Sassafras smells sweet, black birch has an aroma like wintergreen, black walnut emits a sour fragrance, and white pine needles smell...piney.
- Tell them to examine the tree's seedpods or fruit. Ask them to describe the shapes and colors. Some seedpods, such as those of the sweet gum, are spiny-sharp. The maple's "helicopter" seedpod wings twirl when tossed. Sycamore seeds float on the wind like dandelions.

Once you have taught your kids the names and qualities of a few trees at a garden or arboretum, you can have them look at the trees in their everyday lives. No longer anonymous background objects, the trees will have distinct identities, part of the kids' worlds. Knowing the names of trees will give your children a way to take interest in visiting new places, where they can recognize familiar trees and meet new ones.

Visit these Philadelphia-area arboretums and public gardens or places with tree identification trails for further exploration: Awbury Arboretum (Trip 2), Morris Arboretum (Trip 6), Curtis Arboretum (Trip 19), Pool Wildlife Sanctuary (Trip 44), Haverford College Arboretum (Trip 55), Taylor Arboretum (Trip 56), Scott Arboretum (Trip 60), Warwick County Park (Trip 68), and Winterthur Museum and Garden (Trip 79).

Trip 7

Ages
5-8

Smith Memorial Playground & Playhouse

Enjoy old-fashioned fun at a state-of-the-art playground in Fairmount Park.

Address: Smith Day Nursery Drive, Philadelphia, PA
Hours: Playground open April 1 to September 30, Tuesday through Sunday, 10 A.M. to 6 P.M., and October 1 to December 31, Friday through Sunday, 10 A.M. to 4 P.M.; Playhouse open April 1 to September 30, Tuesday through Friday, 10 A.M. to 4 P.M., Saturday and Sunday, 10 A.M. to 6 P.M., and October 1 to March 31, Tuesday through Sunday, 10 A.M. to 4 P.M.
Fee: Free; donations accepted
Contact: smithkidsplayplace.org, 215-765-4325
Bathrooms: At the Playhouse (when open)
Water/Snacks: Vending machines near restroom in Playhouse
Maps: None
Directions by Car: From Center City, take Kelly Drive north. Turn right at the equestrian statue of General Grant onto Fountain Green Drive, and then take the first right onto Mount Pleasant Drive. At a stop sign, turn right onto Reservoir Drive. Bear right into Smith's circular drive. *GPS coordinates:* 39° 58.930´ N, 75° 11.714´ W.
Directions by Public Transit: Take SEPTA bus 32 to 33rd and Oxford streets or bus 3 to 33rd and Cecil B. Moore Avenue and walk one block south to 33rd and Oxford streets. Walk 0.3 mile into Fairmount Park. Smith will be on your left.

Since 1899, Smith Playground & Playhouse have been delighting children by giving them an extraordinary, safe place in which to play. The 6.5-acre playground, redesigned in 2012, is meant for children age 10 and younger. It is beautifully landscaped and tastefully laid out in separate outdoor "rooms" with state-of-the-art equipment. Kids can climb, bounce, swing, ride, and even pretend to be a train engineer. The rubber surface makes jumping and running easy—and tumbling won't hurt a bit.

For generations of Philadelphia children (and their parents), the highlight of the playground has been the 1905 Giant Wooden Slide. Sitting on recycled burlap coffee bags, you slide—fast!—down the wide incline, and before you know it you're at the bottom…and running back to slide again and again. By comparison, contemporary plastic slides are a snooze.

Downhill thrills never grow old: Smith Playground's 1905 Giant Wooden Slide offers a classic ride.

For slightly older kids, the giant spider web will challenge their climbing ability. Old-fashioned swings are here, but so are high-tech items that respond to movement by upping the challenge. Your child may run from place to place, or stay all afternoon at one piece of favorite equipment.

The 24,000-square-foot, three-story Smith Playhouse, for kids age 5 and younger, may look like any number of nineteenth-century Fairmount Park mansions but in fact was designed specifically to be a playhouse. Its rooms contain old-fashioned toys like dollhouses, play kitchens, and ride-on cars and trains.

Smith is located in Fairmount Park, but is run by a nonprofit organization whose mission is to continue to provide a safe space to play for children of diverse backgrounds.

If your kids still have some energy, head for the paved Boxers' Trail that leads down to Kelly Drive from Reservoir Drive (see Trip 8), but the odds are that with all that Smith has to offer, they'll already have run themselves out.

Remember: There are a few picnic tables, but you can also spread out a blanket on the huge lawn in front of the Playhouse.

PLAN B: The multiuse Schuylkill River Trail (Trip 66) along Kelly Drive is great for walking and biking, and is stroller- and pet-friendly.

WHERE TO EAT NEARBY: It's best to pack a picnic.

Trip 8

Schuylkill Banks & East Fairmount Park

It's the best place in the city to enjoy the Schuylkill River: walk, bike, or paddle.

Address: Kelly Drive at Art Museum Circle, Philadelphia, PA
Hours: Park trails and grounds open daily, 8 A.M. to 1 A.M.; Fairmount Water Works Interpretive Center open Tuesday through Saturday from 10 A.M. to 5 P.M., Sunday from 1 P.M. to 5 P.M.
Fee: Free
Contact: schuylkillbanks.org; fairmountwaterworks.org
Bathrooms: At Lloyd Hall on Boathouse Row
Water/Snacks: A water fountain is at the Water Works parking area; also in Lloyd Hall; snack carts are along Boathouse Row
Maps: schuylkillbanks.org/node/8; fairmountparkconservancy.org/downloads/FPMapBrochure.pdf; citymaps.phila.gov/map; museumwithoutwallsaudio.org
Directions by Car: Take Ben Franklin Parkway to Kelly Drive. To park at the Art Museum garage (fee charged), turn left at Art Museum Drive and drive uphill. Free parking is along Kelly Drive (watch for "no left turn" signs) or the side streets. Two-hour free parking is available at the Water Works parking lot (turn left from Kelly Drive onto Water Works Drive, at the traffic light just before Lloyd Hall). *GPS coordinates:* 39° 57.971´ N, 75° 10.760´ W.
Directions by Public Transit: Take SEPTA bus 38 or Philly PHLASH to the Art Museum stop (22nd and Parkway).

The Schuylkill Banks is a newly completed waterfront park that stretches along the eastern banks of the Schuylkill River between the Philadelphia Museum of Art at the Banks' northern end and Locust Street at its southern end. Its 1.2 miles of level, stroller-friendly, paved paths, ideal for waking or biking, swoop along the landscaped riverbanks, protected from traffic, while giving great views of the city skyline. Plans are in place to extend the trails south, eventually connecting to existing trails in Gray's Ferry and Bartram's Garden (Trip 1). Enter the park from the Water Works pathway below the Museum of Art; by crossing Martin Luther King Drive south of the museum; or by crossing the CSX tracks at 23rd and Race Street or 25th and Locust Street.

At the Water Works, a group of repurposed historical structures along the river just northwest of the Museum of Art, you'll find awesome vantage points

*Breathtaking Schuylkill River vistas reward a walk up
steep bluffs to the Water Works overlook.*

of the river and the Fairmount Water Works Interpretive Center, a fun, interactive exhibit space about watersheds that school-age kids will enjoy. The paved walkway up the rock cliffs to the high point is steep but stroller-friendly.

Paddlers can take advantage of the tidal river. A park concessionaire gives scheduled kayak tours of the lower Schuylkill, and it is permissible to put in a kayak or canoe at the Walnut Street dock as long as it does not interfere with organized events. However, there's no motor vehicle access to the Schuylkill Banks, so boats need to be wheeled or carried to the launch.

Young anglers can enjoy several easily accessed fishing locations, under the Walnut Street bridge and elsewhere along the banks.

The Schuylkill Banks' official boundary is at the Water Works, but the path continues into East Fairmount Park. Follow it by walking between the Water Works complex and the rock cliffs, around the circular Water Works parking lot to Water Works Drive, where the path merges into the Schuylkill River Trail (SRT, see Trip 66). The SRT continues along Kelly Drive through East Fairmount Park. Its paved, wide surface along the river is great for kids to bike or walk, and it accommodates strollers. This section of the SRT is very popular not only with families but with bikers, skaters, and runners, so it can get crowded on weekends; a gravel drive that parallels it is good for pedestrians. On the other side of Kelly Drive are more trails to explore. Starting at Fountain Green Drive is the Boxers' Trail, a paved, 3.8-mile bike and hike trail that goes to Strawberry Mansion by way of Smith Playhouse (Trip 7), following the route of a training path reputedly run by boxing legend Joe Frazier. Other easy walking trails meander through Laurel Hill Cemetery (Kelly Drive at Hunting Park Avenue), which overlooks the river from high bluffs.

Remember: Dogs must be leashed.

PLAN B: In the west side of Fairmount Park (Trip 5) you'll find more trails, as well as the Please Touch Museum and the Philadelphia Zoo.

WHERE TO EAT NEARBY: Head up Fairmount Avenue to find many small shops and restaurants.

Trip 9

Schuylkill Center for Environmental Education

Come to a "green island" in the city with easy trails designed for kids to discover nature in the woods, ponds, and fields above the Schuylkill River.

Address: 8480 Hagys Mill Road, Philadelphia, PA
Hours: Trails and grounds open dawn to dusk daily; visitor center open Monday through Saturday, 9 A.M. to 5 P.M.
Fee: Free
Contact: schuylkillcenter.org; 215-482-7300
Bathrooms: At main building
Water/Snacks: Water fountain at main building
Maps: Print maps at the main building; schuylkillcenter.org/publications/trailmap.html
Directions by Car: From City Center, take Kelly Drive north along the river and turn right onto West Hunting Park Avenue (at the Laurel Hill Cemetery). Continue 0.8 mile on West Hunting Park Avenue, and take a left onto Henry Avenue. Continue on Henry Avenue for 5 miles, and turn left onto Port Royal Avenue. Cross Ridge Avenue and turn right onto Hagys Mill Road. The Schuylkill Center driveway is ahead on the left. Parking is at the end of the half-mile drive. *GPS coordinates*: 40° 3.609′ N, 75° 14.685′ W.
Directions by Public Transit: Take SEPTA bus 9 to Ridge Avenue and Port Royal Avenue. Take a left onto Port Royal Avenue and walk 0.2 mile to Hagys Mill Road. Turn right and walk 0.3 mile to the Schuylkill Center driveway on the left.

The 340-acre Schuylkill Center for Environmental Education (SCEE) is a lush ridgetop and hillside forest in the Roxborough section of the city, with exhibits and trails designed to invite kids to learn about nature while enjoying the outdoors.

SCEE was one of the first urban environmental education centers in the country; it is still the "island of green" for urban dwellers as envisioned in 1965. Start your visit at the main building's Discovery Center, which provides low-tech, hands-on nature activities that give kids (especially those of elementary-school age) a great introduction to the plants and wildlife they will discover on

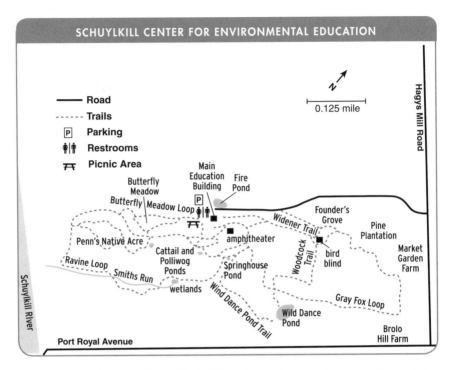

Legend (map):
— Road
----- Trails
P Parking
♦♦ Restrooms
🎋 Picnic Area

0.125 mile

Hagys Mill Road

Butterfly Meadow
Main Education Building
Fire Pond
Butterfly Meadow Loop
Founder's Grove
Pine Plantation
Penn's Native Acre
amphitheater
Widener Trail
bird blind
Market Garden Farm
Ravine Loop
Cattail and Polliwog Ponds
Springhouse Pond
Woodcock Trail
Smiths Run
wetlands
Wind Dance Pond Trail
Gray Fox Loop
Wild Dance Pond
Schuylkill River
Port Royal Avenue
Brolo Hill Farm

the trails outside. Friendly and helpful staff members are happy to share advice that will enhance your kids' experience.

More than 3 miles of well-maintained trails traverse the grounds. They are all suitable for children, though some are steeper than others. The map (available at the visitor center and online) offers detailed descriptions of the trails. The easiest one to begin with is Towhee Trail, which starts behind the main building and leads down to Cattail Pond, where kids can look for frogs and turtles. The very short Butterfly Meadow Loop explores fields of tall grasses and wildflowers in summer and offers a nice view of the city skyline in winter. Widener Trail, a paved, handicap- and stroller-accessible trail, begins in front of the main building, going to a bird blind.

Around the grounds, signs describe interesting environmental features such as the solar panel array and the "green" aspects of the main building.

SCEE has an artist-in-residence and also hosts year-round art and sculpture exhibits inside (and outside) the main building, all with some environmental focus. Call for more details.

Remember: No pets or food are permitted on the trails.

PLAN B: The Schuylkill River Trail (Trip 66) follows along the river below SCEE.

WHERE TO EAT NEARBY: Bring a picnic to the grove near the main building, or head down Ridge Avenue to find shops and restaurants.

Wissahickon Valley Park

If there is "must go" trip in this book, Wissahickon Valley Park is the one. Its rugged beauty in the heart of the city offers endless variety in all seasons.

Address: 300 Northwestern Avenue, Philadelphia PA
Hours: Grounds open 8 A.M. to 1 A.M. daily; Wissahickon Environmental Center open Monday through Friday, 9 A.M. to 4 P.M.
Fee: Free
Contact: fairmountpark.org/WissahickonValleyPark.asp, 215-685-9285; fairmountpark.org/wissahickonec.asp; fow.org
Bathrooms: Next to Valley Green Inn; at Wissahickon Environmental Center; portable or composting toilets along Forbidden Drive
Water/Snacks: A snack bar is at Valley Green Inn
Maps: Map available for purchase at Valley Green Inn or from Friends of the Wissahickon (fow.org)
Directions by Car: To Wissahickon Environmental Center: Take I-76 West (Schuylkill Expressway) to the Green Lane exit. Take the first left onto Main Street, then take the first right onto Leverington Avenue. Turn left onto Ridge Avenue and continue onto Ridge Pike. Turn right onto Church Road, then turn sharply right onto Park Avenue. Make the first left onto Andorra Road to the parking lot on the right. *GPS coordinates:* 40° 5.021′ N, 75° 13.973′ W. (Other parking areas include Forbidden Drive at Northwestern Avenue and at Bell's Mill Road, and Lincoln Drive at Rittenhouse Street.)
Directions by Public Transit: To Wissahickon Environmental Center: Take the SEPTA L bus to Germantown Avenue and Northwestern Avenue and walk 0.2 mile down Northwestern Avenue to Andorra Road.

Wissahickon Valley Park's woods are full of birds and flowers, and the rocky terrain creates a tremendous variety of views, sounds, and experiences. Wissahickon Creek plunges through a rocky, forested ravine on its way to the Schuylkill River.

To get kids acquainted with the 1,800-acre park, walk along Forbidden Drive, a wide, level path that runs along the meandering creek for 5.5 miles from Northwestern Avenue to Lincoln Drive. The gravel path is suitable for strollers and bicycles with thick tires. Helpful maps are placed at intervals along the path.

Wide, level paths follow the rocky, tree-shaded creek through Wissahickon Valley Park.

Forested hills laced with small streams rise steeply on both sides of the creek, with numerous trails—some well marked, others less so. You'll find many spots along the trout-stocked creek for fishing.

For older kids, the trails are a fun challenge, as they go up and down hills, across streams, and along old water supply pipes. Some of the trails are steeper than others; many have small rocks and are slippery when going downhill. Most trails are open to mountain bikers and equestrians.

Special features that kids will love are hidden along these trails. From Rex Avenue, follow the orange and white trails to the 15-foot-high "Indian statue" along the cliff above the creek. Take the orange trail to the Fingerspan Bridge, a sculpture you walk through. Walk through the red Thomas Mill Road covered bridge for a magnificent view of the creek. Near Lincoln Drive, climb the trail behind the stone bridge to reach "Lover's Leap"—a rock parapet high over the creek.

A good introduction to the park for kids under age 8 is the Wissahickon Environmental Center (WEC), in the Andorra Natural Area at the park's northern end. The WEC has educational exhibits and a native-fish aquarium. Trails in this area go through meadows and hills; in general, they're easier than in the other sections. The WEC provides educational programming for families. It's still known as the "Tree House," even though the tree that grew through its front porch has been gone since the 1990s.

Near the park's southern end is Rittenhouse Town, a restored historical village that was the site of the first paper mill in British North America. Tour the visitor center to learn about the history of the town and of papermaking (fee charged, tours weekends only; rittenhousetown.org).

Remember: The nonprofit group Friends of the Wissahickon organizes events, walks, and programs, many suitable for families (fow.org). It also sells an indispensable map of trails, parking, and other structures. Trails in the Andorra section are not open to mountain bikes. Dogs must be leashed. Bring water with you; it's hard to find in the park.

PLAN B: Smith Playground (Trip 7) is a huge playground for young kids.

WHERE TO EAT NEARBY: Go to Germantown Avenue in Chestnut Hill, a busy commercial area.

Trip 11

Pennypack Park

Bike or walk along the banks of Pennypack Creek in this long, linear shaded park.

Address: 8600A Verree Road, Philadelphia, PA
Hours: Trails open dawn to dusk daily; environmental center open Monday through Friday, 9 A.M. to 4 P.M.
Fee: Free
Contact: fairmountpark.org/pennypackpark.asp; pennypackpark.org
Bathrooms: At environmental center
Water/Snacks: Water fountain at environmental center
Maps: pennypackpark.org/ppmap2005
Directions by Car: Take I-95 North to the PA 73/Cottman Avenue exit and merge onto Cottman Avenue. Drive 3.8 miles, then turn right onto Oxford Avenue. Drive 0.3 mile and take a slight right onto Verree Road. Turn into the parking lot. *GPS coordinates:* 40° 5.018′ N, 75° 3.847′ W.
Directions by Public Transit: Take SEPTA bus 67 to Verree Road and Bloomfield Avenue. Walk down Verree Road to the entrance.

Stretching along the steep forested banks of the Pennypack Creek in Northeast Philadelphia, Pennypack Park is one of the most popular areas of the city's treasured Fairmount Park system. Along the banks of the meandering creek are paved, mostly level trails excellent for bicyclists, families with strollers, and walkers. Wooded trails in the hills offer more-challenging hikes; many of these trails are open to horses. Numerous flat spots along the open streambanks are ideal for anglers of various ages.

North of Bustleton Avenue, the natural landscape of the 1,395-acre park is relatively intact. A great place to start your explorations of the park is the Pennypack Environmental Center, near the intersection of Verree Road and Bloomfield Avenue. From behind the center's main building, a trail interspersed with sculptures inspired by the nature writings of Henry David Thoreau winds down to the creek. The creek is remarkably rich in birds and other wildlife; even beavers have been reported to be resettling in this urban refuge.

Other good entrance points with easy parking are located along Pine Road and Krewstown Road. South of Bustleton, the park becomes gradually more open. The restored band shell at Rhawn Street and Rowland Avenue is a fun

Miles of scenic creekside trails wind through Pennypack Park in Northeast Philadelphia.

place for a summer-evening picnic. The 1697 triple-arch Frankford Avenue stone bridge over the creek is the oldest bridge in the United States.

A favorite spot for fishing is a 4-foot dam at Roosevelt Boulevard that creates a picturesque waterfall. Since 2007 several other dams have been removed from the lower stretches of the creek, greatly improving the habitat for fish such as shad, herring, and striped bass.

Picnic tables are at the environmental center, near the parking area at Pine Road, as well as near many other parking lots. A well-shaded, popular tot lot is at Verree Road and Susquehanna Road. Fox Chase Farm, owned by the Philadelphia School District, is across Pine Road from the park. The farm, while not generally open to the public, hosts 4-H (youth farmer) livestock shows, maple sugaring demonstrations, summer Wednesday-evening hayrides, sheep-shearing days, and other events when families can tour the grounds.

Remember: The environmental center offers educational programs for families and children. Call for more details. Pets must be leashed.

PLAN B: Lorimer Park (Trip 13) is northwest of the environmental center (up Bloomfield Avenue and Moredon Road), and offers rock scrambling, fishing, and a rail trail.

WHERE TO EAT NEARBY: Head east on Krewstown Road to find restaurants and shops.

Trip 12

All Ages

FDR Park

Go "down the Lakes" to ride a bike, enjoy a nature walk, or fish in South Philly's green oasis.

Address: South Broad Street and Pattison Avenue, Philadelphia, PA
Hours: Dawn to 9 P.M. daily (6 P.M. from November 1 through March 31)
Fee: Free
Contact: fairmountpark.org/fdrpark.asp, 215-683-0200; fdrpark.org
Bathrooms: At Ashburn Fields; portable toilets throughout park
Water/Snacks: Water fountain at Ashburn Fields
Maps: fairmountparkconservancy.org/downloads/FPMapBrochure.pdf
Directions by Car: Take Broad Street south to Pattison Avenue. Turn right and take left into the park entrance and parking lots. *GPS coordinates:* 39° 54.326′N, 75° 10.430′ W.
Directions by Public Transit: Take the Broad Street Line to AT&T station (formerly Pattison station). Cross Pattison Avenue to the park entrance.

The ponds, woods, and marshes of FDR Park ("the Lakes") in South Philadelphia are unknown to most Philadelphians, who recognize the park only as an alternate parking spot for Eagles and Phillies games. But with a relaxed, family-friendly atmosphere and room for kids to safely roam, it's worth a trip—whether or not you're attending a game.

The 348-acre park is conveniently located at the end of the Broad Street subway line, next to the mammoth sports complex. Originally named League Island Park, it was designed a century ago by the sons of Frederick Law Olmsted, the architect of New York's Central Park. In 1926, it was modified for the nation's Sesquicentennial. The park's designers transformed tidal marshes at the junction of the Schuylkill and Delaware rivers into a serene landscape that includes 77 acres of natural areas where trails wind around lakes, ponds, and lagoons. Birds are abundant, drawn to the mixed forest, marsh, and shoreline habitat. The park is essentially level, so walking or biking is easy for even the youngest kids. Trails explore the shorelines along the lakes and creek, and older kids will enjoy exploring the watery environments. A paved, stroller-friendly bike path loop, about 1.5 miles long, circles the natural areas of the park, beginning at the park entrance. For fun with a different set of wheels,

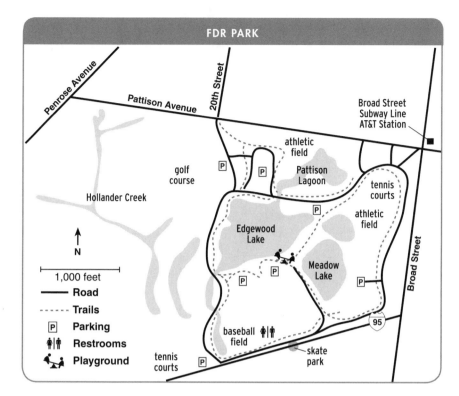

FDR PARK

Penrose Avenue

Pattison Avenue

20th Street

Broad Street
Subway Line
AT&T Station

athletic field

golf course

P

P

Pattison Lagoon

tennis courts

Hollander Creek

P

athletic field

Edgewood Lake

Broad Street

N

1,000 feet

Meadow Lake

P

P

P

Road

Trails

P Parking

Restrooms

Playground

tennis courts

P

baseball field

95

skate park

head to the world-famous skateboarding park in the southern section of the park, under I-95.

For young anglers, Edgewood Lake (the northern of the two lakes) and Meadow Lake are great places to learn the art of fishing. For a nice view of the area, head to the stone gazebo overlooking Meadow Lake. The gazebo is a much-photographed icon of the park. Along the shore, kids will enjoy watching the many ducks that are resident in the lake.

A state-of-the-art playground, including handicap-accessible structures, is near the main entrance, past the tennis courts and baseball fields on the right.

The park is also home to the American Swedish Historical Museum and Bellaire, a Colonial manor house, as well as playing fields and tennis courts. Bike and boat rental facilities are planned for the near future.

Remember: Dogs must be leashed.

PLAN B: The John Heinz National Wildlife Refuge (Trip 4) is a much larger example of the tidal marsh habitat, with 10 miles of walking and biking trails.

WHERE TO EAT NEARBY: The 9th Street Italian Market is open Tuesday through Sunday.

Section 2

Montgomery and Bucks Counties

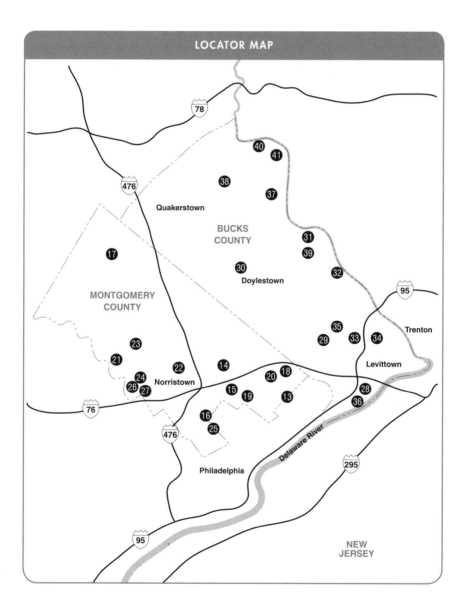

LOCATOR MAP

78

40

41

476

38

37

Quakerstown

BUCKS
COUNTY

31

39

17

30

32

Doylestown

95

MONTGOMERY
COUNTY

35

29   33   34   Trenton

23

Levittown

21

22   14

24   Norristown   20   18

26   27   15   19   13   28

76   16   36

25

466   Delaware River

295

Philadelphia

95

NEW
JERSEY

Trip 13

Ages 9-12

Lorimer Park

Explore rock cliffs, run through tree-lined meadows, fish in the creek, or go sledding at this wooded park on Pennypack Creek.

Address: 183 Moredon Road, Huntingdon Valley, PA
Hours: 8 A.M. to sunset daily
Fee: Free
Contact: montcopa.org/parks, 215-947-3477
Bathrooms: At main-entrance picnic area
Water/Snacks: Water fountain at main-entrance picnic area
Maps: montcopa.org/parks (click on Lorimer Park, then click on Park & Trail map).
Directions by Car: Take I-95 North to the PA 73/Cottman Avenue exit and merge onto Cottman Avenue. Go 3.8 miles, then turn right onto Oxford Avenue. Drive 1.1 miles and turn right onto Pine Road. After 1.5 miles, turn left into Moredon Road. The parking lot is 0.2 mile ahead on the left. The park entrance is across from the lot, on the right. *GPS coordinates*: 40° 5.815′ N, 75° 4.417′ W.

The most distinctive feature of Montgomery County's 230-acre Lorimer Park, along the Pennypack Creek in Abington Township, is the dramatic series of steep rock formations that loom over the creek, the highest of which is known as a "Council Rock," a historical site for Lenape Indian meetings. The steep cliffs of silvery, mica-laden rock (schist and gneiss) provide a beautiful backdrop for walking along the creek. Kids will enjoy scrambling up the rocks via trails that ascend the rocks from the back side near the pedestrian bridge, and looking down from the summit—a definite thrill for (well-supervised, older) children.

In addition to the woods trails, a level, 1.8-mile crushed-stone rail trail is open to walking and biking. Most of the park's 8 miles of trails are open to equestrians and, in winter, cross-country skiers. Kids love sledding down the park's hills when snow is on the ground. Visit in fall for beautiful foliage on the park's huge canopy of trees.

Anglers of all ages can fish from the banks of the creek, which is stocked with trout. The creek runs through the central and north sections of the park, flows past the picnic area, and follows near the rail trail for just over a mile of its length.

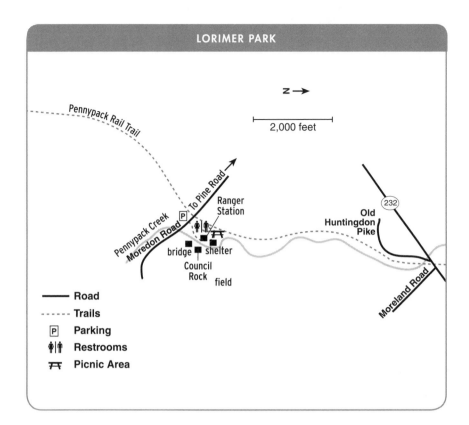

A large picnic area along the creek takes advantage of the pretty views of the cliffs and is a great place to rest after you explore the woods and meadows of the park.

Remember: Pets must be leashed. Swimming is not allowed in the stream, but wading while fishing is OK. The park periodically hosts child-friendly events and programs, such as "Butterflies and Bugs" and bird walks. Check the park's website for schedules and details, or call ahead.

PLAN B: Philadelphia's Pennypack Park (Trip 11), where shaded biking and walking trails follow the creek downstream, is just across Pine Road.

WHERE TO EAT NEARBY: The closest commercial area is along PA 232 (Oxford Avenue, near Rhawn Street). Otherwise, plan to pack a picnic.

Trip 14

All Ages

Green Ribbon Trail

Walk through woods and preserves along the upper reaches of the bucolic Wissahickon Creek.

Address: Four Mills Nature Reserve, 12 Morris Road, Ambler, PA
Hours: Trail open dawn to dusk daily; headquarters open Monday through Friday, 9 A.M. to 5 P.M.
Fee: Free
Contact: wvwa.org, 215-646-8866
Bathrooms: At Penllyn Park, Fort Washington State Park, Evans-Mumbower Mill (when open), Upper Gwynedd Park, and Four Mills Nature Reserve main building (when open)
Water/Snacks: Water fountains at Penllyn Park, Fort Washington State Park, and Upper Gwynedd Park
Maps: Paper maps available at headquarters; wvwa.org/preserves.htm
Directions by Car: Take I-76 West (Schuylkill Expressway) to Exit 331B onto I-476 North. Continue on I-476 to Exit 20. Turn right onto Plymouth Road. After 0.4 mile turn left onto Butler Pike, and continue 4 miles. Turn right onto Morris Avenue. After 0.3 mile turn left into Four Mills Nature Reserve and parking lot. *GPS coordinates:* 40° 8.827′ N, 75° 13.527′ W.
Directions by Public Transit: Take the SEPTA Regional Rail Lansdale/ Doylestown line to the Fort Washington, Penllyn, or Gwynedd Valley stations. From Fort Washington, walk north on Morris Road to Lafayette Avenue, and walk about 0.5 mile to the park entrance. From Penllyn, follow Penllyn Pike south of the station to the GRT trailhead. From Gwynedd Valley, pick up the GRT behind the station.

The Green Ribbon Trail (GRT), 13 miles of mostly level footpaths through young woods along the Wissahickon Creek, links a number of suburban nature preserves and parks, making for a natural area with a variety of hikes for families. Several of the linked parks also offer biking and other activities.

Since the GRT is a linear trail, visitors have various options for access, although parking is limited at some locations. The excellent interactive map on wvma.org indicates parking areas. If driving, a good first stop for families with school-age kids is the Four Mills Nature Reserve, where two 0.5-mile loop trails with interpretive signage help you get oriented to the trail and learn

As you walk Gwynedd Preserve's wide paths, listen for meadowlarks in summer, and bluebirds year-round.

about the preserves. Picnic tables are near the main building, and stepping-stones cross the creek to connect to the GRT.

Just north of the historical, restored Evans-Mumbower Mill, the GRT runs through the 279-acre Gwynedd Wildlife Preserve. There it connects to 5 miles of easy trails that wind uphill from the woods surrounding the creek to extensive hilltop meadows—kids will love the variety of butterflies the meadow attracts in late summer.

For most of its length, the GRT closely follows the creek, with lots of opportunities for checking out the fish and frogs along the banks. At five different points, the trail crosses the creek along specially installed stepping-stones, which kids will enjoy hopping on. Stone bridges and ruins are along the way as well. The trail is well used and, though not consistently blazed, is easy to follow. Signs are posted at road crossings; where the trail is not well defined, green blazes indicate its route.

At Fort Washington State Park (Trip 15), the trail coincides with the Montgomery County multiuse trail that continues to Erdenheim Farm on Stenton Avenus in Flourtown; this 4-mile crushed-stone portion is suitable for biking as well as walking. At Flourtown, the GRT connects via sidewalks along Stenton and Northwestern avenues to the multiuse Forbidden Drive trail through Fairmount Park's Wissahickon Valley Park, adding 8 more miles (see Trip 10).

Remember: An Android field guide app available at wvwa.org shows your position on the trail or any preserve. Dogs must be leashed. The portion of the trail in Fort Washington State Park is stroller-accessible; the rest of the trail is not.

PLAN B: Other good GRT access points with ample parking are at Penllyn Woods, a 77-acre community park with restrooms, a pond, and a picnic pavilion, which is adjacent to the GRT's trailhead at Penllyn Preserve. Upper Gwynedd Park (Parkside Place complex) has restrooms, picnic tables, playground, swimming pool, and other facilities.

WHERE TO EAT NEARBY: North Wales, Ambler, and Flourtown, close to the trail, have commercial areas.

Trip 15

All Ages

Fort Washington State Park

Start with superb views from the Hawk Watch platform before enjoying hiking over wooded hills or fishing in the creek.

Address: Militia Hill Day Use Area, 420 Militia Hill Road, Fort Washington, PA
Hours: 8 A.M. to sunset daily
Fee: Free
Contact: www.dcnr.state.pa.us/stateparks; 215-591-5250
Bathrooms: At Militia Hill and Flourtown day-use areas parking lots
Water/Snacks: Water fountains at restrooms
Maps: www.dcnr.state.pa.us/stateparks (click on Find a Park)
Directions by Car: Take I-76 West (Schuylkill Expressway) to Exit 331B onto I-476 North (Blue Route). Continue to Exit 20 and turn right onto Plymouth Road. After 0.3 mile, turn left onto Butler Pike. Continue 1.6 miles; turn right onto Stenton Avenue, and after 0.7 mile turn left onto Militia Hill Road. The park entrance is approximately 1 mile ahead on the right; continue 0.25 mile ahead to park in Parking Lot 5 for the Hawk Watch platform.
GPS coordinates: 40° 7.255′ N, 75° 13.401′ W.

You'll find no trace of the fort that was here when 12,000 members of George Washington's army camped in winter 1777 before marching to Valley Forge. Nowadays the nearly 500 acres of peaceful wooded hills and streams are alive with families enjoying the fruits of the soldiers' service to a country in the making.

Two day-use areas offer plenty of picnic tables. A good place to start is in the Militia Hill Day Use Area, where the most prominent landmark is the Hawk Watch platform, an observation deck that provides an expansive view of the landscape south toward Philadelphia. Birders flock to the platform in September and October to watch migrating raptors on their southward journey. At all times of the year kids will have fun getting a bird's-eye view of the surroundings. The platform is ADA-accessible and stroller-friendly.

Below the Hawk Watch deck, a short trail winds down to a wide, level footpath paralleling railroad tracks, which connects to the creekside Green Ribbon Trail; this is a pleasant walk for all ages in any season. For older children, unpaved, hiking-only trails of moderate difficulty loop through the woods of

*Watch raptors soar or take in panoramic views from
Fort Washington State Park's Hawk Watch deck.*

Militia Hill west of the Joshua Road crossing. The Wissahickon Creek is trout-stocked in spring and offers warm-water fishing in summer.

In snowy winters, the wide fields and trails in the park are good for skiing or snowshoeing, and the 400-foot slope near Militia Hill is very popular for sledding.

A short trail heads downhill from below the Hawk Watch to a large playground; alternatively, you can drive past the Hawk Watch to Parking Lot 3. The Flourtown Day Use Area has a playground and picnic tables; you can get there on the Green Ribbon Trail but it is easier to drive (see the park map).

Remember: Dogs must be leashed.

PLAN B: From the Flourtown Day Use Area you can gain access to the Green Ribbon Trail along Wissahickon Creek. The level, 2.5-mile paved and hardened trail surface is open to hikers and bikers and is stroller-friendly. The trail continues past PA 73 up the Wissahickon Creek valley to North Wales (see Trip 14). For the remainder of its distance the trail is primarily a natural footpath and is limited to pedestrians.

WHERE TO EAT NEARBY: The commercial area of Fort Washington extends along Bethlehem Pike and Skippack Pike.

Trip 16

Ages 5-8

Riverbend Environmental Education Center

Trails ideal for young children wind through this hillside nature center.

Address: 1950 Spring Mill Road, Gladwyne, PA
Hours: Grounds open dawn to dusk daily; visitor center open Monday through
  Friday, 9 A.M. to 5 P.M. (call ahead for weekend hours)
Fee: Free
Contact: riverbendeec.org, 610-527-5234
Bathrooms: In main building
Water/Snacks: Water fountain in main building
Maps: riverbendeec.org/about (click on Maps & Directions)
Directions by Car: Take I-76 West (Schuylkill Expressway) to the Conshohocken
  exit. Turn right onto PA 23 East. Pass through four lights, and turn left at the
  fifth light onto Spring Mill Road. Pass the Philadelphia Country Club. Follow
  the road downhill, past the No Outlet sign. Turn left at the Riverbend sign,
  and then left into the parking lot. *GPS coordinates*: 40° 4.021′ N, 75° 17.054′ W.

Designed specifically to introduce children to nature, the Riverbend
Environmental Education Center is perfect for young families to get acquainted
with woods, streams, fields, and ponds in a hillside spot above a curve in the
Schuylkill River in Lower Merion Township. Its compact 30 acres harbor a rich
variety of wildlife.

The interconnected, natural-surface trails of dirt or mowed grass are easy
to follow. Because of Riverbend's hillside location, you can't avoid going up-
or downhill, but even the steepest trails are easily navigable by kids (proper
footwear is a must, however). Sassafras Trail climbs from the visitor center
through a small grove of trees; at the top it links to Bluebird Trail, which
heads through the fields. Jack-in-the-Pulpit Trail follows switchbacks down
to a rocky stream and along an old road (which used to go down to the river,
before I-76 was built). For families looking for lengthier hikes, the trails connect to other paths, including Sid Thayer Trail, which offers outstanding views
of the river when the leaves are off the trees.

Some of the structures at Riverbend date from the era when mills thrived
along Lower Merion's numerous swift streams. The visitor center, remarkably,

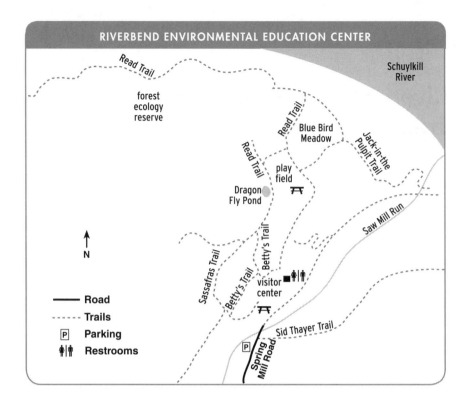

RIVERBEND ENVIRONMENTAL EDUCATION CENTER

is a 1923 Sears catalog barn, which has been renovated and now houses exhibits including live toads, turtles, and other small animals.

In an even earlier era, the native Lenape tribe had a long presence here as well. Informational signs about the history and nature of the land are placed throughout the site.

Remember: Riverbend conducts year-round nature programs for families and a summer camp. Check the website for details. Dogs are welcome but must be leashed.

PLAN B: Rolling Hill Park (Trip 25) is nearby, with hiking trails, as is Valley Forge National Historical Park (Trip 27), with more extensive trails, plus biking and fishing.

WHERE TO EAT NEARBY: Gladwyne center (east on PA 23) has a small commercial area.

Trip 17

Green Lane Park

Many options abound for enjoying wildlife-rich woods and meadows and lakes.

Address: 2144 Snyder Road, Green Lane, PA
Hours: 8 A.M. to sunset daily
Fee: Trails and grounds free; boat rentals and camping require fees
Contact: parks.montcopa.org, 215-234-4528
Bathrooms: At park office parking lot and at day-use areas
Water/Snacks: Water fountain at Deep Creek Day Use Area parking
Maps: parks.montcopa.org (click on Green Lane Park)
Directions by Car: Take I-76 West (Pennsylvania Turnpike) to Exit 331B onto I-476 North (Pennsylvania Turnpike Northeast Extension) to Exit 31 for PA-63. Turn right at the light onto PA-63 West, Sumneytown Pike. Follow it for 9.6 miles, then turn left onto PA-29. After 1.8 miles, take the first right onto Deep Creek Road, then turn right onto Snyder Road to reach the parking area for the main office and Deep Creek Day Use Area. *GPS coordinates:* 40° 19.937′ N, 75° 28.987′ W.

Green Lane Park is a splendid family destination. Surrounding its three forested lakes are miles of trails that take full advantage of the beauty of the park's rugged upper Montgomery County setting, and accommodate all levels of hikers, from beginners to old hands. The woods are rich in birds and wildlife.

A paddle in the quiet Green Lane Reservoir is a great way to take in the scenery. Kayaks may be rented at the Hill Road Day Use Area. The smaller, less scenic Deep Creek Lake can be paddled from the Deep Creek Lake boat rental area, where canoes, kayaks, and paddleboats are available. Both lakes also provide opportunities for fishing; Deep Creek is stocked with trout in spring.

On land, 25 miles of hiking trails wind through the woods. For young kids, easy options are the 2-mile Hemlock Point Trail, a woods trail loop with several lakeside openings in the seldom-used Hemlock Point Day Use Area, and the 1-mile Whitetail Nature Trail, a self-guided nature loop that heads up a stream valley in the Hill Road Day Use Area. In the Deep Creek Day Use Area, the Orange Trail is a long but easy loop that is primarily a woods walk

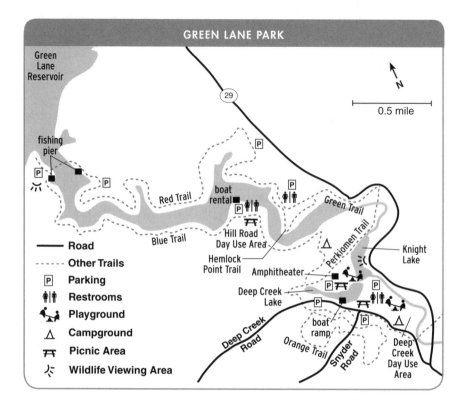

with some creek crossings. For older kids, try parts of the more challenging Blue and Red trails around the reservoir's rocky perimeter; see the park map for details about reaching these trails. (Note: Mountain bikes and horses are permitted on all trails except for Hemlock Point Trail.)

In snowy winters, the trails are popular for snowshoeing and skiing, as they offer great lake views through the woods.

Biking in the park is also popular. A 4-mile section of the multiuse, natural-surface, 20-mile Perkiomen Trail begins in Green Lane and passes through the Deep Creek Day Use Area; this section is suitable for kids 8 and up. A 1.5-mile connector trail leads to it from Hemlock Point (this route offers easy riding, though there is one steep, paved hill that may be difficult for young bikers).

The park also features 30 primitive family tenting campsites, picnic areas, playgrounds, and playfields. Green Lane even has an equestrian campground limited to campers with horses.

Remember: Swimming and private boats are prohibited in the lakes.

PLAN B: Explore the Perkiomen Trail (Trip 26).

WHERE TO EAT NEARBY: It's best to bring snacks and a picnic.

Kids in the Philadelphia area are lucky to be surrounded by one of the largest stretches of open space in the Mid-Atlantic region: the Pennsylvania Highlands.

The 1.9 million acres of the Pennsylvania Highlands offer a wealth of opportunities for outdoor recreation close to home. Beginning along the Delaware River, between Bethlehem and New Hope, the Highlands region arches southwest to the Maryland border in south-central Pennsylvania. Parts of thirteen counties, including Bucks, Northampton, Lehigh, Montgomery, Chester, and Berks, make up this region. This beautiful area boasts extensive forests, many rivers and creeks, and varied terrain, from rugged mountains to rolling hills. Abundant with wildlife, and easily reached by major highways, the parks, nature preserves, and trails throughout the Highlands are must-explore destinations in any season.

Trips in this book that are in the Pennsylvania Highlands are indicated within the trip descriptions. The rivers and streams of the Highlands draw kids' attention with their ever-moving beauty. Kids will get a kick out of looking way down on the mighty Delaware River from the Highlands bluffs at the Mariton Wildlife Sanctuary (Trip 42), or having a snack sitting on the big flat rocks that jut into the rushing Tohickon Creek at Tohickon Valley Park (Trip 37). Roll through the Highlands landscape along a pretty stream by taking a family bike ride on the Perkiomen Trail (Trip 26), which follows the tree-shaded Perkiomen Creek.

Highlands destinations are excellent places for kids to spot wildlife. As spring begins to warm up the woods, kids will love trying to find the tiny frogs that call loudly from hidden ponds in lush Highlands forests, like those along the trails in French Creek State Park (Trip 64). Follow the tracks of white-tailed deer on a winter snowshoe hike through a Highlands preserve such as Green Lane Park (Trip 17). Rent a canoe or kayak at Nockamixon State Park (Trip 38), paddle around the shorelines where the rocky Highlands ridge meets the water, and spot the graceful great blue herons fishing along the quiet shore.

The Appalachian Mountain Club has made the Pennsylvania Highlands a focal area of its conservation work. To find information about where to go and what to do in the region, visit hikethehighlands.outdoors.org. There you can find trip ideas not only for hiking, but also for paddling, biking, fishing, camping, and horse riding. Interactive maps of water trails and footpaths, descriptions of highlight locations, and features including a free app for smartphones help in your trip planning. You can also find out how you can get involved in helping to protect the Pennsylvania Highlands.

Trip 18

Pennypack Preserve

Walk or bike in meadows, in woods, and along old roads in the beautiful upper Pennypack Creek valley.

Address: 2955 Edge Hill Road, Huntingdon Valley, PA
Hours: Trails open dawn to dusk daily; visitor center open Monday through
    Friday, 9 A.M. to 5 P.M., Saturday, 10 A.M. to 2 P.M., Sunday, 1 P.M. to 4 P.M.
Fee: Free
Contact: pennypacktrust.org, 215-657-0830
Bathrooms: Outside visitor center
Water/Snacks: Water fountain outside visitor center
Maps: pennypacktrust.org (click on Trails & Maps)
Directions by Car: Take I-95 North to PA 63 West (Woodhaven Road exit).
    After Woodhaven Road ends, merge left. Turn left at the end of the concrete
    median barrier onto Evans Street, then turn right (north) at the traffic light
    onto Byberry Road. After 5.0 miles, turn left onto Masons Mill Road. At
    Huntingdon Road, turn left. At the rise of a hill, turn right onto Edge Hill
    Road. The entrance is on the left; park in the parking lot. *GPS coordinates:*
    40° 8.635′ N, 75° 5.026′ W.

The 800-plus acres of the Pennypack Preserve are remarkable for their diverse natural beauty and variety of family activities. The grounds are a mosaic of meadows, farm fields, and woods along the Pennypack Creek, interlaced with 11 miles of trails, including 2.6 miles of multipurpose trails open to bikes and horses as well as hikers.

The preserve is owned by the nonprofit Pennypack Ecological Restoration Trust, which has restored many acres of meadows and forest here. Start at the visitor center, which has several small exhibits on local wildlife and nature. Below the visitor center is a pond with an observation deck and openings along the banks where youngsters can look for frogs and turtles.

Creek Road (closed to vehicles), along the creek, is a level, pleasant, multipurpose trail that runs between the creek and woods, and past ruins of mill structures and a historical stone bridge. The trail continues onto Pennypack Creek Trail and Pennypack Parkway (trail). The entire stretch is easily walkable and is open to bikes. Small parking areas are at either end, at

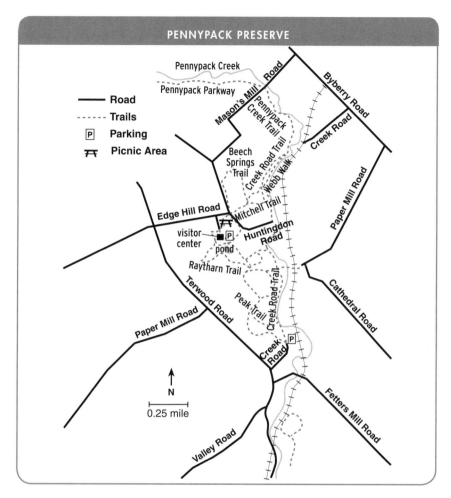

PENNYPACK PRESERVE

——— Road
- - - - - Trails
P Parking
🛆 Picnic Area

Pennypack Creek
Pennypack Parkway
Mason's Mill Road
Pennypack Creek Trail
Byberry Road
Creek Road
Beech Springs Trail
Creek Road Trail
Webb Walk
Paper Mill Road
Edge Hill Road
Mitchell Trail
visitor center
P
Huntingdon Road
pond
Raytharn Trail
Creek Road Trail
Cathedral Road
Terwood Road
Peak Trail
Paper Mill Road
Creek Road
P
N
0.25 mile
Fetters Mill Road
Valley Road

Mason's Mill and Creek roads, providing direct access. Anglers will find many flat, shaded, sandy areas along the creek.

Other trails and natural footpaths traverse the woods and meadows. Most sections are gently hilly, easily hiked by young children; the steeper, rockier Peak Trail offers older kids more of a challenge.

Along the trails are informational signs that describe many of the preservation and restoration projects. The Pennypack Trust offers educational nature programming throughout the year. Call or visit its website for details.

Remember: Dogs are permitted only on designated trails.

PLAN B: Briar Bush Nature Center (Trip 20) has trails and a small museum (fee charged), both of which are good for young children.

WHERE TO EAT NEARBY: The closest commercial area is west on PA 63. Pack a picnic to enjoy at picnic tables near the visitor center.

Trip 19

Ages
0-4

Curtis Arboretum

Enjoy a quiet afternoon strolling through the beautiful woods, open lawns, and paved paths of Curtis Arboretum.

Address: 1250 Church Road, Wyncote, PA
Hours: 8 A.M. to 8:30 P.M. daily, May through August, and 8 A.M. to 6 P.M., September through April
Fee: Free
Contact: 215-887-1000
Bathrooms: None
Water/Snacks: Water fountains (for both people and dogs) at the dog park
Maps: None
Directions by Car: Follow PA 611 north (this starts as Broad Street in Philadelphia and continues on Old York Road) for about 8 miles. Make a left onto Church Road. Cross Washington Lane; the main entrance to the arboretum will be on your left, about a half-mile ahead. *GPS coordinates:* 40° 5.227′ N, 75° 8.920′ W.
Directions by Public Transit: Take the SEPTA Regional Rail to the Jenkintown-Wyncote station, and walk about 1 mile south on Greenwood Avenue to Church Road.

Curtis Arboretum (also known as Curtis Hall) is a 45-acre park in Cheltenham Township located on the former Curtis Estate. The landscaping was designed by Frederick Law Olmsted, who designed New York's Central Park, among other landscapes. Especially good for young children, the park is a friendly, open location for exploring the outdoors. The blue sky doesn't get any bluer nor the green grass any greener for a kid rolling down the long lawn at Curtis Arboretum.

The beautiful grounds include a historical mansion (used for special events) and adjacent grassy terraces where younger kids will enjoy jumping from one level to the next. Wide-open lawns spill down a long hill that provides plenty of room for running, as well as winter sledding. Stroller-friendly, easily walked paved paths wind down to two pretty ponds and end near Rock Creek. In autumn, the township hosts a harvest festival in the park, complete with hayrides.

*Pretty ponds, wide, sloping lawns, and a variety of trees
give Curtis Arboretum a four-season appeal.*

The wooded perimeter of the arboretum is a haven for birds and wildlife in this residential area. More than 50 types of trees grow throughout the park, creating natural picnicking spots with beautiful vistas. Many trees are labeled; for school-age kids it's an opportunity to compare leaf shapes, or fall colors, of the different species. The park is especially lovely in spring, when the hillside offers dramatic views of the flowering trees.

Remember: Fishing is not permitted in the ponds. A leash-free dog park is at the bottom of the hill.

PLAN B: Briar Bush Nature Center (Trip 20) is nearby; although it's not stroller-friendly, the easy trails offer young kids a chance to explore nature.

WHERE TO EAT NEARBY: Head to Glenside Avenue, where you'll find restaurants and shops.

Trip 20

Briar Bush Nature Center

Young kids will enjoy exploring nature along hillside trails and at a large pond, and climbing the Nature Playscape.

Address: 1212 Edge Hill Road, Huntingdon Valley, PA
Hours: Trails open dawn to dusk daily; museum, pond, and bird observatory
 open Monday through Saturday, 9 A.M. to 5 P.M., Sunday, 1 P.M. to 5 P.M.
Fee: Adults, $3; children ages 2 through 17, $2; children under age 2, free
Contact: briarbush.org, 215-887-6603
Bathrooms: In the bird observatory
Water/Snacks: None
Maps: briarbush.org (click on About Us, then Grounds and Facilities)
Directions by Car: Take Broad Street north to Old York Road and continue on
 PA 611 4.5 miles, then turn left onto Susquehanna Road. At the traffic light at
 the top of the hill, turn right onto Edge Hill Road. After 0.25 mile, Briar Bush
 will be on the left at the intersection of Edge Hill Road and Tyson Avenue.
 GPS coordinates: 40° 7.335′ N, 75° 7.677′ W.
Directions by Public Transit: Take the SEPTA Regional Rail Warminster line or
 bus 22 and exit at Roslyn Station (Easton and Susquehanna roads). Walk up
 the hill on Susquehanna Road, and turn left onto Edge Hill Road at the traffic
 light. Briar Bush will be on your left after a few blocks.

Briar Bush Nature Center packs a great deal into only 12.5 acres in the midst of a residential neighborhood in Abington Township. It's a wonderful place for young children to get acquainted with the outdoors in a safe, contained environment.

From the backyard of the nature center, wide, wood-chipped trails meander down a wooded hillside to a big pond where green frogs try to disguise themselves as mud along the shores. The trails total only 1 mile, but that's plenty for the young children for whom this nature center was created.

Along the way, kids can stop at the Nature Playscape, a play area inspired by natural structures, such as logs to balance on and a tunnel to crawl through. The playscape is constructed out of branches, boulders, and other materials found in the woods.

For young children, a natural playscape multiplies the fun of exploring Briar Bush's trails.

In a screened Butterfly House (open seasonally), kids can stand amid flying monarch and painted lady butterflies, and if they're lucky, get one to land on a shoulder. The area around the Butterfly House is stroller-friendly.

The trails are open during winter, which is a good time to look for animal tracks in the snow.

Two indoor spots on the grounds are open for nominal fees. The Griscom Bird Observatory, in a cottage, is a comfortable place to look out onto naturalistic bird-feeding areas. The Nature Museum features interactive exhibits about nature designed for young children. Briar Bush hosts numerous programs throughout the year for families. Check the website or call for more details.

Remember: No pets are permitted.

PLAN B: Pennypack Preserve (Trip 18) is nearby; school-age kids will enjoy its variety of trails along ponds, a creek, meadows, and woods.

WHERE TO EAT NEARBY: Easton Road at Edge Hill is a commercial area with shops and restaurants.

Schuylkill Canal Park/Lock 60

A historical canal is now an inviting spot for easy paddling, walking, and fishing, with connections to a tree-shaded stretch of the Schuylkill River.

Address: 400 Towpath Road, Mont Clare, PA
Hours: 8 A.M. to sunset daily
Fee: Free
Contact: schuylkillcanal.org; montcopa.org/parks, 610-917-0021
Bathrooms: Portable toilets near parking areas
Water/Snacks: None
Maps: schuylkillcanal.org (click on Recreation at the Canal)
Directions by Car: Take I-76 West (Pennsylvania Turnpike) to Exit 328A for US 422 West. Take US 422 West to the Collegeville/Phoenixville exit. At the bottom of the exit ramp, make a left onto PA 29 South and follow it for approximately 3 miles to Mont Clare. Proceed through the traffic light at Produce Junction and cross the bridge to Phoenixville. Look to the right for Towpath Road and a large green sign for Lock 60. Make the right and follow the road to the end, about 1 mile. Parking lots are ahead on the left. *GPS coordinates*: 40° 8.473′ N, 75° 30.491′ W.

Schuylkill Canal Park parallels the Schuylkill River for 2.5 miles from Mont Clare to Port Providence. Built in the early nineteenth century, the canal originally ran for 108 miles. Mule-drawn barges transported coal from Port Carbon to Philadelphia, passing through 92 locks along the way. Today, the Lock 60 section is a quietwater-centered recreation area, managed by the Schuylkill Canal Association.

The canal's steady, slow current makes it easy for families to paddle either up- or downstream. Boat launches are at both ends. You cannot rent boats in the park, but a commercial outfitter is at Fitzwater Station. Along the banks, you'll frequently encounter turtles and ducks unfazed by passing boats.

More-experienced paddlers can portage to the Schuylkill River at Lock 60 and Port Providence (under the high-tension wires that cross the river) for a 5-mile loop.

The Schuylkill River Trail (SRT), a long-distance multiuse trail mostly used by bikes (see Trip 66), can also be accessed here, using the paved towpath that extends to the PA 29 bridge.

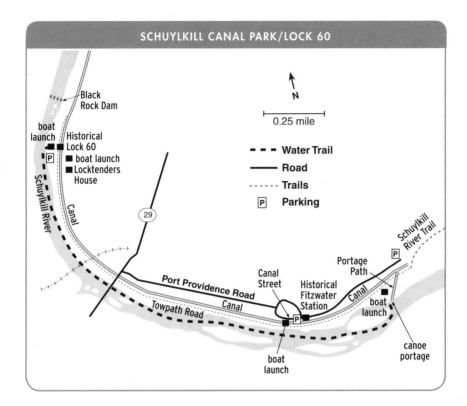

Black
Rock Dam

boat
launch
Historical
Lock 60
boat launch
Locktenders
House

Schuylkill River

Canal

29

N

0.25 mile

Water Trail

Road

Trails

P Parking

Schuylkill River Trail

Port Providence Road

Towpath Road

Canal

Canal
Street

Historical
Fitzwater
Station

Canal

Portage
Path

P

boat
launch

canoe
portage

boat
launch

A fishing dock is located right along the canal at Lock 60. A pleasant, flat path, good for walking, also follows along the canal. More-challenging hiking trails go up into the ravines surrounding the park and over to the Upper Schuylkill Valley Park, which features a Wildlife Center where kids can enjoy up-close experiences with native animals and raptors (see Plan B below).

Remember: The historical Locktenders House at Lock 60 is open to visitors on the third Sunday of every month; here kids can learn about canal history through exhibits and from helpful staff. The lock itself has been restored to working condition and is opened at least once a year for recreational paddlers to experience the up-and-down ride.

PLAN B: To drive to Upper Schuylkill Valley Park, take PA 29 north and turn left onto Black Rock Road, then left onto PA 113 south. You can continue over the river on PA 113 to Black Rock Sanctuary, a 119-acre Chester County park where a 0.75-mile trail descends to the river at Black Rock dam.

WHERE TO EAT NEARBY: Head south on PA 29 to Phoenixville to find restaurants.

Trip 22

All Ages

Norristown Farm Park

Bike or hike on paths that wind around the fields, woods, and streams of a historical working farm.

Address: West Germantown Pike and Barley Sheaf Drive, Norristown, PA
Hours: Grounds open sunrise to sunset daily; visitor center open Monday through Friday, 7 A.M. to 4 P.M.
Fee: Free
Contact: parks.montcopa.org, 610-270-0215; www.dcnr.state.pa.us/stateparks; farmpark.org
Bathrooms: At visitor center (when open) and Picnic Pavilion; portable toilet at Whitehall Parking Lot
Water/Snacks: Water fountain outside visitor center
Maps: www.dcnr.state.pa.us/stateparks (click on Find a Park)
Directions by Car: Take I-76 West (Schuylkill Expressway) to Exit 329 and turn right onto South Henderson Road. After 1.4 miles, turn right onto East Dekalb Pike. In 0.5 mile, turn right to stay on Dekalb Street. Continue 2.6 miles, then continue onto Dekalb Pike. After 1.1 miles, turn left onto West Germantown Pike. After 1.3 miles, turn left onto Barley Sheaf Drive. Continue and take a slight right onto Upper Farm Road. Follow the road to the main parking lot. (Many additional lots are available; see park map.) *GPS coordinates*: 40° 8.939′ N, 75° 20.090′ W.

Norristown Farm Park's unusual history creates a quirky context for its many opportunities for biking, hiking, and fishing in both natural and agricultural areas. The 690-acre park has been farmed continuously since Colonial times. In 1876, the property was purchased by the state, and for nearly a century it was farmed by patients at the adjacent state psychiatric hospital, providing all the food used at the facility. Nowadays, the state still owns the land (it's technically a state park) but the park is operated by Montgomery County and its 450 acres are farmed by a tenant farmer.

Eight miles of trails cover the park, seven of them paved and suitable for bikes, strollers, and wheelchairs. Start at the main parking lot and follow the trail along Upper Farm Road in either direction. On a hilltop west of Upper Farm Road is the large (1-acre) Farm Pond where there is a bird blind.

The perimeter biking and hiking path at Norristown Farm Park passes by fields of growing crops.

Open farm fields predominate in the park's western section. A 2-mile paved route starts across the creek from Parking Lot 3 (near the High Arch Bridge) and goes along Whitehall Road (where there's an alternate entrance and parking lot) and around the reservoir. This is a good biking route for younger kids, though note that there's no shade around the farm fields. Stony Creek and Kepner Creek wind through and eventually join together through the middle of the park, where the trails are steeper and more forested. Follow the trail down Stony Creek Road or Lower Farm Road to cross the creek and get to a connector trail to the Schuylkill River Trail (see Trip 66).

A hiker-only nature trail leads along Stony Creek and can be reached from the Spring House. Both the Stony Creek and Kepner Creek are trout-stocked. Farm Pond is also good for fishing.

Plenty of picnic tables can be found in the park. In winter the trails are open for cross-country skiing or snowshoeing. Kids also enjoy sledding off Upper Farm Road near Shannon Mansion.

Remember: Dogs must be leashed. Any of the roads or paved trails can be used by park or farm equipment; exercise caution and pay attention.

PLAN B: Elmwood Park Zoo, adjacent to the park, is a great little zoo for young kids.

WHERE TO EAT NEARBY: Shops and restaurants are on West Germantown Pike.

Trip 23

Evansburg State Park

Shady Skippack Creek is the centerpiece of this linear, forested park where visitors can hike, ride mountain bikes, and fish.

Address: 851 Mayhall Road, Skippack, PA
Hours: 8 A.M. to sunset daily
Fee: Free
Contact: www.dcnr.state.pa.us/stateparks; 610-409-1150
Bathrooms: At most parking areas
Water/Snacks: Water fountains at many restrooms
Maps: www.dcnr.state.pa.us/stateparks (click on Find a Park)
Directions by Car: Take I-76 West (Schuylkill Expressway) to Exit 328A and merge onto US 422 West. After 9.3 miles, merge onto PA 29 North. After 2.6 miles, turn right onto East Main Street, which becomes Ridge Pike; take a slight left onto Germantown Pike. After 1.3 miles, turn left onto Skippack Road, then after 1 mile turn left onto Mill Road, and continue to the park entrance on Mayhall Road. There are many parking lots. The "Pines" lot is past the office near a large playground. *GPS coordinates:* 40° 12.008′ N, 75° 24.061′ W.

Evansburg State Park is a long, linear park that follows the path of its central natural feature, the Skippack Creek. Although it is in the midst of a populous area, the park seems less crowded than other state parks in the region. It's a quiet, peaceful creekside refuge where families can relax and enjoy the essential beauty of southeastern Pennsylvania—a place where people and nature are on the same scale.

The park is set in a narrow woodland valley. In wet weather visitors can expect trails along the creek to be quite muddy. Trails that are open to horses and mountain bikes get even muddier. Use hiking-only trails for the best experience with kids. The main park area off of Mayhall Road, which features several picnic pavilions and a large, popular playground, is the best place to start. For young kids, a good short (1.5-mile) out-and-back hike descends from the trailhead near the restrooms at the "Pines" picnic pavilion (look for the sign for Skippack Creek Loop Trail), crosses a small footbridge, and follows the yellow-and-blue-marked trail through woods along high ground above the old mill race, to a recently refurbished bridge over the creek at Mill Road

Wooly bear caterpillars tickle your fingers when you pick them up to move them off the trail.

(closed to vehicles). There are great views of the very pretty creek here, and it's a popular fishing spot. For older children, you can head over the bridge to continue on the 5-mile Skippack Creek Loop Trail, which gives access to the creek along the way.

Young anglers will enjoy fishing year-round; the creek is trout-stocked in spring. An ADA-accessible fishing pier is located in the Lewis Road picnic area.

The Friedt Visitor Center is an eighteenth-century house that features exhibits on the German Mennonites who owned the home for almost two centuries. Call ahead to schedule a visit.

Remember: Hunting is permitted in certain areas of the park. During hunting season, exercise caution on trails in these areas; wear blaze orange or go to the park on Sundays, when hunting is prohibited.

PLAN B: You can gain access to the multiuse Perkiomen Trail (Trip 26) in Collegeville and Graterford; also nearby is the John James Audubon Center at Mill Grove (Trip 24), with hiking trails.

WHERE TO EAT NEARBY: Take the Germantown Pike north a short distance to Collegeville at the PA 29 intersection, or go north on PA 73 to the village of Skippack, where diverse commercial areas feature a variety of shops and restaurants.

Trip 24

John James Audubon Center at Mill Grove

Take a hike or a bike ride to be inspired by the woods, fields, and creeks that shaped the career of naturalist and artist John James Audubon.

Address: 1201 Pawlings Road, Audubon, PA
Hours: Grounds open Tuesday through Sunday, dawn to dusk; museum open Tuesday through Saturday, 10 a.m. to 4 P.M., Sunday, 1 to 4 P.M.
Fee: Grounds, free; museum admission fee: adults, $4; children ages 2 to 17, $2; children ages 2 and under, free
Contact: pa.audubon.org, 610-666-5593
Bathrooms: At the pavilion
Water/Snacks: Water fountain outside the pavilion
Maps: In kiosks at parking area and trailhead
Directions by Car: Take I-76 West (Schuylkill Expressway) to Exit 328A and merge onto US 422 West. After 3.6 miles, take the PA 363N/Trooper Road exit. Merge onto South Trooper Road and make an immediate left onto Audubon Road. Go 1.2 miles to the third left onto Pawlings Road, and follow it to the parking lot. *GPS coordinates:* 40° 7.361′ N, 75° 26.278′ W.

Mill Grove was the first American home of John James Audubon, the Haitian-born naturalist and artist whose name is now virtually synonymous with American birding. The 175-acre site preserves the house where Audubon lived as a young man from 1803 to 1806, along with the surrounding forests and fields along the Perkiomen Creek, where he first encountered the landscape that inspired his love for wildlife.

The main attraction of the site for families is the network of trails. About 6 miles of natural footpaths wind through the property. From the parking lot you can follow Wetherill Trail a short distance to the green-blazed John's Trail, a rocky path that finds its way down to the shallow creek, where kids can splash and look for fish. John's Trail connects to the blue-blazed Copper Mine Trail, along which you'll see remnants of historical mine structures. For a gentler walk, head uphill from the parking lot to the blue-blazed Lucy's Trail, which goes through wildflower meadows and fields.

Exploring sunny wildflower meadows is twice as fun when you go with a friend.

A paved bike trail, the 4.5-mile Audubon Loop, circles the perimeter of the property along Pawlings Road and above the Perkiomen Creek. It is suitable for kids but does include a few steep hills. Gain access to the trail near the property entrance at Pawlings Road. Audubon Loop connects to the Schuylkill River Trail (see Trip 66) and the Perkiomen Trail (see Trip 26), if you're looking for a longer ride.

The three-story stone house Mill Grove, built in 1762, is now a museum that includes displays of Audubon's art, including *Birds of America*, the book that first earned him fame with its life-size paintings of birds.

Picnic areas are near the pavilion, across from the parking lot. Throughout the year, Mill Grove (owned by Audubon Pennsylvania) sponsors educational programs and events for families. Visit the website or call for details.

Remember: Dogs are not permitted on the trails, though leashed dogs are permitted on the paved Audubon Loop.

PLAN B: Valley Forge National Historical Park (Trip 27) has bike and hiking trails, as well as several historical buildings and an interpretive center.

WHERE TO EAT NEARBY: Return to Trooper Road to find restaurants.

Birds are everywhere. They're easily seen, colorful, and vocal. Year-round inhabitants of every environment—from cities to countryside, woods to seashore—birds are the most widely observed wildlife.

Introduce your kids to the fun of watching birds and they'll have a hobby that will last a lifetime, traveling with them whenever they are outdoors.

Bird-watching can be as simple as pointing to a bird and asking your kids what color it is, then comparing it to another bird. Ask them to describe what the bird is doing: Eating? Flying? Singing? Can they sing the bird's song? When you get back home, get out the crayons and have your children draw the bird.

As your child gets older, you can encourage a closer look at birds. Invest in a good, sturdy pair of binoculars; test them first to make sure they feel good in your child's hands. If they're waterproof, all the better. Both of you will be amazed at how much more detail you'll see through the lenses. A good portable bird field guide will help you further your investigation. Contemporary field guides are also interactive, including apps you can download that have facts, pictures, and even bird sounds. For an online guide to learning about birds, check the Audubon Society's website, audubonbirds.org.

In identification, a bird's sound is as definitive as its plumage. Start by having your child listen for the songs of common, year-round, backyard birds, like the chick-a-dee-dee-dee of the chickadee or the cheer, cheer of the cardinal. After picking up some songs, kids can graduate to forest-dwelling or water-loving birds. For these, you may need a sound-capable field guide. Lots of portable gadgets and smartphone apps can help your child identify bird calls and songs.

Knowing which bird you're looking at helps you understand what it is you're watching. But bird-watching is much more than identifying the bird—and for some kids that may be the least interesting part. What's the bird doing, and why? In nesting season, watch the birds as they court, stake out territory, gather food for chicks, and teach their fledglings to fly.

A great place for kids to watch birds is Peace Valley Park (Trip 30), which has a bird blind with multiple feeders around a small pond. Ducks, gulls, herons, and ospreys can be seen at Silver Lake Nature Center (Trip 28), where an observation deck fronts a quiet stretch of water. At the John Heinz National Wildlife Refuge (Trip 4), a bird-watching deck crosses the impoundment pond. The Wetlands Institute (Trip 81) and the DuPont Environmental Education Center (Trip 77) feature great views of marshland from boardwalks and observation decks.

Trip 25

Ages
5-8

Rolling Hill Park

Walk in the woods through a hideaway park with historical ruins and a sparkling creek at the bottom of the hill.

Address: 1301 Rose Glen Road, Gladwyne, PA
Hours: Sunrise to sunset daily
Fee: Free
Contact: lowermerion.org, 610-645-6220; lmconservancy.org; bridlewildtrails.org
Bathrooms: None
Water/Snacks: None
Maps: A map is posted in the parking lot
Directions by Car: Take I-76 West (Schuylkill Expressway) to Exit 337 for Gladwyne; merge onto Hollow Road and follow it to Conshohocken State Road (PA 23) west. Continue into Gladwyne center and turn right at the traffic light onto Youngsford Road, then take the first right onto Rose Glen Road. Follow this road to the park entrance on the right. *GPS coordinates:* 40° 2.456′ N, 75° 16.321′ W.

The 103 wooded acres of Rolling Hill Park are mostly hidden behind meadows until you start exploring the eponymous hill. The park, owned by Lower Merion Township and also the headquarters of the nonprofit Lower Merion Conservancy, spills down a steep forested ravine, at the bottom of which is Mill Creek. The trails are of varying difficulty. The blue-blazed trail is recommended for kids due to its more-gradual slopes. It connects to the white trail, which begins near the off-leash dog area at the top of the hill.

Mill Creek is wide, shallow, and rocky—a nice place to splash, look for tadpoles, or try a bit of fishing. Along the creek are ruins of old mill buildings and some informational signage about the history of this creek: It's a bucolic waterway now, but its name reveals its past glory as a thriving industrial center during the water-powered era.

Around the conservancy's headquarters building—a nineteenth-century cottage at the end of a driveway off the parking lot—is a natural playscape.

The park was once the estate of Walter C. Pew (of the prominent Philadelphia Pew family, founders of Sun Oil). Much of the estate was destroyed by fire in 1958, but remnants of the mansion, the pool, and associated stone structures

Half-hidden ruins peeking from Rolling Hill's trails evoke the early history of Mill Creek.

grace the top of the hill; terrace walls serve well as picnic benches. Here you will also find a lovely wildflower butterfly garden full of colorful flowers that attract just as colorful—but more elusive—butterflies for kids to watch during summer.

The park's trails connect to an extensive trail system in the township that is owned and maintained by the private Bridlewild Trails Association (which also maintains Rolling Hill's trails); a map is available to members (see website).

Remember: Dogs must be leashed if not in the off-leash area.

PLAN B: Riverbend Environmental Education Center (Trip 16) is nearby; its trails are suitable for children of various ages.

WHERE TO EAT NEARBY: The closest commercial area is on Conshohocken State Road in Gladwyne.

Trip 26

All Ages

Perkiomen Trail

Walk or bike this easy, pretty rail trail through a historical rural creek valley.

Address: Pawlings Road (near US 422), Audubon, PA
Hours: Dawn to dusk daily
Fee: Free
Contact: trails.montcopa.org/trails, 610-287-6970
Bathrooms: At Pawlings Road and some other trailheads
Water/Snacks: Water fountains at bathrooms
Maps: trails.montcopa.org/trails; schuylkillrivertrail.com
Directions by Car: For the Pawlings Road trailhead, take I-76 West (Schuylkill Expressway) to Exit 328A and merge onto US 422 West. After 3.6 miles, take the PA 363 North/Trooper Road exit. Merge onto South Trooper Road and make an immediate left onto Audubon Road. Go 1.2 miles to the third left onto Pawlings Road, and follow it 1.2 miles, over US 422, to the parking lot on your right. *GPS coordinates*: 40° 6.883´ N, 75° 27.327´ W.

The Perkiomen Trail is a 21-mile multiuse trail that runs from Oaks to Green Lane in Montgomery County. The trail generally follows the route of an old railbed in the Perkiomen Creek valley, through a varied and pretty rural landscape of woods, farmland, and historical towns and villages, with the creek a constant companion below.

The trail surface is mostly crushed stone, making it suitable for walking, bicycles (with thick tires), and strollers. Because it follows a converted railbed, the trail is level with an overall gentle grade (uphill going north, downhill going south), making it an easy ride or walk for kids of various ages. With the ever-moving creek on one side and bucolic scenery of woods, meadows, or towns on the other, the trail is a stimulating yet calming place for kids, and the wide, level trail lets them put on some speed comfortably.

The Pawlings Road trailhead is a good spot to gain access to the trail. Eleven other trailheads, including the northern end at Green Lane, are along the trail (see website for details of location and parking).

The trail passes by some towns, including Arcola, Collegeville, Schwenksville, and Spring Mount, and several parks, including Valley Forge

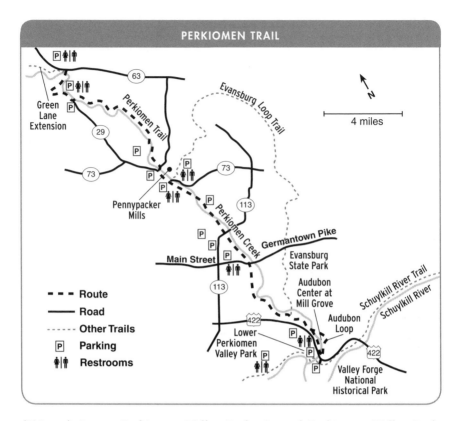

Route
Road
Other Trails
P **Parking**
Restrooms

Green Lane Extension

Perkiomen Trail

Pennypacker Mills

Evansburg Loop Trail

4 miles

Perkiomen Creek

Main Street

Germantown Pike

Evansburg State Park

Audubon Center at Mill Grove

Schuylkill River Trail

Schuylkill River

Audubon Loop

Lower Perkiomen Valley Park

Valley Forge National Historical Park

(Trip 27), Lower Perkiomen Valley Park, Central Perkiomen Valley Park, Pennypacker Mills Historic Site, and Green Lane Park (Trip 17).

Remember: The trail may be crowded on summer weekends, making it difficult to navigate with strollers. There are a fair number of ungated road crossings, so kids need to be supervised on the ride. Dogs must be on a leash 6 feet or less in length.

PLAN B: Perkiomen Trail connects with the Schuylkill River Trail (see Trip 66) and Audubon Loop Trail (see Mill Grove, Trip 24) near the Pawlings Road trailhead, and with the Evansburg Loop Trail, which goes to Evansburg State Park (Trip 23).

WHERE TO EAT NEARBY: Bring snacks or explore one of the trailhead towns.

Trip 27

Valley Forge National Historical Park

Experience history outdoors in this huge park with hike and bike trails.

Address: 1400 North Outer Line Drive, King of Prussia, PA
Hours: Grounds open 7 a.m. to dusk; visitor center open 9 A.M. to 5 P.M.
Fee: Free
Contact: nps.gov/vafo
Bathrooms: At visitor center (when open), main parking lot, and Washington's Headquarters; portable toilets at northside (Betzwood) parking area
Water/Snacks: Water fountain in visitor center (when open)
Maps: At visitor center; nps.gov/vafo (click on Plan Your Visit)
Directions by Car: Take I-76 West to Exit 328A and merge onto US 422 West. After 2.8 miles, take the Valley Forge exit onto PA 23 west. Turn left at the exit ramp and merge into the center lane. The park entrance is straight through the first set of traffic lights, at the intersection with North Gulph Road. Follow signs to the main parking lot. *GPS coordinates:* 40° 6.109′ N, 75° 25.342′ W.

Valley Forge National Historical Park, with its wide variety of popular hiking and biking trails, is a great place for kids. While it can be enjoyed for its natural beauty alone, its history gives the experience a special charge.

The park commemorates the harsh winter encampment of 1776–77 that transformed George Washington's ragtag soldiers into a disciplined fighting force. The visitor center has excellent exhibits that describe this turning point of the American Revolution. More exhibits are at Washington's Headquarters and in re-created soldiers' huts. The park also offers guided walking tours, a cell phone tour, and occasional re-created encampments.

Valley Forge has a diverse landscape on both sides of the Schuylkill River. South of the visitor center, the park spreads over hilltop grassy fields. Closer to the river the terrain is more steep and wooded. Two high hills, Mount Misery and Mount Joy, flank Valley Creek between the Covered Bridge and the river. North of the river is a level, forested floodplain. More than 28 miles of trails, 19.5 of which are designated for hiking, traverse the park. The 1.5-mile Valley Creek Trail, with an easy, flat, gravel surface good for hiking or biking, runs along the tree-shaded creek; pick it up across PA 23 from Washington's Head-quarters and continue to the Covered Bridge. The trail connects at both ends

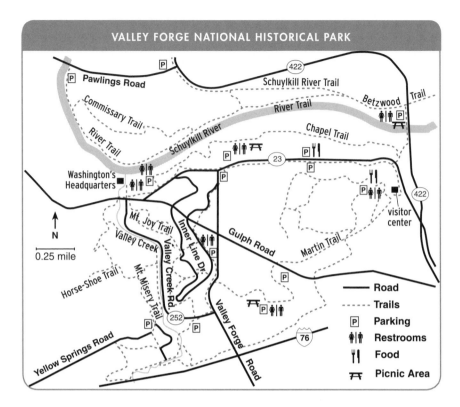

VALLEY FORGE NATIONAL HISTORICAL PARK

to trails over Mount Misery that, while rocky and steep in parts, are suitable for kids used to hiking. Across PA 252 are similar trails that go over Mount Joy. On the north side (Betzwood trailhead), the 3-mile, level, gravel-surface River Trail, open to hiking and biking, parallels the Schuylkill under huge old trees, ending at the Pawlings Road trailhead.

Bicycles can be rented at the visitor center parking lot, and 21 miles of trail are open to bikes. The paved Joseph Plumb Martin Trail, reached from the visitor center, has a 5-mile loop that parallels roads and drives, offering a good way to see the park's historic sites. The path has some hills but they are not steep.

Valley Creek is trout-stocked; many good fishing spots are along its wide banks south of the Covered Bridge (catch-and-release only). For paddlers with experience, a tranquil 3-mile stretch of the Schuylkill River can be accessed from boat launches at Betzwood and Pawlings.

Remember: Dogs must be leashed. Fishing is not permitted in Valley Creek south of PA 23.

PLAN B: At the Pawlings Road trailhead, gain access to the multiuse, 21-mile Perkiomen Trail (Trip 26) or Schuylkill River Trail (Trip 66).

WHERE TO EAT NEARBY: King of Prussia Mall is close by (take US 422 East).

Trip 28

Ages 5-8

Silver Lake Nature Center

Flat, peaceful trails and small, sun-splashed lakes invite families to spend time together exploring nature.

Address: 1306 Bath Road, Bristol, PA
Hours: Trails open sunrise to sunset daily; nature center open 10 A.M. to 5 P.M. Tuesday through Saturday, noon to 5 P.M. Sunday
Fee: Free
Contact: silverlakenaturecenter.org, 215-785-1177
Bathrooms: In the nature center
Water/Snacks: Water fountain at nature center
Maps: silverlakenaturecenter.org (click on About Us)
Directions by Car: Take I-95 North to Exit 40 and turn left onto PA 413 North (Veterans Highway). After 0.6 mile, turn right at the first cross street, Ford Road. Follow Ford Road 0.3 mile and take a slight right onto Bath Road. Continue 1.3 miles to the nature center entrance on your left. (Note: Just after the nature center entrance is the entrance to Silver Lake County Park. The two lots are not connected.) *GPS coordinates*: 40° 6.780´ N, 74° 51.817´ W.

At Silver Lake Nature Center, families can enjoy a variety of activities suitable for different ages and interests, in a well-cared-for setting of woods, lakes, pond, and marsh.

The park's landscape looks a lot like that of South Jersey and southern Delaware—flat and sandy, with lots of hollies and pines sprinkled in the hardwood forests. There's a good reason for the similarity: The park sits on Pennsylvania's tiny sliver of coastal plain, so it is in fact the same flat, sandy soil. This makes for easily walkable trails, which are natural footpaths or boardwalks in marshy spots. Two small lakes connected by the Mill Creek flank the nature preserve. Magnolia Lake was a by-product of Pennsylvania Turnpike construction, while Silver Lake is a descendant of a centuries-old mill pond.

Begin your visit at the nature center, which features small but fascinating exhibits about local plants and animals, as well as the coastal plain. Two miles of well-marked trails fan out from the center through 60 adjoining acres. They include a handicap-accessible trail, a half-mile of stroller-friendly, paved trails, and a "Kids Krawl" designed to give children a close-to-the-ground experience of the woods. Adjacent to a picnic area is a children's play area that

Watch for herons, egrets, and gulls from the deck over the water at Silver Lake.

encourages young kids to explore "off-trail" in a safe, contained space, featuring interactive natural apparatus such as a teetering bridge and a sand "fossil pit." Older kids can watch for ducks, egrets, and occasional eagles from wildlife observation platforms that overlook the lakes along the stream. Young anglers will enjoy fishing in the lakes themselves, from boats or along the banks.

Across Bath Road from the nature center is the 175-acre Delhaas Woods section of the property. The 2.5 miles of trails here are not difficult, but they are more suited for the experienced trail walker. The trails are not quite as well marked or as open as those on the nature center side.

The nature center sponsors several hundred family-oriented programs every year. Visit the website or call for details.

Remember: No pets or bikes are permitted in the nature center. Nonmotorized boats are permitted; the best launch site is from the Silver Lake County Park parking lot. Fishing is prohibited in the stream and from the observation platform.

PLAN B: Silver Lake County Park, next to the nature center, has 200 additional acres of wide-open spaces, ball fields, and picnic areas.

WHERE TO EAT NEARBY: Along PA 413 or US 1 are plenty of places to eat.

Trip 29

Churchville Nature Center

Intimate trails and a welcoming staff invite young children to explore nature.

Address: 501 Churchville Lane, Churchville, PA
Hours: Trails open sunrise to sunset daily; visitor center open 10 A.M. to 5 P.M. Tuesday through Sunday; Lenape village open to the public for tours on Sundays from 1 to 4 P.M., April through October
Fee: Free
Contact: churchvillenaturecenter.org, 215-357-4005
Bathrooms: In the visitor center
Water/Snacks: Water fountain at visitor center
Maps: churchvillenaturecenter.org (click on About Us)
Directions by Car: Take I-95 North to the exit for PA 132/Street Road. Turn left onto PA 132 West and follow it 6 miles to Bustleton Pike. Turn right onto Bustleton Pike and get into the left lane. At the second traffic light, get into the left turn lane. Turn left to continue on Bustleton Pike. After 2 miles, at the next traffic light, cross over Bristol Road; you are now on Churchville Lane. Continue 1 mile to the nature center on your left, just after you cross over the reservoir. *GPS coordinates:* 40° 11.153′ N, 74° 59.574′ W.

If little 54-acre Churchville Nature Center seems specifically designed to make young kids feel at home outdoors, that's because it is.

While nearby Tyler State Park offers wide-open spaces and plenty of room for hiking, biking, fishing, and other activities, Churchville's intimate trails are perfect for getting young children comfortable exploring nature.

The 2 miles of trails are color-coded and easy to follow; all start at the visitor center. They take you to a diverse set of habitats to explore—woods, marsh, meadows, pond, lake, even an apiary. For children ages 8 and under, the trails offer numerous opportunities to explore nature just by doing what comes naturally. They can watch birds from a bird blind, imagine they're living in the woods in a re-created Lenape village, or search for frogs under lily pads.

Churchville feels a bit larger than it is because it's adjacent to the Churchville Reservoir, as well as to several hundred acres of open space (county and local parkland and private lands), which contribute to the abundant wildlife that can be found at the nature center.

Discover how trees are drilled for sap at Churchville's annual maple syrup demonstration.

The enthusiastic and knowledgeable staff of this Bucks County park, who can be found both at the visitor center and along the trails, are eager to talk with kids. Numerous programs are designed to entertain youngsters while acclimating them to the outdoors. Visit the website or call for more details.

Remember: Paths are handicap-accessible and wheelchairs are available. Yellow Trail, behind the main building, is paved; all-terrain strollers can traverse the other paths, which are dirt. No fishing is permitted in the reservoir. Bicycles and pets are not permitted. Bring snacks and have a picnic at one of the many picnic tables.

PLAN B: Tyler State Park (Trip 35) and Core Creek Park (Trip 33) are nearby, offering hiking, biking, and paddling.

WHERE TO EAT NEARBY: Follow Bustleton Pike, becoming PA 232, north to Richboro, where there are several shopping areas.

Peace Valley Park

Peace Valley's size and variety of activities make it "just right" for families.

Address: 170 North Chapman Road, Doylestown, PA
Hours: 8 A.M. to sunset daily; fishing pier open 24 hours a day
Fee: Grounds, free; fee for boat rental in season
Contact: buckscounty.org, 215-822-8608; peacevalleynaturecenter.org,
215-345-7860
Bathrooms: At boat rental building, Sailors Point, and other park locations;
composting toilets at nature center
Water/Snacks: Water fountain at boat rental building and nature center
Maps: buckscounty.org (click on Living & Working to find the Parks and
Recreation page); peacevalleynaturecenter.org/trailmap
Directions by Car: Take I-76 West (Schuylkill Expressway) to Exit 331B and
merge onto I-476 North (Blue Route). After 4.4 miles, take the exit onto
I-276 East toward New Jersey, then take Exit 343 onto PA 611 North toward
Doylestown. Continue 13 miles to the exit for PA 313 West. Turn left onto PA
313, continue for 2.2 miles, and then turn left onto New Galena Road. Proceed
0.7 mile to Chapman Road on the left. The parking area is ahead on the left.
GPS coordinates: 40° 20.423′ N, 75° 10.272′ W.

Peace Valley Park's central Bucks County location and variety of activities have
made it one of the most popular family destinations in the region. It's a fun
locale for biking, hiking, and boating that is not overly challenging for young
kids, but still interesting enough for adults to enjoy too.

Its 1,500 acres surround Lake Galena, a reservoir that offers boating
and fishing. The lake is big enough to provide boaters with a few hours of
exploration, but small enough to make novices feel comfortable, and its
shoreline of grass and woods is indeed a peaceful valley. In season, kayaks,
canoes, and sailboats are available for rent at the Boat Rental Pavilion.

A 6.5-mile, paved, multiuse path circumnavigates the lake, with access
points at several parking areas. Mostly level, it is a great family bike trail, and
is also popular with walkers and strollers.

There are numerous locations for fishing, including the pier on the south-
western side of the lake, and Sailors Point on the northwestern side.

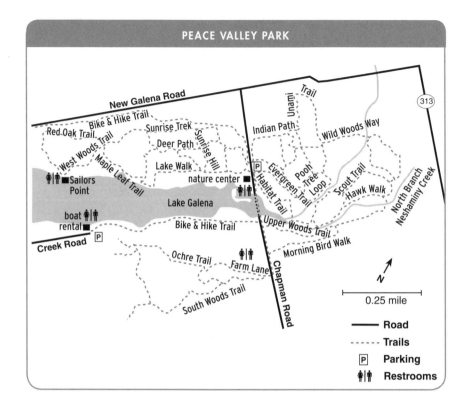

New Galena Road

313

Bike & Hike Trail

Red Oak Trail

Sunrise Trek

Indian Path

Wild Woods Way

Deer Path

West Woods Trail

Sunrise Hill

Maple Leaf Trail

Lake Walk

nature center

Unami Trail

Pooh Tree Loop

Evergreen Trail

Scout Trail

Hawk Walk

North Branch Neshaminy Creek

Sailors Point

Lake Galena

boat rental

Habitat Trail

Bike & Hike Trail

Upper Woods Trail

Creek Road

Ochre Trail

Farm Lane

Morning Bird Walk

Chapman Road

South Woods Trail

N

0.25 mile

—— Road

----- Trails

P Parking

Restrooms

The northeastern portion of the park is given over to the nature center, where you'll find a network of easy loop trails through woods and fields. Don't miss Pooh Tree Loop; follow it to the gigantic hollowed-out sycamore where kids will adore pretending they're Pooh and Piglet living in the tree. Make sure to bring water shoes for children to splash in the North Branch Neshaminy Creek, since the trails cross it in many places. At the Chapman Road Bridge, enjoy beautiful views of the lake. Along with turtles and fish, birds are abundant: ducks, herons, and cormorants are here year-round; ospreys and eagles are regular visitors. The nature center offers many programs and events for families; call ahead for details. Its main building has a few exhibits on local nature, as well as a large bird blind.

Remember: Swimming is not allowed in Lake Galena.

PLAN B: Nockamixon State Park (Trip 38) is north on PA 313. In Doylestown, south on PA 313, are some unusual museums.

WHERE TO EAT NEARBY: The borough of Doylestown, south on PA 313, is a lively commercial and cultural center.

Trip 31

All Ages

Delaware Canal State Park

A 60-mile-long park along the historical Delaware Canal and the forested Delaware River offers many options for hiking, biking, paddling, or fishing.

Address: Virginia Forrest Recreation Area, River Road (near Paxson Road), Solebury, PA
Hours: Sunrise to sunset daily
Fee: Free
Contact: www.dcnr.state.pa.us/stateparks, 610-982-5560; fodc.org; canals.org
Bathrooms: At Virginia Forrest Recreation Area, Theodore Roosevelt Recreation Area, and park office
Water/Snacks: Water fountains at bathrooms
Maps: www.dcnr.state.pa.us/stateparks (click on Find a Park)
Directions by Car: Take I-95 North into New Jersey, to Exit 1, and turn left onto NJ 29 North for 9.4 miles into Stockton. Turn left onto Bridge Street and cross into Pennsylvania. Turn right onto PA 32 North (River Road). Continue about 1.5 miles to the entrance and parking lot on the right. *GPS coordinates*: 40° 24.370´ N, 75° 0.192´ W.

Delaware Canal State Park is a 60-mile linear park that follows the Delaware Canal's mule-barge towpath along the Delaware River. From below Easton to above Morrisville, the river is largely undeveloped. Along the length of the park, the level, compact-surface towpath is stroller-friendly and provides excellent opportunities for easy hiking and biking (with thick tires), most of it in a beautiful, natural riverside landscape. Along the park's northern section, five river bridges connect to the Delaware and Raritan (D&R) Canal State Park on the New Jersey side (Trip 95). The park also links to state and local parks and recreation areas along its length.

Visitors can gain access to the park from many points. A good starting place is the Virginia Forrest Recreation Area at mile 29, about the midpoint. From here, you can walk or bike on the towpath and enjoy great views of the wide river, which is bordered by woods and cliffs in this section. Make an 8-mile loop by going north about 2 miles to Lumberville, crossing the river on the Roebling pedestrian bridge to Bulls Island State Park in New Jersey, then going south on the D&R Canal path to Stockton, crossing back to Pennsylvania at Centre Bridge, and returning to Virginia Forrest. It's a short, easy bike ride for

You never know what you'll discover outdoors when you stop, look, and listen.

kids. Walking this loop is easy but long; you can shorten the trip by going to the pedestrian bridge and back. This bridge itself is great fun. It's a miniature version of a suspension bridge and provides the thrill of standing above the river with your feet in two different states.

At Virginia Forrest and elsewhere along the canal are put-ins to the Delaware River, appropriate for families with paddling experience.

Numerous other points of interest are along the canal. At the path's start in Easton, visit the National Canal Museum in Hugh Moore Park, where you can take a ride on a canal boat and learn about its history from costumed interpreters (fee charged). In the lively river town of New Hope is a visitor center where you can learn more about the canal's history, or visit the headquarters of Friends of Delaware Canal, which sponsors many programs and offers detailed information on hiking, biking, and paddling around the canal. Near Upper Black Eddy, Giving Pond Recreation Area (Trip 41) is a small pond with easy trails and paddling. Near Washington's Crossing, Bowman's Hill Wildflower Preserve (Trip 32) has easy trails through woods.

An enormous variety of programs are offered through the state park, from boating instruction to wildlife classes to nature walks. Call ahead for details.

Remember: Dogs must be leashed. The canal is not always deep enough to permit boating; check with the park office before setting out.

PLAN B: In Easton, visit the Easton Dam & Fish Ladder to see how shad running upstream get over the dam.

WHERE TO EAT NEARBY: Bring water and snacks. You may pass through small towns where you can get supplies, depending on which part of the canal you are on.

Trip 32

Bowman's Hill Wildflower Preserve

In a beautifully maintained nature preserve, follow flower-lined paths through rich woods and take in a bird's-eye view of the Delaware River.

Address: 1635 River Road, New Hope, PA
Hours: Grounds open 8:30 A.M. to sunset; visitor center open Tuesday through Sunday, 9 A.M. to 5 P.M.
Fee: Members, free; nonmembers: adults, $5; children ages 4 to 14, $2
Contact: bhwp.org, 215-862-2924
Bathrooms: In visitor center (when open)
Water/Snacks: None
Maps: Paper copies available at visitor center; bhwp.org/map.htm
Directions by Car: Take I-95 North to Exit 51 (New Hope) and turn left (north) onto Taylorsville Road. Go north on Taylorsville Road for 7 miles. Turn left (north) onto River Road/PA 32 and go 2.5 miles. The entrance to the preserve is on your left. Follow the drive to the gates, which open automatically (if not, press the button). Proceed to the parking lot at the end of the drive.
GPS coordinates: 40° 19.883´ N, 74° 56.352´ W.

Bowman's Hill Wildflower Preserve is a lovely, small nature preserve near the northern end of Washington Crossing Historic Park. The 134-acre preserve is dedicated to growing native wildflowers and promoting their use in the landscape. Although kids will probably be less interested in the message than adults, they'll delight in the many paths that wind through the woods along Pidcock Creek. Nature-curious kids can read the labels on the more than 800 species of native plants grown on the site.

All the trails are well maintained and easy to follow, with trail names posted at the crossings. The rich collection of native plants in the preserve attracts a wide variety of birds and other wildlife.

Young kids will enjoy following the gentle trails down by the creek, which all lead somewhere fun: to a stone bridge, a pond, or a stream. Steeper trails lead from the visitor center down to the creek and up the hillside on the opposite bank. Almost all of the 2.5 miles of trails are natural footpaths, though Wood's Edge Walk is wheelchair- and stroller-accessible; this paved path connects to the drive (an old road) that leads from the parking area to the exit gate. You can also take the paved path down to the creek at the stone bridge.

As you cross the bridge at Bowman's Hill, look for fish shimmering in Pidcock Creek.

Trails meander through the meadows outside the front exit gate (kids will enjoy pressing the button to open the gates, which surround the preserve and keep out deer to protect the wildflowers). In summer these meadows are a kaleidoscope of color, full of dipping, fluttering butterflies and other pollinators.

The steepest trail goes outside the back gates and up the drive to Bowman's Hill Tower, a stone structure high on the bluffs overlooking the Delaware River, where George Washington's lookout may have been posted. You can climb the tower for a fabulous view all around the river valley (the tower is part of Washington Crossing Historic Park; open Tuesday through Sunday, 10 A.M. to 4 P.M.; $5 fee charged).

The visitor center has a few exhibits on native plants; helpful staff will be happy to give advice on your visit. During the year, the preserve hosts many family-oriented nature programs and events for the public. Call ahead for details.

Remember: Dogs are not permitted inside the fenced portion of the preserve.

PLAN B: Giving Pond Recreation Area (Trip 41) in Upper Black Eddy, part of Delaware Canal State Park (Trip 31), has short trails and a pond for paddling.

WHERE TO EAT NEARBY: The town of New Hope is north up River Road. If you bring a picnic, enjoy it at the large picnic area located next to the meadows (outside the fence).

Trip 33

All Ages

Core Creek Park

Room to roam and paddle too: The whole family will enjoy Core Creek's peaceful lakeside location.

Address: 901 E. Bridgetown Pike, Langhorne, PA
Hours: Trails, sunrise to sunset daily; fishing, 24 hours a day; see website for boathouse season (usually May through September) and hours
Fee: Grounds, free; fees for boat rental
Contact: buckscounty.org, 215-757-0571; Core Creek boat rental, 215-757-1225
Bathrooms: At picnic areas and boathouse
Water/Snacks: Water fountains at picnic areas
Maps: buckscounty.org (click on Living & Working to find the Parks and Recreation page)
Directions by Car: Take I-95 North to Exit 44. Merge onto PA 413 North. After 0.8 miles turn left onto North Flowers Mill Road. Continue 0.6 miles; turn slightly right onto Winchester Avenue, which becomes Langhorne Yardley Road. After 0.4 miles turn left onto Bridgetown Pike. The park entrance is 0.2 miles on the right. Continue past the park office on the park road, following signs for the boathouse, and park in the adjacent lot. *GPS coordinates:* 40° 12.274′ N, 74° 55.152′ W.

Core Creek Park is a 1,200-acre Bucks County park that surrounds serene Lake Luxembourg. A bit off the beaten track, Core Creek is not crowded as often as nearby Tyler State Park, a virtue in itself in this densely populated region. With its combination of wide-open grassy areas and pockets of woods, the park provides families with many options to enjoy the changing seasons. Indeed, while Core Creek is lovely year-round, it is especially magical in snowy winters, when there's plenty of room for skiing, sledding, and snowshoeing along the shores overlooking the lake.

The centerpiece lake lives up to its grand name as a small but "rich" destination; its wealth is in its beauty. The calm waters provide beautiful, quiet recreational opportunities particularly appropriate for young or beginner boaters. Many fishing spots are along the shore.

A cartop boat launch is near the boathouseboathouse (reached most easily through a second entrance off Tollgate Road). Kayaks, canoes, rowboats, and paddleboats are available to rent during warmer months. The boat rental

*At Core Creek Park's free fishing event, kids and adults
learn fishing skills together; no license required.*

concession also conducts classes in boating and fishing. Visit the website or call for more details.

On land, walking trails wind around two wooded sections of the park. Stroller-friendly, paved walkways closely following the lake offer lovely views and easy biking. Some trails are open to horses. There are plenty of places to picnic, and kids will enjoy visiting the playgrounds by the lake.

Bring your dog along to enjoy the off-leash dog park, or take advantage of the tennis courts.

Remember: Dogs should be leashed outside of the dog park.

PLAN B: Tyler State Park (Trip 35) and Churchville Nature Center (Trip 29) are both a short drive away.

WHERE TO EAT NEARBY: Follow PA 413 south to Langhorne or north to Newtown.

Trip 34

Five Mile Woods Nature Preserve

These woods are made for walking, with easy, interesting trails in a quiet location off US Route 1.

Address: 1305 Big Oak Road, Yardley, PA
Hours: Dawn to dusk daily
Fee: Free
Contact: lmt.org; 215-493-6652
Bathrooms: At main building
Water/Snacks: None
Maps: lmt.org/park-fivemilewoods.php
Directions by Car: Take I-95 North to Exit 46A, and merge onto US 1 North. Continue 0.6 mile to the Oxford Valley exit. Turn left onto Oxford Valley Road. Take the next right onto Big Oak Road, and continue 1 mile to the nature preserve on the right; park in the lot. *GPS coordinates:* 40° 12.270′ N, 74° 50.986′ W.

Five Mile Woods is a delightful nature preserve, easily reached from major highways, with easy but interesting walking trails for young families or those new to the outdoors.

The 300-acre forest, owned by Lower Makefield Township, is open only to pedestrians. The trails close to the main building are all level, winding through open woods, around ponds, and along small streams where kids can look for tadpoles and salamanders. Many of the trails follow along a boardwalk, since the woods can be somewhat muddy in wet seasons. The abundant sweet gum trees litter the forest floor with their spiky seed balls.

The woods feature a distinctive half-flat/half-rocky geography. They strad-dle the fall line—the border between the level, gravelly coastal plain (which underlies South Jersey) and the more rocky Piedmont (which is what most of southeastern Pennsylvania looks like). So, as you walk farther from the main building along Creek Trail or Five Mile Trail, you'll start to come across large boulders strewn in the woods. Here the trees are taller and the trails no longer flat as beach sand. Fall Line Trail itself goes up and over the literal fall line, a rocky ridge that is no problem for older kids to traverse.

Salamanders nestle in the moist soil under decaying logs at Five Mile Woods.

Although US 1 forms the southern boundary of the preserve, its noise is not intrusive except for a short stretch of trails adjacent to the highway. The woods are rich in bird life and spring wildflowers.

The trails are exceptionally well marked, with beautiful wooden signs at all crossings, and easy-to-follow maps are usually available at the kiosk outside the main building. Signs indicate "HQ" when a trail leads back to the main building. The network of trails makes this a place you can go with kids often yet never take the same route twice.

Remember: The preserve hosts nature programs for families throughout the year, and a summer camp.

PLAN B: Core Creek Park (Trip 33) has playgrounds, bike and hike trails, and boating and fishing, and is dog-friendly and stroller-friendly.

WHERE TO EAT NEARBY: Plenty of shops and restaurants are in the vicinity of the intersection of Oxford Valley Road and US 1.

Trip 35

Tyler State Park

Walk, bike, fish, or canoe in this popular park along the lower Neshaminy Creek.

Address: 101 Swamp Road, Newtown, PA
Hours: Sunrise to sunset daily; fishing and boating are permitted 24 hours; see
    website for seasonal boat rental hours
Fee: Free
Contact: www.dcnr.state.pa.us/stateparks; 215-968-2021
Bathrooms: At Mill Dam parking area and several playgrounds; at canoe rental
    and boathouse areas
Water/Snacks: Water fountain at playground
Maps: www.dcnr.state.pa.us/stateparks (click on Find a Park)
Directions by Car: Take I-95 North to Exit 49 (Newtown/Yardley), then drive
    west on the four-lane bypass around Newtown. The park entrance is on the
    left at the intersection of Swamp Road and the four-lane bypass. To park at
    boathouse area, follow signs. *GPS coordinates*: 40° 14.008′ N, 74° 57.075′ W.

Tyler State Park is justly popular. Easily reached by car, it is a large and vibrant
green space along the Neshaminy Creek in lower Bucks County. Packed into
its 1,700 acres is more than enough space for diverse outdoor activities, including hiking, fishing, boating, swimming, and biking. The park is a mosaic of
natural woods, grassy areas, and fields that are actively farmed, with the creek
bisecting the grounds. Families will find options for kids of various ages.

Start at the boathouse parking area, which is central to many activities.
Kids can walk along (or in) the creek. Its broad, flat banks are easily negotiable
and perfect for practicing the ancient art of skipping stones. For beginner
boaters the creek is a good place to learn about navigating currents; head to
the boathouse area, where you can put in a canoe or kayak at the public boat
launch and paddle above the dam. In season, a canoe rental concession is at
the same spot. It's calm on the creek; only nonpowered and electric boats are
permitted. Fishing along the banks is popular too.

The trail system is diverse. More than 10 miles of paved multiuse trails
accommodate bikes, strollers, and walkers. An additional 9 miles of dirt bridle
paths are open to equestrians and hikers. Horse trailer parking is available.

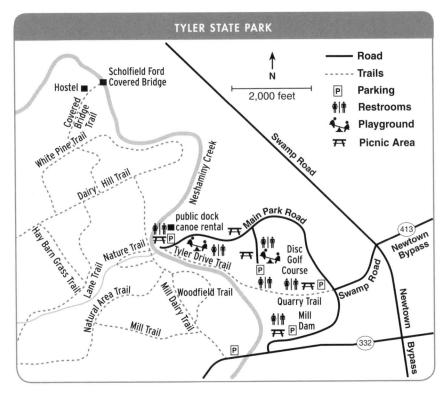

The trails wind through the woods and around farm fields, with the flatter trails being near the creek. The Mill Dam area is convenient to a lovely trail overlooking the creek. In winter, kids can enjoy sledding on the disc golf course or by the hostel, and ice skating near the boathouse area. The equestrian trails, hiking trails, and biking trails are great for cross-country skiing.

There are numerous picnic areas, playfields, and playgrounds. At the northernmost part of the park, a historical covered bridge crosses the creek. Here too is Tyler Hostel, operated by Hostelling International and open to overnight visitors; for more information, see hi-dvc.org.

Remember: Pets must be leashed.

PLAN B: Core Creek Park (Trip 33) and Churchville Nature Center (Trip 29) are nearby. Core Creek is a quiet park with a variety of trails and a large lake for boating and fishing; Churchville is a small nature center with trails for young children.

WHERE TO EAT NEARBY: Take the Newtown Bypass (532) east a short distance to Durham Road, where there is a commercial district.

Trip 36

Ages 9-12

Delaware River

Paddle or float down the big, wide river, combining the thrill of a ride with the serenity of nature.

Address: Delaware River between Easton, PA/Phillipsburg, NJ and Washington Crossing, PA/NJ
Hours: All hours
Fee: Free if you own your own paddling equipment; rental fees at outfitters vary
Contact: nps.gov/lode; delawareriverwatertrail.org
Bathrooms: At various points along the river
Water/Snacks: None
Maps: delawareriverwatertrail.org/water-trail-map/lower
Directions by Car: See Appendix B for information about commercial outfitters.

Just a few miles north of Philadelphia, the banks of the Delaware River are thick with forests. Silence is punctuated by birdsong, and fish glint in clear water that rushes over smooth stones. Gone are the highways and refineries. Canoes replace freighters. Eagles and osprey soar overhead.

From just south of Easton north to Morrisville, the lower Delaware River has been designated part of the National Wild and Scenic River System, protected by the National Park Service.

There is little development in this section, mainly because the Falls of Trenton—a line of boulders—blocks navigation, so industry and cities never came this far upstream. Instead, quaint towns hug the banks. The riverside roads are scenic byways.

To really experience the river, you have to get out on it. Follow the Delaware River Water Trail and journey downstream. Kids who are old enough to pay attention can accompany adults in a canoe or raft. Older children can pilot their own kayak or tube.

You can rent canoes, kayaks, or tubes from an outfitter, who will ferry you upstream so that you travel down to where you left your car. (Outfitters are in Point Pleasant, Pennsylvania, and Stockton and Frenchtown, New Jersey.) Be sure to call ahead, as some outfitters do not rent boats to children under age 12.

Tubing is an easy introduction to the ways of a big river: Kids can learn how to float with the current, ride the rapids, and make small adjustments to

All you need is a tube to float down the wild and scenic Delaware River.

change course. Tubing is extremely popular on the river between Tinicum and Point Pleasant, where the current is reliable and there are just a few areas of relatively easy rapids. In some sections, the water is calm and deep enough to swim in (but keep your life jacket on). Depending on distance, and how often you stop, a tubing trip can take anywhere from two to five hours.

Canoeing and kayaking allow much more control over your ride, so you can explore the river, its inlets, and islands. Boats make it easier to pack a lunch, water, or extra sunblock.

If you have your own boat, you can put in at launches along the river; some good locations are Upper Black Eddy (PA Fish & Boat), Tinicum Park (Bucks County), and Bulls Island State Park in New Jersey. If you are boating on your own, it is imperative that you research the river conditions for your route. Note that the wing dam at Lambertville creates whitewater.

Remember: On summer weekends the river can be downright crowded with floating parties. Bring plenty of water and snacks. Wear sneakers, water shoes, or other footwear that will not come off your feet. Do not wear flip-flops. Also note that the river is open to powerboats and Jet Skis, which heavily use some areas of the river.

PLAN B: Visit one of the many parks along the river, including Giving Pond Recreation Area (Trip 41), where you can put in a boat to paddle around, or fish or hike, or Delaware Canal State Park (Trip 31), where you can bike or walk along the level towpath.

WHERE TO EAT NEARBY: It's best to pack a picnic.

Trip 37

Tohickon Valley Park/Ralph Stover State Park (High Rocks)

Enjoy the dramatic beauty of the swift, rocky Tohickon Creek from high above or right beside it.

Address: Cafferty Road, Point Pleasant, PA
Hours: Trails open sunrise to sunset; pool open Memorial Day through Labor Day (see website for hours)
Fee: Trails are free; cabins and campsite require rental fee; pool requires usage fee
Contact: buckscounty.org, 215-297-0754 (in season)
Bathrooms: At pool; in campgrounds
Water/Snacks: Water fountain at pool (when open)
Maps: buckscounty.org (click on Living & Working to find the Parks and Recreation page)
Directions by Car: Take I-95 North into New Jersey for about 30 miles. Take Exit 1 onto NJ 29 North/River Road. After 9.4 miles, take a slight right onto PA 165, then turn left onto Bridge Street, then right onto North Main Street. Continue onto NJ 29 North/River Road. After 2.5 miles, turn left onto Bridge Street into Pennsylvania. Turn right onto PA 32 North/River Road. After 5.2 miles, turn right onto PA 32 North/Point Pleasant Pike/River Road. Take the first left onto PA 32N/River Road, then take a slight left onto Cafferty Road. The main parking lot for the park is at the entrance. *GPS coordinates:* 40° 26.721´ N, 75° 4.986´ W.

Tohickon Valley Park takes full advantage of its location on the steep gorge of the rocky Tohickon Creek. Hiking trails in the woods (some open to mountain bikes and horses) parallel the creek, so they are easy to follow even though they are not well marked. A steep paved path, navigable by strollers, leads from the main parking area down to the creek, where flat rocks are perfect for picnicking. Twice a year, the banks are jammed with onlookers as whitewater kayakers paddle in the torrents released from Tohickon's upstream dam at Lake Nockamixon. Most of the rest of the year the creek is swift, with quiet pools and eddies where young anglers can fish for trout (the creek is stocked annually). The creek is swift and rocky—not recommended for swimming—

With proper equipment and supervision, young climbers can tackle High Rocks at Tohickon Valley Park.

but in summer the public pool, at the top of the hill next to the main parking lot, is very popular.

Families can camp here in tents or rent a cabin. There are 22 family tentsites near the field next to the main parking lot.

For the adventurous members of the family, the 200-foot sheer cliff known as High Rocks (part of adjacent Ralph Stover State Park) is one of the Philadelphia region's best-known rock-climbing locations. For those not wanting to rock-climb, the overlook from the top of the cliffs provides a series of awesome views of the creek below. Follow the trails from the campgrounds along the top of the ridge; it's about a 2-mile walk to High Rocks. Or drive to Tory Road, where parking is available right at the overlook.

Remember: Rock climbing here requires supervision and skill. Dogs must be leashed.

PLAN B: If it's a bigger stream you want, paddle or go tubing down the Delaware (Trip 36). Ralph Stover Park also extends along the creek beyond High Rocks and offers more picnic areas along quieter sections of the creek.

WHERE TO EAT NEARBY: The village of Point Pleasant, at the intersection of PA 32 and Cafferty Road.

Just because it's raining doesn't mean kids can't go outdoors. In the Philadelphia region it rains on average 120 days every year—and the wettest months are in summer! Instead of despairing, turn the rain into a fun element of your trip.

Of course, dress children, and yourself, for the weather. Remember the saying, "There's no such thing as bad weather, only bad clothing choices." Waterproof shoes or boots are a must; rain jackets too, and gloves in cold weather. Rain pants are a better choice than jeans or other cloth pants that get cold and heavy when wet. Bring a dry change of clothes in case of a wardrobe malfunction.

Other handy items to have along on rainy day trips are large plastic trash bags, to put wet clothes in, or to spread out on a damp picnic bench. Toss towels of various sizes into the car; bring small towels in plastic bags in your day pack. A folding umbrella is useful to create temporary shelter when you're looking at a map (carry the map in a clear plastic bag). Bring rainproof snacks that won't get soggy while you're eating, such as fresh cut carrots. On cold, wet days, a thermos full of hot chocolate warms young bodies from the inside.

Once everyone's protected against getting soaked, you're ready to go. A walk in the woods becomes a chance to listen to the music that rain makes on leaves, and compare it to the sounds it makes on a pond, or a bridge railing, or an umbrella. If you're walking along the ocean or bay shore, look for cool patterns in the sand that rain creates.

How fast is it raining? Ask your kids to try and count by catching raindrops as they fall from the sky. Rain brings worms squirming out of their burrows, and it invites shy frogs and toads to sit out in the open, soaking up their favorite element. Rain makes tiny streams where kids can launch leaf rafts with acorns to pilot them. Rain makes mud that you can draw pictures in with sticks. And rain makes puddles to jump in! (Luckily there's that change of clothes....)

Remember:

- Rain can turn normally placid streams into raging torrents, and water is powerful when moving.
- Stepping-stones may be underwater. Don't let kids wade across a stream that's above their knees.
- Be careful above the stream too; wooden boardwalks and footbridges may be slippery when wet.
- If rain is accompanied by thunder or lightning, seek shelter immediately, preferably in a structure or vehicle. If you're on the water, get to shore. (See page xli for tips on lightning safety.)

Trip 38

All Ages

Nockamixon State Park

With loads of options for boating, fishing, and hiking, families won't tire of Lake Nockamixon, no matter how often they visit.

Address: 1542 Mountain View Drive, Quakertown, PA
Hours: 8 A.M. to sunset daily
Fee: Grounds free; fee charged for pool and boat rental
Contact: www.dcnr.state.pa.us/stateparks; 215-529-7300
Bathrooms: At the marina, Tohickon and Haycock boat launches, fishing pier, and elsewhere
Water/Snacks: Water fountains at restrooms (but may be inoperative); snack bar at day-use area/pool in season
Maps: www.dcnr.state.pa.us/stateparks (click on Find a Park)
Directions by Car: Take I-76 West (Schuylkill Expressway) to Exit 331B and merge onto I-476 North; continue on I-476 to the Pennsylvania Turnpike Northeast Extension. Continue to Exit 44, and take a left onto PA 663 North toward Quakertown. At PA 309 continue straight, onto PA 313 East. Take PA 313 East to PA 563 South on the left. The park office is 3.5 miles farther, on the right. To get to the marina, continue on PA 563 for 1 mile, then turn right onto Harrisburg School Road and follow it to its end at a large parking area. *GPS coordinates:* 40° 27.853′ N, 75° 14.488′ W.

Nockamixon State Park, like many other lake-centered parks in the region, is a by-product of an engineering project. Lake Nockamixon was created in the late 1960s by the damming of the Tohickon and Haycock creeks and Three Mile Run. Today it seems like it has always been here, enclosed as it is by deep green forests. Stone ruins hidden in the woods reveal its history as a mill valley.

The huge lake attracts boaters and anglers from afar. There's a 20-horsepower limit on motor craft so paddlers can feel safe on the busy lake. You can rent canoes, kayaks, rowboats, and sailboats at the marina boat rental concession in season. For the youngest anglers, a children's fishing pond in the day-use area makes a good starting point before trying out the big pond.

Lake Nockamixon's size might make it intimidating for a novice solo boater, especially when a big breeze kicks up, but Nockamixon's rewards are abundant enough for a lifetime. The long, quiet, mostly undeveloped shoreline is a

Woods covered with freshly fallen snow create a natural playground.

haven for birds, fish, and other wildlife that kids can spot from a boat or look for on a trail. Despite the proximity of a nearby highway, the lake is quiet enough to hear the splash of fish from the far shore, and the songs of birds in the woods.

Hiking trails thread through these woods. The Sterner Mill hiking area is designated for foot traffic only and has an easy-to-follow set of loop trails that go down to the lake and back, good for school-age kids. Other trails in the park in the Old Mill area are more rugged and rocky, suitable for older kids, though they are also always easy to follow.

Many of the park's other unpaved trails are open to mountain bikes and horses. A paved trail around the day-use area is a nice, short lakeside route for bikes and strollers.

A half-acre swimming pool, with two waterslides as well as a shallow end with fountains for young children, is located in the day-use area and open seasonally.

Remember: In hunting season, some hiking areas may be open to hunters; check a map and always wear blaze orange in hunting season (hunting is prohibited on Sundays). Swimming is not permitted in the lake.

PLAN B: Peace Valley Park (Trip 30) is south, off of PA 313; it has trails, boating, and fishing. Its Lake Galena, which also has a boat rental, is a smaller, less intimidating alternative to Lake Nockamixon.

WHERE TO EAT NEARBY: Continue down PA 563 South to a small commercial area near PA 413, or go to Quakertown, north on PA 313.

Trip 39

Honey Hollow Environmental Education Center

Explore woods, ponds, and meadows in a preserved watershed surrounded by working farms.

Address: 2877 Creamery Road, Solebury, PA
Hours: Trails open 9 A.M. to 5 P.M. daily; visitor center open Monday through Friday, 9 A.M. to 5 P.M.
Fee: Free
Contact: bcas.org, 215-297-5880
Bathrooms: At visitor center (when open)
Water/Snacks: None
Maps: bcas.org/documents/HHtrailmap.ai.pdf
Directions by Car: Take I-95 North into New Jersey to Exit 1, and turn left onto NJ 29. Continue on NJ 29 into Lambertville. Turn left onto Bridge Street (NJ 179), and cross into New Hope, Pennsylvania. Continue on PA 179 to a right turn on North Sugan Road. After 0.6 mile, turn right onto Sugan Road. Take the second left onto Meetinghouse Road. After 0.6 mile, take the first right onto Creamery Road; go 0.4 mile to the entrance on left. Continue to the parking area next to the visitor center. *GPS coordinates:* 40° 22.361′ N, 75° 0.614′ W.

Headquarters of the Bucks County Audubon Society (BCAS), the Honey Hollow Environmental Education Center has 7 miles of trails through woods, in meadows, and near ponds that surround agricultural fields. Set among rolling hills, the trails are relatively easy but still interesting for kids as they traverse a variety of habitats.

Honey Hollow is a National Historic Landmark. In the 1930s, six farmers banded together to protect 700 acres in the Honey Hollow Creek watershed, including their homesteads, as a way to reduce erosion caused by severe drought. Today, the property still includes working farmland and private residences. A 55-acre portion of the watershed is open to the public as part of the BCAS mission to promote conservation and education.

Trails are marked with posts in colors that correspond to colors noted on maps at the trailhead kiosk outside the visitor center and online. This is a good opportunity for kids to learn map-reading to follow the route. For almost

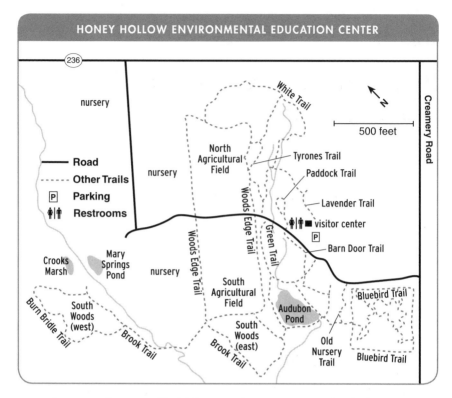

immediate gratification of kids' desire to be near water, take the lavender trail immediately off the main parking lot (stopping at the bird blind along the way) to the white trail, which leads down into woods and across a small stream on rocks. It continues through the woods and ends at the yellow trail, which goes around two farm fields. To stay mostly in the woods, turn off white onto orange, which connects to blue/green then green; follow the green trail down to another stream before arriving at the large, tree-shaded Audubon Pond.

Honey Hollow's diverse, protected landscape makes it a rich habitat for wildlife—especially frogs, birds, and butterflies and other pollinators.

The visitor center is in a converted old stone barn. It has exhibits on local wildlife including "please touch" installations. The BCAS sponsors walks and educational programs at the preserve.

Remember: No pets are permitted. Trails on the west side of the preserve are closed weekends and holidays; these are the private residential areas.

PLAN B: Giving Pond Recreation Area (Trip 41) has a pond for paddling and fishing, and an easy walking trail around the large pond.

WHERE TO EAT NEARBY: Bring snacks to enjoy in the picnic area next to the visitor center, or you can return to New Hope for supplies.

Trip 40

Ages
9-12

Ringing Rocks Park

Bring your hammers to play music on acres of boulders, and clamber over rocks below a plunging, year-round waterfall at this natural playground in the woods.

Address: Ringing Rocks Road, Upper Black Eddy, PA
Hours: Sunrise to sunset daily
Fee: Free
Contact: buckscounty.org, 215-348-6114
Bathrooms: Portable toilet next to the parking lot
Water/Snacks: None
Maps: None
Directions by Car: From the Pennsylvania Turnpike (I-276), take Exit 343 onto PA 611 North. Drive about 27 miles to Revere, then bear right onto Marienstein Road, which after 3 miles becomes Bridgeton Hill Road. Continue 1.4 miles to Ringing Rocks Road on the left; the park's parking lot is 0.4 mile straight ahead. *GPS coordinates*: 40° 33.631′ N, 75° 7.712′ W.

Music doesn't get any more basic than the notes you make by hitting rocks with hammers. The 128-acre Ringing Rocks Park is named for its distinctive boulders, which ring like bells when tapped. Kids will love making the rocks ring, comparing the notes, and climbing from one boulder to the next. The boulder field next to the parking lot, spread across 4 acres and surrounded by woods, formed over millions of years, as extreme freeze–thaw cycles fractured a huge block of dark volcanic rock called diabase. Why the rocks ring has been the subject of much research and even more conjecture; so far there is no definitive answer.

An unmarked but easily followed trail starts at the boulder field entrance and winds a quarter-mile through the woods down to High Falls Creek, named for the waterfall that plunges into a deep ravine. It's the highest waterfall in Bucks County. Kids can climb down to the creek and, in drier months, even play below the waterfall. The falls offer a lesson on the dramatic geologic history of the park—kids can examine the layered rocks, where the dark volcanic rock meets the flat red shale. The trail continues along the creek down the ravine.

Bring a hammer to make music at Ringing Rocks.

Both the rocks and the falls are good year-round destinations; in cold winters the falls freeze into icy beauty, and even in the driest summers, walking in the rocky creek bed is fun. Wildflowers abound in the moist woods surrounding the ravine.

Remember: Bring a hammer and wear sturdy shoes. The trails are not stroller-friendly, and the boulder field is challenging for kids under 5.

PLAN B: Lake Warren (State Game Lands 56) is about a half-mile south on Lake Warren Road (off Marienstein Road) and offers fishing and hiking trails. (Wear bright colors in hunting season.)

WHERE TO EAT NEARBY: The best option, at least in warmer months, is to bring a picnic. Otherwise, continue down Marienstein Road to Bridgeton Hill Road, where the village of Bridgeton has a general store. Just across the Delaware River, Milford, New Jersey, is a bigger town with more restaurants, or there are options along PA 611.

Trip 41

Giving Pond Recreation Area

This large, wildlife-rich pond between the Delaware Canal and Delaware River is a great place to learn paddling skills.

Address: River Road, Upper Black Eddy, PA
Hours: 8 a.m. to sunset daily
Fee: Free
Contact: www.dcnr.state.pa.us/stateparks, 610-982-5560
Bathrooms: Portable toilet at parking area
Water/Snacks: None
Maps: None
Directions by Car: Take I-95 North into New Jersey to Exit 1, and turn left onto NJ 29 North. Continue on NJ 29 for approximately 15 miles into Frenchtown. Turn left onto Bridge Street and cross into Uhlerstown, Pennsylvania. Turn right onto PA 32 North (River Road). Continue 0.8 mile to the Giving Pond entrance on the left, and park in the gravel parking area. (For the boat launch and the pond, continue walking past the parking area.) *GPS coordinates*: 40° 32.378´ N, 75° 4.162´ W.

Giving Pond, a 90-acre pond between the Delaware Canal and Delaware River, is a wonderful place for kids to learn how to canoe or kayak, or to spend time fishing. It also provides opportunities for easy short walks around the pond, and it connects to the Delaware Canal towpath for longer walks.

The pond was reclaimed from a disused quarry in 2002, and became part of the Delaware Canal State Park. It has a long, unobstructed central area and smaller offshoot ponds, as well as several islands. Trees and shrubs line the shores. Over the years that the quarry was not used, water seeped in and eventually rose to ground level. As it did so, it drowned many trees that had been growing on quarry ledges. These snags are still standing along the outer edges of the pond.

For the paddler, the pond combines protected, enclosed areas, a wide-open stretch, and natural obstacles (dead standing trees) to maneuver around. The open area can get windy on days when the weather is changeable, but powerboats (other than those with electric motors) are prohibited. (Note that there is no boat rental at the pond. See Appendix B for nearby outfitters.)

Green frogs are common, though well camouflaged, in vegetation along shallow pond banks.

The pond's inlets, islands, and standing trees are enticing to explore by boat, which makes learning how to get there fun. It's excellent for novice paddlers to practice how to steer, stop, and reverse a canoe or kayak, and how to read the currents and wind. Even for experienced paddlers the pond is an enjoyable trip. It is full of wildlife, attracting ducks, cormorants, herons, and other waterfowl; sightings of eagles and ospreys are not uncommon. Turtles are abundant, basking on the numerous fallen logs in quiet coves. Kids will enjoy spotting and seeking out wildlife as they explore the pond.

Giving Pond's standing trees provide excellent habitat for fish. The brushy shoreline near the boat launch is popular with anglers, as is casting a line from a slow-moving boat.

On dry land, you can follow a level and easy trail around the pond, in summer passing through dense patches of wildflowers that attract butterflies. A picnic area overlooks the pond.

From June to October, park staff conduct public paddling programs at Giving Pond on the first and third Saturdays of each month. Call ahead for details.

Remember: Swimming is not permitted. Dog must be leashed. Note that in deer hunting season, bowhunting is permitted. If you're on the trails, wear blaze orange, or go on Sundays when hunting is prohibited.

PLAN B: Giving Pond is part of Delaware Canal State Park (Trip 31); the canal towpath connects to the pond's trails.

WHERE TO EAT NEARBY: Return to Frenchtown to find a variety of places to eat.

Section 3

Lehigh and Northampton Counties

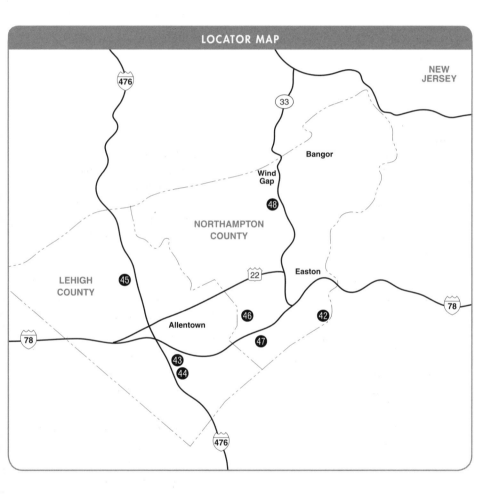

LOCATOR MAP

Trip 42

Ages 5-8

Mariton Wildlife Sanctuary

High on a rocky bluff overlooking the Delaware River, look for wildlife along trails in woods and meadows.

Address: 240 Sunnyside Road, Easton, PA
Hours: Dawn to dusk daily
Fee: Free
Contact: natlands.org, 610-258-6574
Bathrooms: Outside the nature center
Water/Snacks: None
Maps: natlands.org (click on List of Preserves, then Mariton)
Directions by Car: Take I-76 West (Schuylkill Expressway) to I-476 North, then take the exit onto I-276 East (Pennsylvania Turnpike). Take Exit 343 and merge onto PA 611 North toward Doylestown. Continue on PA 611 for 34 miles, then turn left onto Spring Hill Road. Take the first right onto Sunnyside Road. Proceed up the hill about 0.5 mile to the entrance on the left. The parking lot is ahead. *GPS coordinates*: 40° 36.597′ N, 75° 12.271′ W.

Natural Lands Trust's Mariton Wildlife Sanctuary is a 200-acre nature preserve on the bluffs overlooking the Delaware River just north of Riegelsville, at the line between Bucks and Northampton counties. Its 4 miles of well-maintained trails are sure to entertain kids; they range from gentle old roads bordered by stone walls to steep, rocky climbs. All are short and easily followed, marked by color-coded posts. This is a nice place for kids to practice map-reading because the trail system is not complicated, but it has enough choices to make it interesting.

The small nature center is a good place for families to get oriented. You'll find exhibits about the many different kinds of wildlife to be spotted here during every season, from songbirds to butterflies. Mariton features lovely trails that traverse a wide variety of habitats, from old mature woods with towering trees, to young woods, to hilltops maintained as meadows. Kids will especially enjoy climbing onto rock outcrops to take in the views. River Lookout Trail, which connects to Main Trail next to the nature center, features the most dramatic vista, looking down onto the river from the top of an east-facing cliff (supervise children closely here). Chimney Rock, a little farther along Main

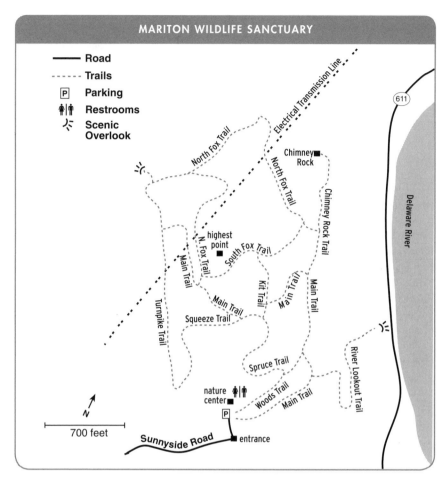

Road
Trails
P Parking
Restrooms
Scenic Overlook

North Fox Trail

Electrical Transmission Line

611

Chimney Rock

North Fox Trail

Chimney Rock Trail

Delaware River

highest point

N. Fox Trail

South Fox Trail

Main Trail

Kit Trail

Main Trail

Main Trail

Turnpike Trail

Main Trail

Squeeze Trail

Spruce Trail

River Lookout Trail

nature center

Woods Trail

Main Trail

P

N

700 feet

Sunnyside Road entrance

Trail, has views through the woods from large boulders perched on a rise in the woods. Take Main Trail in the opposite direction to reach North Fox Trail and the Pine Circle overlook, from which you can see the woods from a steep, north-facing angle. While views are best in winter and early spring when the leaves are off the trees, Mariton's woods are beautiful in fall when the leaves are turning color. The meadows are best in summer when the wildflowers are out.

Remember: Dogs must be leashed. Stay on trails.

PLAN B: Take in the views of the river from a different vantage point: Walk along the Delaware Canal Towpath (Trip 31).

WHERE TO EAT NEARBY: Go back downhill to the borough of Riegelsville, on PA 611, where there are a few small stores and cafés.

Trip 43

· ·

Lehigh Parkway

Feed the fish and enjoy a walk or bike ride on paved paths along the Little Lehigh Creek, in one of the prettiest urban parks in the region.

Address: 2901 Fish Hatchery Road, Allentown, PA
Hours: Sunrise to sunset daily
Fee: Free admittance; small fee for fish food
Contact: allentownpa.gov, 610-437-7627
Bathrooms: At fish hatchery and disc golf course
Water/Snacks: Water fountains at picnic areas
Maps: allentownpa.gov (click on Parks & Recreation, then Park Maps & Inventory)
Directions by Car: Take I-76 West (Schuylkill Expressway) to Exit 331B and merge onto I-476 North; continue on I-476 to the Pennsylvania Turnpike Northeast Extension. Take Exit 56 toward Lehigh Valley. Follow US 22 East for 0.6 mile and take the exit onto PA 309 South toward Quakertown. Continue 1.8 miles to exit onto I-78/PA 309 South toward Allentown/Quakertown. Drive 1.8 miles to Exit 55 for PA 29 South. Turn right onto PA 29 South/South Cedar Crest Boulevard, and then left onto Fish Hatchery Road (PA 2010).The parking lot is on the right. *GPS coordinates:* 40° 33.864′ N, 75° 30.781′ W.

Lehigh Parkway, a delightful multiuse trail along both sides of the Little Lehigh Creek in Allentown, provides many opportunities for family recreation, including walking, hiking, biking, and fishing.

The shaded creek itself is lovely, and young children love the Lil-Le-Hi Trout Nursery. Opened in 1883, it is the nation's only city-owned fish hatchery. Here, for a small fee, you can buy fish food that kids toss into the pools. The fish twist and spin to get to the food; the water seems to churn and boil with the flash of fins. The hatchery is open year-round.

Several parking areas are along the parkway. If you park at the hatchery, you can walk or bike along either side of the creek. The parkway extends for 3 miles on both sides, but you can loop back across the creek at one of several bridges. The stroller-friendly cinder path is mostly flat, though it traverses some small hills when it goes through woods.

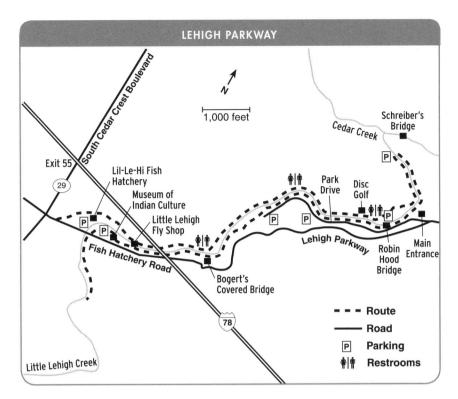

LEHIGH PARKWAY

South Cedar Crest Boulevard

N

1,000 feet

Cedar Creek

Schreiber's Bridge

Exit 55

29

Lil-Le-Hi Fish Hatchery

Museum of Indian Culture

Little Lehigh Fly Shop

Park Drive

Disc Golf

Fish Hatchery Road

Lehigh Parkway

Robin Hood Bridge

Main Entrance

Bogert's Covered Bridge

78

Little Lehigh Creek

- - - Route
——— Road
P Parking
Restrooms

In the cold-water limestone spring creek itself, the many pools and riffles make for ideal trout habitat, so fly fishing is popular—popular enough that a fly-fishing shop provides instruction in the sport for kids ages 11 and up. The shop is located near Fireman's Bridge (contact Heritage Fly Shop, 610-248-8836).

Also along the parkway are the small Museum of Indian Culture, the 1841 Bogert's Covered Bridge, a log cabin, and other historical structures. At Klein's Bridge, look for Planet Walk, a model that gives a sense of the scale of the solar system; it will likely be "over the heads" of young kids, but will appeal to older children.

Picnic areas are located along the creek, including a large area adjacent to the disc golf course.

Remember: Dogs must be leashed.

PLAN B: Cedar Creek Parkway's universally accessible destination playground is nearby in Cedar Beach, on Hamilton Street at Ott Street.

WHERE TO EAT NEARBY: Proceed down South Cedar Crest Boulevard to a commercial area with restaurants and shops.

Trip 44

Ages 5-8

Pool Wildlife Sanctuary

Kid-friendly trails welcome even the youngest children to explore nature.

Address: 3701 Orchid Place, Emmaus, PA
Hours: Dawn to dusk daily
Fee: Free
Contact: wildlandspa.org; 610-965-4397
Bathrooms: Composting toilets near parking area
Water/Snacks: Water fountain near bathroom
Maps: Trail map painted on kiosk at parking area
Directions by Car: Take I-76 West (Schuylkill Expressway) to Exit 331B and merge onto I-476 North; continue on I-476 North to the Pennsylvania Turnpike Northeast Extension. Take Exit 56 onto US 22 East toward Allentown. After only 0.5 mile on US 22, exit onto PA 309 South and continue 1.7 miles to I-78 East/PA 309 South toward Allentown. Continue 1.8 miles to Exit 55 onto South Cedar Crest Boulevard/PA 29 South toward Emmaus. Go 1.6 miles to a left on Riverbend Road, then take the first right onto Orchid Place. At the bridge (on the right), turn right and cross the bridge into the sanctuary to the parking lot. *GPS coordinates*: 40° 32.502′ N, 75° 30.739′ W.

Pool Wildlife Sanctuary welcomes children to explore upland woods, meadows, and floodplain forest with easy trails along the Little Lehigh Creek. For young kids or families not experienced with the outdoors, the preserve is a great place to get out and get comfortable in nature.

The 77.5-acre sanctuary is headquarters for Wildlands Conservancy, a nonprofit organization that works to preserve natural areas and educate the community on environmental protection in the Lehigh Valley. The conservancy runs family programs such as guided wildlife walks, instructional paddling trips, and stargazing evenings throughout the year at Pool and other locales.

Although the only trail map is painted on the parking lot kiosk, the trails are not hard to follow. All the trails are loops and are level or gently sloped. Floodplain Trail, an elevated boardwalk, is easy enough even for toddlers to follow. Starting near the covered bridge, it goes along the creek, through the woods, and over a natural footbridge crossing a pond. A short tree-

Connected bridges and boardwalks on Pool Wildlife Sanctuary's Floodplain Trail make water crossings fun.

identification trail branches off from it; designed to teach kids how to tell common trees apart by their leaves and bark, it's a fun way to engage them in their surroundings. On the opposite side of the parking area, younger children will enjoy the Woodland Loop and Urban Forest trails that wind through a young forest. On these short trails, it's easy to see into the woods and test your new tree knowledge, or just try to spot the chipmunk that's making such loud noises.

A small pond where very young kids can look for frogs and fish (and butterflies and dragonflies in summer) is at the parking area. Just the right size for them, they may want to stay there all day.

Remember: The Little Lehigh Creek can be reached from the trails, but depending on water conditions, it may not be open for access for splashing or fishing.

PLAN B: The Lehigh Parkway (Trip 43), including the Lil-Le-Hi Trout Nursery, is nearby in Allentown.

WHERE TO EAT NEARBY: Travel south on South Cedar Crest Boulevard to Main Street in Emmaus to find a commercial area.

Trip 45

Trexler Nature Preserve

Discover animals (native and not-so-native) while you hike along the trail.

Address: 5150 Game Preserve Road, Schnecksville, PA
Hours: North Range, dawn to dusk daily; Central Range, April 1 through October 31, 9:30 A.M. to 5 P.M., November 1 through March 31, 9:30 A.M. to 4 P.M.
Fee: Free
Contact: trexlernaturepreserve.org; 610-871-1444
Bathrooms: Outside environmental center; at the zoo; portable toilets at Jordan Creek ford
Water/Snacks: Water fountain and snack bars at the zoo
Maps: May be available at the environmental center and at the zoo, and at kiosks around the preserve
Directions by Car: Take I-76 West (Schuylkill Expressway) to Exit 331B and merge onto I-476 North; continue on I-476 to the Pennsylvania Turnpike Northeast Extension. Take Exit 56 onto US 22 East. After 0.8 mile, merge onto PA 309 North and continue into Schnecksville. You will pass Lehigh Carbon Community College and come to a light at Sand Spring Road. After the light, continue past Game Preserve Road. When you come to a Y in the road, stay to the left on PA 309. After approximately 1.75 miles, turn left onto Mill Creek Road. Follow this road until you come to a T intersection with Game Preserve Road. Turn left onto Game Preserve Road. Go approximately 0.25 mile and turn right into the main entrance gate, following signs for the Lehigh Valley Zoo. *GPS coordinates:* 40° 39.485′ N, 75° 37.602′ W.

The 1,108-acre Trexler Nature Preserve was originally a game preserve established by Colonel Harry Clay Trexler, father of Allentown's park system, to protect bison, elk, and white-tailed deer. Herds of bison and elk still graze here in protected areas and can be viewed from the trails. (The deer, though, are not protected and roam the preserve freely.) Centuries ago, elk and bison were native to southeastern Pennsylvania; nowadays they live here only in captivity.

The preserve is divided into North, Central, and South ranges. Only two are open, the North and Central. The Jordan Creek flows through all of the ranges. The preserve's extensive forests and network of streams interspersed with open fields create a habitat rich for diverse wildlife—and ripe for exploring.

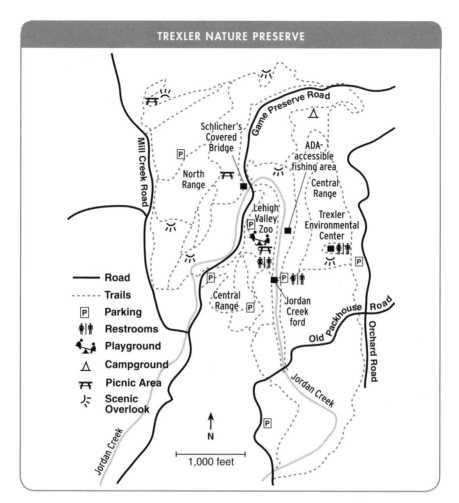

Road

---- **Trails**

P **Parking**

🚹🚺 **Restrooms**

Playground

△ **Campground**

🎏 **Picnic Area**

🔆 **Scenic Overlook**

1,000 feet

N

A good place to start and a favorite spot for kids at the preserve has long been the Jordan Creek ford, where the main road crosses the creek; it's fun to watch cars roll through the stream, and you can walk across the ford too, if you've brought your water shoes. Kids can also explore the creek, looking for frogs and fish.

The recently built environmental center, which has many "green," energy-efficient features, is perched on a high hill in the Central Range, near Orchard Road. An observation deck—in between the solar panels on the vegetative roof—affords a great view of the preserve.

More than 18 miles of trails are at the preserve, many open to mountain bikes and horses. Trails are color-blazed, and numbered kiosks orient you to where you are on the trail map. The trails range from easy to difficult; most are short and can be combined into longer hikes or loops. A 0.3-mile Observation Trail loop goes around the environmental center. The 1.2-mile, double-red-blazed Covered Bridge Trail in the Central Range is ADA-accessible; it ends at a fishing area on the Jordan Creek (near the ford) for kids and physically challenged anglers. You'll find the trail off of Old Packhouse Road at a parking lot near Geiger's Covered Bridge. The moderately difficult, 1.5-mile Elk Viewing Trail offers views of bison as well as elk.

The longest trail, and the only one rated "difficult" for hiking, is the 8.5-mile, red-blazed Trexler Border Trail that loops around the outer edges of the Central and North ranges.

In winter the preserve's open hills are good for cross-country skiing and the trails in the woods make good snowshoe paths.

Remember: Dogs must be leashed. The North Range is open to bowhunting in deer season. The Jordan Creek Greenway, a trail under development, will eventually connect the preserve to Allentown, to the south, and the Appalachian Trail, to the north.

PLAN B: Young kids will love the Lehigh Valley Zoo in the Central Range (fee charged; lvzoo.org). The exhibits feature a small but diverse collection of animals—both domestic and exotic. Kids can watch the penguins feeding and then feed goats and birds. There is also a playground.

WHERE TO EAT NEARBY: It's best to bring a picnic.

Trip 46

All Ages

Sand Island Park

This urban park along the Lehigh Canal offers great views of the Lehigh River, in addition to trails, tennis courts, and level biking.

Address: Main Street and River Street, Bethlehem, PA
Hours: 6 A.M. to 6 P.M. daily (to 9 P.M. during daylight saving season)
Fee: Free
Contact: bethlehem-pa.gov, 610-865-7081
Bathrooms: Near the tennis courts
Water/Snacks: Water fountain near the bathrooms
Maps: wildlandspa.org/lrwt; delawareandlehigh.org
Directions by Car: Take I-76 West (Schuylkill Expressway) to Exit 331B and merge onto I-476 North; continue on I-476 to the Pennsylvania Turnpike Northeast Extension. Take Exit 44 onto PA 663 toward Quakertown, and continue for 3.4 miles to PA 309 North. Take PA 309 for 6.3 miles to PA 378 North, and continue for 6.4 miles to the Main Street Bethlehem exit. Continue on Main Street, crossing over the canal. Parking is available on the left. *GPS coordinates*: 40° 36.948′ N, 75° 22.984′ W.

Sand Island Park is a narrow peninsula between the Lehigh Canal and the Lehigh River in downtown Bethlehem. At this city park, you'll find easy walking and biking along the water, as well as access to the canal for fishing and paddling (and the river, for experienced boaters).

The Lehigh Canal, created in the nineteenth century to transport coal by mule-drawn barges, ran from White Haven to Easton, passing through Bethlehem. Today, the canal is used for recreation. Its level towpath has been converted to a paved, stroller-friendly trail, which is part of the D&L Trail, a planned 165-mile route from Wilkes-Barre to Bristol.

On Sand Island, the level canal towpath trail is crushed stone suitable for any hybrid or mountain bikes. You can pick up the trail below the Main Street overpass and continue about a half-mile to the end of the island, passing a historical lock and the Ice House (now converted to a performing arts center) over an iron bridge. At the end of the island, you get a nice view of the Lehigh River through the trees, and the Bethlehem Steel plant across the river. The trail makes a loop with Sand Island Trail, which runs along the middle of the island with occasional river views. For longer biking or hiking, you can follow

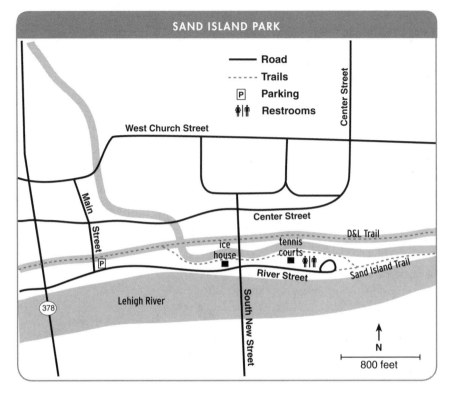

SAND ISLAND PARK

Road
Trails
P Parking
Restrooms

West Church Street

Center Street

Main Street

Center Street

D&L Trail

ice house

tennis courts

River Street

Sand Island Trail

Lehigh River

South New Street

378

N

800 feet

the canal towpath 4 miles north from Sand Island to Allentown, or south 3.6 miles to Freemansburg, or beyond, to Easton.

The slow-moving, protected canal can be paddled upstream over a short section beginning from the cinderblock building next to the railroad trestle at the western end of Sand Island. After about a mile, it encounters Lock 41. Portage around the lock to continue upstream about 3 miles to Allentown's Canal Park, and return via the same route. Kids old enough to handle their own boats will enjoy this paddle. For more-experienced paddlers, a loop can be made using the Lehigh River to return to Sand Island.

The canal's best fishing access on the island is around Lock 41 where Sand Island Trail and the D&L Trail towpath diverge.

The park also has picnic tables and a playground.

Remember: Dogs must be leashed.

PLAN B: Nearby, Allentown's Lehigh Parkway (Trip 43) features an easy, paved path along the Little Lehigh Creek for bikes and walking, and a trout nursery.

WHERE TO EAT NEARBY: Walk up Main Street to explore downtown Bethlehem.

Trip 47

Ages 5-8

Saucon Rail Trail and Lost River Caverns

Walk or bike an easy creekside trail, then explore an underground cave.

Address: West Water Street (between Front Street and Creek Road), Hellertown, PA
Hours: Dawn to dusk daily
Fee: Trail, free; Lost River Caverns: adults, $11; children ages 3 to 12, $7
Contact: hellertownborough.org; lostcave.com
Bathrooms: at Upper Saucon Township Community Park; portable toilet at Water Street Park
Water/Snacks: Water fountain near Upper Saucon Township Community Park restroom
Maps: hellertownborough.org/railtrailmap.pdf; uppersaucon.org/parks/SRT_Map.pdf
Directions by Car: To the Hellertown trailhead: Take I-76 West (Schuylkill Expressway) to Exit 331B onto I-476 North; continue on I-476 to the Pennsylvania Turnpike Northeast Extension. Continue to Exit 44 onto PA 663 toward Quakertown. Take PA 663 North for 3.4 miles to PA 309 North. Take PA 309 for 5.8 miles to a right turn onto Passer Road (PA 2028). Take an immediate left onto Flint Hill Road. After 0.5 mile, turn left onto Taylor Drive, and continue onto Apples Church Road. Turn left onto PA 412 North; after 1.6 miles, turn left onto West Water Street. After 0.1 mile, turn left into the park entrance and parking lot. *GPS coordinates*: 40° 34.742′ N, 75° 20.675′ W.

The Saucon Rail Trail, a 4.5-mile trail between Water Street Park in Hellertown and Upper Saucon Township Community Park, is a wide, crushed-stone trail good for bikes (with thick tires), strollers, and easy walking.

The trail parallels the tree-shaded Saucon Creek, offering a rural landscape for much of its length. A good starting point is the Hellertown trailhead at Water Street Park, which features walking trails, a playground, picnic tables, and a volleyball court.

Combine the hike or bike ride with a visit to the Lost River Caverns in Hellertown, a short distance uphill from Water Street Park. A 40-minute, family-oriented guided tour of the cave explores the underground labyrinth, where water is still dripping from the limestone.

Look for traces of the old railroad line on Saucon Rail Trail.

Afterward, you can pick up the Saucon Rail Trail on the eastern edge of Water Street Park and head south for a pleasant, easy bike ride or walk. Posts every quarter-mile along the way indicate how far you've come, but with a twist: They refer to the mileage of the old rail line from its terminus in Philadelphia, so you have to calculate. The Water Street trailhead is mile 53.

At Walnut Street, a half-mile from your Water Street start, the trail passes the Hellertown Historical Society's museum. The museum consists of a restored barn, house, and gristmill depicting early American industrial and home life. (Open Tuesdays, Thursdays, and Saturdays, 9 to 11:30 a.m. and by appointment.) Also here is the moved and restored 1860 "Pony Bridge," a cast-iron truss bridge; crossing it is a fun diversion for kids (even though it now just crosses land).

At Upper Saucon Township Community Park, at the other end of the trail, you'll find picnic tables, playing fields, 2 miles of walking paths, basketball courts, and a tot lot. In winter, the trail is open for cross-country skiing.

Remember: Dogs must be leashed. The trail will soon be extended another 2 miles to Coopersburg.

PLAN B: In nearby Bethlehem, bike or walk on the D&L Trail, a converted towpath along the Lehigh Canal. Sand Island Park (Trip 46) is a good place to gain access to the trail.

WHERE TO EAT NEARBY: Walk up Water Street to Hellertown, where you'll find many shops and restaurants.

Trip 48

All Ages

- -

Jacobsburg Environmental
Education Center

Hike from high to low—look way down on a creek from the top of the ravine, then cool off by wading into it.

Address: 835 Jacobsburg Road, Wind Gap, PA
Hours: Dawn to dusk daily
Fee: Free
Contact: www.dcnr.state.pa.us/stateparks; 610-746-2801
Bathrooms: At Henrys Woods trailhead and main parking lot
Water/Snacks: Water fountain near Henrys Woods restroom
Maps: www.dcnr.state.pa.us/stateparks (click on Find a Park)
Directions by Car: Take I-76 West (Schuylkill Expressway) to Exit 331B and merge onto I-476 North; continue on I-476 to the Pennsylvania Turnpike Northeast Extension. Continue to Exit 44, and take PA 663 North for 3.4 miles to PA 309 North. Take PA 309 to I-78 East. Continue on I-78 to the exit for PA 33 North toward Stroudsburg, and take PA 33 to the Belfast exit. At the end of the exit ramp, turn left onto Belfast Road. Take the first right into the park entrance and parking lot. *GPS coordinates:* 40° 47.432′ N, 75° 18.074′ W.

The beautiful Bushkill Creek is at the heart of the 1,168-acre Jacobsburg Environmental Education Center, part of the Pennsylvania State Park system. The creek winds through a lush forested ravine, traversed by a web of trails—18.5 miles in the park altogether.

The premier hiking route is the 1.9-mile Henrys Woods Trail. Although you can gain access to the trail from the main parking lot on Belfast Road, a less crowded option is the lot near the Boulton Historic Site on Henry Road. The trail loops around the creek through an old-growth forest with immense oak, pine, and hemlock trees that date back several centuries. The trail has a high side that climbs to the top of the bluffs overlooking the creek, and a low side on the opposite bank that has lots of access points to the water where kids can wade, fish, or look for crayfish. To get to the high side, you cross the bridge over the creek after entering the park from Henry Road; the low-side trail is on the near side of the creek. While the cliff-side trail may not be appropriate for toddlers, it's great fun for kids who have some experience hiking; be sure to supervise in the narrow spots.

The historical site, open seasonally, is a museum and educational center focused on eighteenth- and nineteenth-century American crafts and industry. For older kids, this site may be fun to visit during scheduled reenactments and demonstrations of the small firearms manufactured here by the Henry family.

Henrys Woods Trail is for hiking only. Many of the other trails in the park are open to horses and bikes, and for cross-country skiing. The lower section of Henrys Woods Trail is wide and easy enough to accommodate strollers.

Bushkill Creek is trout-stocked, and is extremely popular with anglers.

Remember: Dogs must be leashed. Other than the Henrys Woods Trail area, the park is open to hunting in season. Swimming is not permitted in the creek.

PLAN B: Homestead Trail, on dirt and grass surfaces, can be reached from the main parking lot and is not too difficult for children 8 and up (or younger, experienced hikers). It provides great views from the upland meadows.

WHERE TO EAT NEARBY: It's best to pack a picnic. Numerous picnic areas are in the park, including one by the main parking lot.

Section 4

Berks County

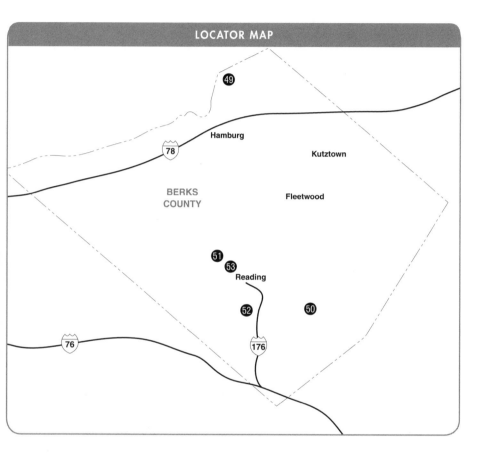

Trip 49

Ages 9-12 $ 🛒 🚶

Hawk Mountain Sanctuary

Introduce kids to the magnificent vistas of the rugged Appalachian ridge and the soaring majesty of raptors.

Address: 1700 Hawk Mountain Road, Kempton, PA
Hours: Trails open dawn to dusk daily; visitor center open daily (hours vary by season)
Fee: Members, free; nonmembers: adults, $6; children ages 6 to 12, $3; weekends in September, October, and November and national holidays: adults, $8; children ages 6 to 12, $4
Contact: hawkmountain.org, 610-756-6961
Bathrooms: In visitor center
Water/Snacks: Water fountain in visitor center; snacks at visitor center gift shop
Maps: At visitor center
Directions by Car: Take I-76 West (Schuylkill Expressway) to Exit 331B and merge onto I-476 North; continue on I-476 to the Pennsylvania Turnpike Northeast Extension. Continue on I-476 to Exit 56 (Lehigh Valley). Get on US 22 West toward Harrisburg (becomes I-78 West), and continue to Exit 35 for Lenhartsville. Take PA 143 North, and drive 4 miles to a gas station on the right. Turn left at the blue Hawk Mountain sign onto Hawk Mountain Road. Continue along the road, and turn left into the parking lot. *GPS coordinates:* 40° 38.056′ N, 75° 59.265′ W.

For many people, Hawk Mountain is the most family-friendly path to the Appalachian range. Although you have to pay admission, the fee not only supports an essential conservation organization, but it buys an exceptional family hiking experience: a self-guided trail that provides a controlled environment for making an ambitious climb. Kids will laugh with delight as they scramble up rocks and gaze out over valleys, watching hawks and vultures spiral against the clouds.

Hawk Mountain Sanctuary was founded in the 1930s to save hawks at a time when raptors were hunted nearly to extinction. Today the sanctuary offers numerous family programs designed to broaden understanding of why and how to protect wildlife.

The best introductory route for families is the 1-mile Lookout Trail. After passing through the admission booth, follow Lookout Trail to South Lookout. (This groomed trail to South Lookout is the only wheelchair-accessible and

Below Hawk Mountain's South Lookout, the River of Rocks winds through a glacier-carved valley.

stroller-accessible trail at the sanctuary.) The view below is the River of Rocks boulder field. Return to Lookout Trail, which leads to successive overlooks, each with a vista more breathtaking than the last. The trail gradually becomes rockier and steeper as you proceed. Follow signs to the North Lookout, climbing a set of rock stairs with handrails to the top. The North Lookout, and Sunset Overlook just beyond, are promontories that offer magnificent views of the valley below and the continuation of the Kittatinny Ridge northward.

In the fall hawk migration season, the lookouts are the place to observe thousands of raptors in a day as they soar on rising columns of sun-warmed air and glide on invisible currents of wind. It's fun, but at these times the mountain can be crowded, so it may not be the ideal first visit for kids who want to explore the rocks.

To get an even better view of the scenery and the birds, bring binoculars, or rent them at the visitor center.

Along Lookout Trail are posts with QR codes, so you can use a smartphone to access additional details about the natural features.

Remember: Wear proper footwear: hiking shoes or sturdy athletic shoes. On fall days, be prepared for wind on the lookouts even if it seems calm in the woods; bring jackets. Bring water and snacks, and carry trash out with you.

PLAN B: For more-ambitious hikers, the River of Rocks and the Appalachian Trail can be accessed from the trails at Hawk Mountain. More information is available at the visitor center.

WHERE TO EAT NEARBY: It's best to bring snacks.

Although we take kids outdoors to have fun in nature away from their usual surroundings, digital media can sometimes enhance their experience, and even help kids to feel comfortable.

Finding your way or keeping track of where you've been requires map and compass skills. In addition to practicing these skills, you can use a GPS (global positioning system) device, which uses satellites to locate the exact latitude and longitude coordinates of your location. You can use a handheld GPS unit (different from the car units), or a smartphone GPS app with equivalent features. Kids can use the GPS to track a hike, bike ride, or paddle, and see in real time on a topographic map or satellite photo exactly where they went, how far, and how high. They can mark points that are special enough that they'll want to come back to them. Kids can upload and share GPS maps with friends. While no substitute for a trail map, a GPS may help you feel less trepidation about taking your kids to unfamiliar territory.

A GPS is also used for the game of geocaching: finding hidden boxes identified by their GPS coordinates. Websites such as Geocaching.com list cache locations; players use the GPS to show direction and distance to the target location. Often, the path to the cache is in stages and the player finds clues to decipher along the way in order to get to the next stage. It's a great game for kids and adults to play together, and it's a different way of exploring the outdoors than by following a set trail. Kids won't be bothered by how long they've been hiking when they're hot on the trail of a geocache! (Note that off-trail geocaching is prohibited or discouraged in many parks and preserves.)

Field guides to common birds, flowers, trees, and butterflies are available as apps for smartphones or tablets. Kids, especially older ones, may be reluctant to tote around bulky paper field guides. An app that tells the name of a tree by taking a picture of a leaf or identifies birds by playing the songs you hear couldn't be easier to use. These apps open up the natural world to kids: formerly unfamiliar things outdoors now have names and stories.

Parks, preserves, and nature centers are beginning to use apps to engage young people with nature. It can be as simple as the use of QR codes on posts along a trail that, when scanned by a smartphone, bring up information on natural features. Try this out at Hawk Mountain Sanctuary (Trip 49). An example of a more sophisticated app is Natural Lands Trust's SCVNGR app (natlands.org). Designed for children up to age 10, it enables kids to share their experiences with other kids by providing comments or uploading photos. Download this app to use at the Stroud Preserve (Trip 72).

Trip 50

Daniel Boone Homestead

Walk in the footsteps of the young man who became the eighteenth century's most famous frontier explorer.

Address: 400 Daniel Boone Road, Birdsboro, PA
Hours: Grounds open sunrise to sunset daily; visitor center open Tuesday to Friday, 9 A.M. to 5 P.M.; Saturday, 10 A.M. to 5 P.M.; Sunday, 11 A.M. to 5 P.M.
Fee: Trails, free; paths in Historic Area require fee when visitor center is open: adults, $3; children, free; guided tours require an extra fee
Contact: danielboonehomestead.org, 610-582-4900
Bathrooms: Outside the visitor center
Water/Snacks: None
Maps: danielboonehomestead.org (click on Visit Us, then Recreation)
Directions by Car: Take I-76 West to Exit 328A and merge onto US 422 West. Continue for about 35 miles. After Pottstown, look for a brown sign with white letters reading Daniel Boone Homestead on the right. Make the first right after the sign at the traffic light onto Daniel Boone Road. After 0.5 mile, use the jug handle to turn left into the Daniel Boone Homestead. Drive past the gate to the visitor parking area. (After hours, when the grounds are open but the buildings are closed, park outside the gate.) *GPS coordinates*: 40° 17.843′ N, 75° 47.646′ W.

The 579-acre Daniel Boone Homestead gives kids a chance to experience the structures and setting of an eighteenth-century colonial farm. In this serene Oley Valley landscape, kids can discover the woods and fields where frontiersman Daniel Boone grew up. The future wilderness explorer was born here in 1734 and lived at the homestead until his family moved to North Carolina in 1750. If your family is interested in American history, this spot is worth a trip.

In the Historic Area next to the visitor center, the Colonial farm buildings and house are open for self-guided tours of the exterior. Walk around the easy gravel paths to see the house, barn, blacksmith shop, sawmill, and other buildings. Kids will get a kick out of how different these buildings are from the modern ones they're used to. Paved paths in this area are great for bikes and strollers, and a picnic area is near the visitor center.

At the Daniel Boone Homestead, walk in the childhood footsteps of the famed frontier explorer.

Outside the Historic Area, a network of easy hiking and bridle trails extends through the meadows and woods. To gain access to the start of these trails, drive past the South Picnic Area to the parking lot at the end of the road. The trails are marked by numbered posts that are noted on the equestrian trail map available on the homestead's website. The trails are a good way for kids to explore the rest of the homestead and imagine being a young Daniel Boone exploring the frontier in his backyard.

Young anglers will enjoy fishing in the Historic Area in Daniel Boone Lake, a long lake that is dammed by the sawmill. Also near the sawmill is a pleasant little picnic grove.

Remember: Dogs must be leashed. Biking is discouraged on the bridle trails.

PLAN B: South of Birdsboro, French Creek State Park (Trip 64) has an extensive network of trails for hiking and a small lake for paddling. To the north, Green Lane Park (Trip 17) similarly offers hiking biking and paddling.

WHERE TO EAT NEARBY: Follow PA 422 west to find restaurants and shops along the road.

Trip 51

Blue Marsh Lake

This huge lake surrounded by forests provides endless outdoor recreational opportunities.

Address: 1268 Palisades Drive, Leesport, PA
Hours: Day-use areas, 8 A.M. to sunset unless otherwise posted; grounds open sunrise to sunset daily, except that hiking, fishing, and boating are permitted 24 hours
Fee: Free, except at day-use areas, where fees are $3 per vehicle or $1 per person for walk-ins; annual passes available for $30
Contact: www.nap.usace.army.mil, 610-376-6337
Bathrooms: Outside visitor center, and at Dry Brooks Day Use Area and Dry Brooks Boat Launch (in season); portable toilets at many parking areas
Water/Snacks: Water fountain at visitor center; concession stands at Dry Brooks Day Use Area (in season)
Maps: www.nap.usace.army.mil (click on Missions, then Civil Works)
Directions by Car: Take I-76 West (Schuylkill Expressway) to Exit 328A and merge onto US 422 West. Continue to the Spring Ridge Drive exit. Turn left onto Spring Ridge Drive, take the first right onto Paper Mill Road, and continue 1.4 miles. Turn right onto Rebers Bridge Road. Go 0.6 mile, then turn left onto Palisades Drive. The visitor center is ahead on the left. *GPS coordinates*: 40° 23.408′ N, 76° 1.928′ W.

Blue Marsh Lake is an amazing recreational resource, well worth many a family trip. The visitor center on Palisades Drive is a terrific place to get oriented. A wraparound deck boasts a panoramic view of the lake; inside are exhibits on the nature and history of the region.

Thirty-six miles of natural footpaths wind around the lake, threading through woods and fields. An unpaved, multipurpose trail—open to bikes and horses—loops all the way around the lake. You can gain access to the trails from many places, including the day-use areas. These trails feature great views of the lake; they are of varying terrain with some long climbs, suitable for older kids or for short walks with young kids. There's a stroller-friendly, universally

Broad reaches, winding inlets, and tree-lined shores invite boaters to expansive Blue Marsh Lake.

accessible sensory trail, an orienteering trail, and nature trails suitable for young children within the Dry Brooks Day Use Area.

The 8-mile lake offers families a variety of opportunities to enjoy being on the water. The middle of the lake can be quite crowded with powerboats, but canoes, kayaks, or fishing boats can launch into a no-wake zone from the Sheidy Boat Launch, off Bernville Road toward the northern end of the lake, or at the launch on Old Church Road. From here, explore broad expanses of the lake, as well as quiet, shaded arms. At the northern end of the lake, you can paddle up the Tulpehocken Creek for quite a distance.

Fish are abundant in the lake. Blue Marsh attracts hordes of anglers from boats, docks, and along the shores. An ADA-accessible fishing dock is at Stilling Basin.

Swimming is allowed in the lake. A popular beach is in the Dry Brooks Day Use Area, where there's a bathhouse (note, no lifeguard). You can also slip into the water anywhere in the lake from your boat. The best places to do this are along the shores of the main lake, or in the narrower arms, where cold springs continuously replenish the water.

Remember: Dogs must be leashed and are prohibited in certain areas. Swimming is permitted sunrise to sunset.

PLAN B: In the nearby Oley Valley is the Daniel Boone Homestead (Trip 50); the Union Canal Towpath bike trail (Trip 53) connects to Blue Marsh bike trails at Stilling Basin and the Swiftwater Road parking area.

WHERE TO EAT NEARBY: Bring a picnic to enjoy at the picnic areas with standing grills.

Trip 52

Nolde Forest Environmental Education Center

Hike a variety of trails through a remarkably rich forest.

Address: 2910 New Holland Road, Reading, PA
Hours: Trails open sunrise to sunset; park office open Monday through Friday,
8 A.M. to 4 P.M.
Fee: Free
Contact: www.dcnr.state.pa.us/stateparks; 610-796-3699
Bathrooms: At Sawmill trailhead parking lot, Boulevard trail crossing, and near
Fire Gate 5
Water/Snacks: None
Maps: www.dcnr.state.pa.us/stateparks (click on Find a Park)
Directions by Car: Take I-76 West (Schuylkill Expressway) to Exit 328A onto
US 422 West. Continue to the Morgantown Expressway (I-276), then, after
less than a mile, take Exit 10 onto PA 724 West toward Shillington. Remain
on PA 724 for about 2.5 miles; turn left onto PA 625. The Sawmill trailhead
and parking lot are about 1.7 miles ahead on the right. *GPS coordinates*: 40°
16.606′ N, 75° 56.956′ W.

At the 665-acre Nolde Forest, 10 miles of trails lead through a remarkable
woodland that combines native hardwoods with conifer plantations, for year-
round green. Several of the trails—gravel-surface former fire roads—combine
the ease of walking in a park with the wild surroundings of a forest. Others—
narrow, dirt footpaths—follow winding courses along streams and wooded
hills, and to ponds. The beauty of the former Nolde family estate is preserved
in the converted mansion that serves as a park office and picnic pavilion, and
in stone bridges and walls.

The trails are generally well marked, well maintained, and easy to follow.
Trail maps are available at trailhead kiosks. From the Sawmill trailhead, go up
stairs and cross the dam to get onto Watershed Trail, which leads up a small
creek called Punches Run, passes the mansion, and intersects Boulevard Trail.
Follow Boulevard Trail, an easy old fire road, to loop around the eastern half
of the park for 2 miles, passing over a large rock outcrop that's fun for kids to
climb on. Or take Watershed Trail to Kissinger Trail, another old fire road,

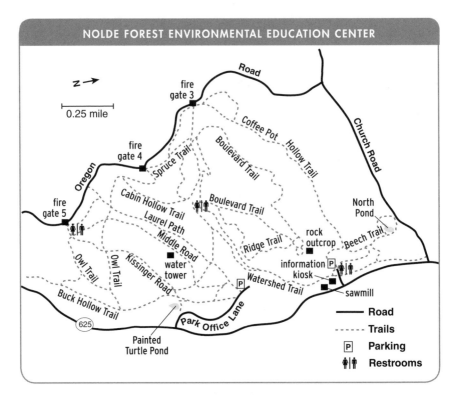

which takes you to the Painted Turtle Pond by way of Chestnut Trail. This wide pond, bordered by meadows, attracts turtles, frogs, and salamanders, as well as butterflies and dragonflies. Benches here offer a good spot for a picnic lunch.

Whichever trail you choose, make sure to visit the stone mansion. It has whimsical detailed stone carvings, iron work, and leaded glass windows that kids will enjoy discovering (especially around the entrance to what was the Nolde children's nursery). A covered stone arcade with picnic tables is a perfect place to sit on a hot day. A stroller-friendly, ADA-accessible trail loops around the mansion. An unpaved old road with an easy grade, suitable for strollers, connects the Sawmill area (at the bathrooms) to the mansion.

There's good fishing in the trout-stocked Angelica Creek, below the Sawmill. In snowy winters, the wide trails are great for cross-country skiing or snowshoeing, and the forest is a silent wonderland.

Remember: Dogs must be leashed. Bikes are not permitted on trails.

PLAN B: At Blue Marsh Lake (Trip 51) you can hike, bike, swim, fish, or paddle.

WHERE TO EAT NEARBY: Nolde is a good picnic spot, but if you follow PA 422 in either direction you will find restaurants and shops.

Trip 53

Union Canal Towpath

Hike or bike a level path along the lovely Tulpehocken Creek.

Address: 2201 Tulpehocken Road, Wyomissing, PA
Hours: 8 A.M. to sunset daily
Fee: Free
Contact: co.berks.pa.us, 610-372-8939
Bathrooms: None
Water/Snacks: None
Maps: None
Directions by Car: Take I-76 West (Schuylkill Expressway) to Exit 328A and merge onto US 422 West. Drive 41.6 miles to West Shore Bypass. Continue onto US 222 North, to the PA 183 exit. Turn left onto PA 183 and continue 3 miles to Palisades Drive. Follow Palisades Drive to Rebers Bridge Road. The trailhead is on the right. For fishing, park in the lot on the left side of the road. *GPS coordinates:* 40° 22.374′ N, 76° 0.524′ W. For hiking or biking parking, continue on Palisades Drive across Rebers Bridge Road, and take the next left at Swiftwater Lane, where the parking lot is. The connector path to Union Canal at Rebers Bridge (0.9 mile) begins here.

Union Canal Towpath is a level biking and hiking trail that follows the Tulpehocken Creek for 4.2 miles between Rebers Bridge and the Stonecliffe Recreation Area. The gravel path is suitable for hybrid bikes; road bikers might find it slippery.

Start at Rebers Bridge by crossing Plum Creek over a historical truss bridge (Rush's Mill Bridge, relocated here in 1980), and continue downstream. The beautiful tree-lined path winds along the banks, passing historical structures dating from when the trail was a towpath along the 79-mile Union Canal. Wertz's Covered Bridge area , about 1.9 miles from Rebers Bridge, is an interpretive center (fee charged), a great place to learn about Berks County history, including a museum devoted to the history of canals, as well as a gristmill and wagon works. The 204-foot red covered bridge is a remarkable sight, the longest of the state's existing single-span bridges. About 3 miles from Rebers Bridge is Gring's Mill and Homestead, which now serves as a visitor center for the park and offices for the Berks County parks department.

Union Canal Trail crosses Plum Creek via the historical iron Rush's Mill Bridge.

At the end of the trail is Stonecliffe Recreation Area, an active park that includes playgrounds, a picnic area, a fishing dock, and a skatepark.

An out-and-back journey is a pleasant and easy bike ride for families, or take a long walk (which can, of course, be shortened).

Fishing is popular in trout-stocked Tulpehocken Creek. Gain access to the creek from the trailhead or below the Rebers Bridge parking area.

Remember: No pets permitted. Bike rentals are available for drop-off at Blue Marsh Lake trails; check local outfitters.

PLAN B: At Rebers Bridge, the connector trail continues along the creek and links to the extensive trail system of Blue Marsh Lake (Trip 51), where you can hike, bike, swim, fish, or paddle.

WHERE TO EAT NEARBY: A snack bar is at Gring's Mill along the trail.

Section 5

Delaware and Chester Counties

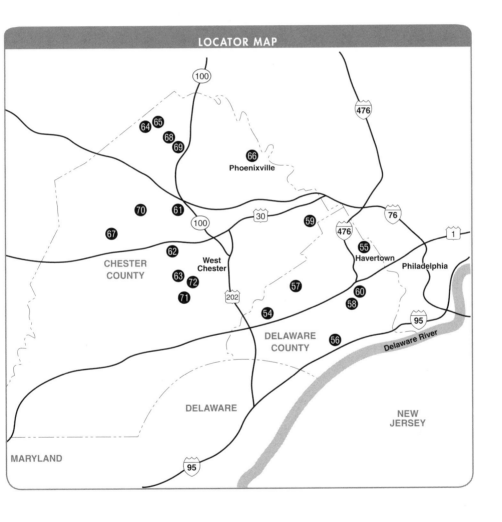

LOCATOR MAP

MARYLAND

Newlin Grist Mill

Get started fishing in made-for-kids ponds at a water-powered operating gristmill.

Address: 219 South Cheyney Road, Glen Mills, PA
Hours: Grounds open 8 A.M. to dusk daily; office open 9 A.M. to 4 P.M. daily; trout-fishing pond open weekends, 9 A.M. to 4 P.M.
Fee: Trails, free; fee for fishing, $5 per person and $4 per fish; mill tours, $5 per person
Contact: newlingristmill.org, 610-459-2359
Bathrooms: In the office (when open)
Water/Snacks: Water fountain in the office (when open)
Maps: newlingristmill.org/information/parkmap.html
Directions by Car: Take I-95 South to Exit 3A and merge onto US 322 West toward West Chester for 7.4 miles. Turn right onto Baltimore Pike/US 1 North. After 1.3 miles, turn right onto South Cheyney Road. The entrance to Newlin Grist Mill is immediately on the right. Park in the lot.
GPS coordinates: 39° 53.433′ N, 75° 30.375′ W.

Newlin Grist Mill is a fun family outing along the West Branch of the Chester Creek. It's a privately owned, 150-acre park known both for its historical working gristmill and its kids' trout-pond fishing; less well-known are its extensive grounds, with 8 miles of hiking trails through woods and fields.

For young kids, fishing in the stocked trout ponds may "hook" them on fishing for a lifetime. Open during trout season (weekends only), the small ponds are typically lined with kids trying out their angling skills, guided by a parent, grandparent, older sibling, or adult mentor. There's a fee to fish, and a fee for every fish caught (and you must keep the fish), but the park lends cane fishing poles if you don't have your own. Bait is available for sale. Once the kids gain confidence in their fishing, the ponds may seem a little tame, but for generations these ponds have been a place to get started.

A network of 8 miles of trails winds through the natural areas of the park. Gain access to the trails by walking along the mill race past the log cabin. These pedestrian-only paths lead uphill, through woods to open fields. A trail map is not yet available, but the trails are not difficult to follow.

Kid-sized and easily accessible, Newlin Grist Mill's trout ponds are perfect for learning how to fish.

The historical 1704 gristmill continues to operate as it has for over 300 years: Powered by the flowing creek, a waterwheel turns a series of gears that spin a millstone, which grinds corn into cornmeal. Kids will be fascinated to watch the moving machinery powered only by running water. Cornmeal from the mill can be purchased in the park store. Past the historical complex, by the mill race, are several pleasant picnic areas and a playground.

The mill complex also includes other restored or re-created historical buildings, including a blacksmith shop where you can see demonstrations of the traditional techniques to forge implements using the anvil. The park conducts children's workshops during summer for kids to get hands-on experience with everyday Colonial activities such as cooking, soap making, and games.

Remember: Dogs are welcome on the trails but must be leashed. No wading in the pond, mill race, or creek. Fishing in the creek is permitted only to members of the Newlin Grist Mill Fly-Fishing Club; inquire at the office about membership.

PLAN B: At Ridley Creek State Park (Trip 57), you'll find plenty of fishing access on Ridley Creek, as well as hike and bike trails.

WHERE TO EAT NEARBY: South on US 1 is Concordville, a commercial area.

Trip 55

Haverford College Arboretum

Haverford College offers a safe, extensive green space and nature walk in a close-in Main Line suburb.

Address: 1 College Lane, Haverford, PA
Hours: Sunrise to sunset daily; Whitehead Campus Center open during academic year
Fee: Free
Contact: haverford.edu/arboretum, 610-896-1101
Bathrooms: In Whitehead Campus Center (when open)
Water/Snacks: Water fountain in Whitehead Campus Center; café open Monday through Friday, 8 A.M. to 2:30 P.M. during academic year
Maps: haverford.edu/visiting/campusmap.php
Directions by Car: Take I-76 West (Schuylkill Expressway) toward Valley Forge. Stay in the far left lane, and take the exit for City Avenue (US 1 South). Turn right onto City Avenue and proceed 2.5 miles. Turn right onto Lancaster Avenue (US 30 West) and drive about 3 miles; turn left at the main entrance of the Haverford campus (just past South Wyoming Avenue). Follow signs to the visitor parking lot. *GPS coordinates:* 40° 0.720´ N, 75° 17.966´ W.
Directions by Public Transit: Take the SEPTA Regional Rail Thorndale/Paoli line to Haverford station. Walk down Haverford Station Road, across Lancaster Avenue, and then turn left and walk a short distance to the main entrance of the Haverford campus. The walk should take less than 10 minutes.

Haverford College's beautiful 200-acre campus, tucked off of busy Lancaster Avenue on the Main Line, is a hidden green haven that has been around since 1834. Like Scott Arboretum at Swarthmore College (Trip 60), the Haverford Arboretum covers the entire college campus. It's a great spot for families—especially those with young children—to get outdoors in a safe, controlled environment, and it offers a surprising variety of quiet natural experiences.

Near the visitor parking area, signs mark a nature walk, a short but interesting natural footpath along a small, wooded stream. Elsewhere on campus, stroller-friendly paved paths wind through open grassy areas and between groves of trees. A large duck pond near the main entrance is a favorite spot for kids to explore; it is home to a giant snapping turtle. A small playground is next to a spectacularly twisted tree that looks almost human.

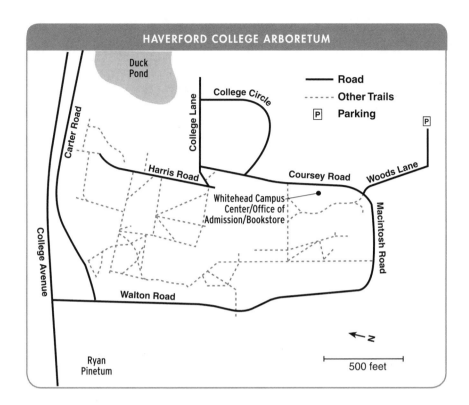

Encourage your kids to smell, touch, and even listen to the different trees around the campus. A pinetum—a grove of various pine trees—covers an 18-acre northwest corner.

There's a historical scion (descendant) of the "Penn Treaty Elm," the elm tree under which William Penn supposedly entered into a 1682 treaty with the Lenape Chief Tamanend.

Remember: Although there is plenty of room and open space for running and expending excess energy, this is a place of study. Supervise children. Also note that bikes are permitted on campus, but not on the nature trail.

PLAN B: Rolling Hill Park (Trip 25) has a natural playscape for young children, and more extensive trails and creek access for older children.

WHERE TO EAT NEARBY: The vicinity of Haverford in either direction along US 30 is a venerable commercial area, with plenty of food and beverage options.

Trip 56

Ages 5-8

Taylor Memorial Arboretum

Take quiet walks in a small, little-known naturalistic arboretum along the Ridley Creek in Delaware County.

Address: 10 Ridley Drive, Nether Providence, PA
Hours: 9 A.M. to 4 P.M., Monday through Friday
Fee: Free
Contact: taylorarboretum.org, 610-876-2649
Bathrooms: In visitor center
Water/Snacks: Water fountain in visitor center
Maps: taylorarboretum.org/map.htm
Directions by Car: Take I-95 South to Exit 7. Merge onto I-476 North toward Plymouth Meeting. Immediately take Exit 1 and continue onto MacDade Boulevard West, which becomes East 22nd Street. After 0.8 mile, take the right turn onto Chestnut Street. After 0.5 mile this becomes Chestnut Parkway; immediately turn left onto Ridley Drive. The entrance is a short distance ahead on your left. Proceed to the parking area. *GPS coordinates:* 39° 52.387′ N, 75° 22.074′ W.

Is Taylor Arboretum the best-kept secret in Delaware County? Often confused with the much bigger (and fee-based) Tyler Arboretum, this free, peaceful, pretty preserve is focused on maintaining a beautiful contemplative landscape suitable for all ages. Kids, especially younger ones, will enjoy the paths that meander to the Ridley Creek, where fishing is permitted. A wide variety of flowering shrubs and trees, as well as exotic evergreens, create a naturalistic woodland landscape that is always beautiful in a different way, no matter the season.

The unpaved paths are easy to follow and easy to navigate. The preserve is owned by a private trust that seeks to perpetuate the founder's wife's Quaker principles of quiet simplicity.

From the small visitor center, follow the trail that goes through the azalea garden (follow signs). It leads gently downhill to a meadow, where in summer a maze is mowed through the tall wildflowers. Continue downhill to get to the creek, where kids can wander along and wade in the water. The arboretum ends at the creek, but the other side is tree-shaded too; it's part of Chester Park.

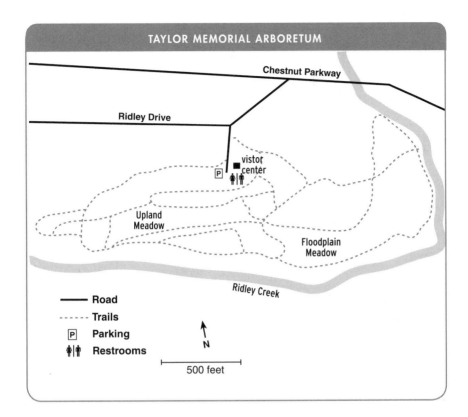

TAYLOR MEMORIAL ARBORETUM

Chestnut Parkway

Ridley Drive

vistor center

P

Upland Meadow

Floodplain Meadow

Ridley Creek

Road
Trails
P   Parking
Restrooms

N

500 feet

You can follow the creekside trail upstream, where there are other access points to the creek. The paths lead uphill back to the visitor center, but you can wander the trails in the middle to explore groves of different species of trees. A kids' favorite photo op is the giant, twisty-armed musclewood tree with its skin-smooth bark.

Remember: Dogs must be leashed.

PLAN B: Farther upstream, Ridley Creek State Park (Trip 57) provides trails for hiking and biking.

WHERE TO EAT NEARBY: Continue west on Chestnut Parkway to the commercial area at PA 352.

Trip 57

Ridley Creek State Park

This beautiful state park welcomes the whole family to enjoy diverse activities.

Address: 351 Gradyville Road, Newtown Square, PA
Hours: Sunrise to sunset daily
Fee: Free
Contact: www.dcnr.state.pa.us/stateparks, 610-892-3900; hiddenvalleyhorsefarm.
com
Bathrooms: At parking area for park office and at many picnic areas
Water/Snacks: None
Maps: friendsofrcsp.org/trailmap.html; www.dcnr.state.pa.us/stateparks (click on
Find a Park)
Directions by Car: Take I-76 West (Schuylkill Expressway) to Exit 331A for I-476
South (Blue Route) to Exit 5 onto US 1 South. After 5.9 miles, turn right onto
PA 252 North. After 0.2 mile, turn left onto Providence Road. Drive 4.0 miles,
and then take a left onto Gradyville Road and follow signs to the park office
and parking lot. *GPS coordinates:* 39° 57.151′ N, 75° 26.868′ W.

Ridley Creek State Park is a beautiful and popular—but not overcrowded—
state park close to the city and the western suburbs, where people of all ages
can enjoy the attractions of woods and streams. The woods are full of wildlife
and the trails lead you up and down hills, along and across streams, and over
and under bridges. At 2,606 acres, the park is a major green space in the midst
of a densely populated area.

Paved multiuse trails wind through the park; they're perfect for bikers,
walkers, and strollers. A network of paved, non-bike trails connect to the park
office parking area and provide more secluded walks through the woods for
strollers and young children. It's pleasant to walk or take a snack break in the
remnant formal gardens that surround the historical mansion that now houses
the park office.

If your family is ready for a more challenging hike, the park has many
miles of well-maintained trails that traverse the wooded hills (note that bikes
are not allowed on unpaved trails). These are well marked in different colors
that correspond to the trail names on the trail map. For a good introduction to
these trails, start at Parking Lot 7 next to the main office parking area and pick
up Yellow Trail; it passes through meadows and downhill through woods to a

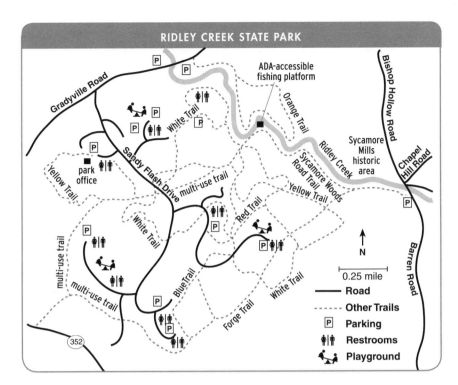

RIDLEY CREEK STATE PARK

ADA-accessible fishing platform

Gradyville Road

Bishop Hollow Road

Orange Trail

White Trail

Sandy Flash Drive

park office

Yellow Trail

Ridley Creek

Sycamore Woods

Sycamore Mills historic area

Chapel Hill Road

multi-use trail

Yellow Trail

Red Trail

N

0.25 mile

Barren Road

multi-use trail

White Trail

White Trail

multi-use trail

Blue Trail

Forge Trail

352

Road

Other Trails

P Parking

Restrooms

Playground

small stream. After walking along the stream, you can leave the trail and loop back across a bridge via the paved drive to the mansion. In winter, these trails are fun to snowshoe or ski on, and a sledding slope is outside the main office. About 5 miles of trails are open to horses; trailers can be parked at Lot 8. Hidden Valley Horse Farm, in the park, offers riding lessons.

Fishing is popular along the creek, notably in the historical Sycamore Mills area (Chapel Hill Road parking). The creek is stocked with trout in season. Along the trails are several ruins of old mill buildings, with signs describing the history of the site. An ADA-accessible fishing dock is here too. Numerous picnic areas and several playgrounds are throughout the park.

Remember: The Chapel Hill Road parking lot can get crowded because of its easy access to the multiuse trails and Ridley Creek. Fishing in Ridley Creek south of Sycamore Mills Dam is fly fishing, catch-and-release only. Dogs must be leashed.

PLAN B: The Colonial Penn Plantation, on the park grounds, is a 300-year-old working farm that vividly demonstrates what it was like to live in Colonial Pennsylvania (fee charged; open weekends April to November; colonialplantation.org).

WHERE TO EAT NEARBY: West Chester Pike (PA 3), on the northwest border of the park, is a commercial thoroughfare.

Winter in Philadelphia is never the same from one year to the next. Some years the snow falls and falls and never melts; some years it never snows. Most years winter seems to start slowly, shyly, before settling in for so long it seems spring will never get here. Whatever winter brings, it is an opportunity for outdoor fun that you can't have in any other season:

- Snow transforms the landscape—city, suburb, or rural—however briefly, into an amusement park. For really special sledding, go to a park or preserve where the wide-open hills are surrounded by snow-glazed woods, such as Fort Washington, Tyler, or Ridley Creek state parks (Trips 15, 35, 57).

- Snow lets you make tracks, and likewise shows where animals have walked; it clothes trees in sunlit sparkles; and it makes everything so quiet you can hear snowflakes hissing as they fall.

- Hiking through the snow can be fun—if you're properly equipped. Dress kids in layers; be prepared to remove them as kids warm up. Hats and gloves are obvious accessories, but keeping kids dry is critical. Snowpants and water-proof boots make a big difference. Hand warmers, available at hardware stores, are small packets that, when exposed to air, generate heat for hours; tucked into mittens or gloves, they can turn a sad, cold hike into a happy, warm one. When snow melts and refreezes, it can get slippery; ice creepers that attach to boots improve traction immeasurably.

- Consider trying snowshoes when the snow gets deep enough. Hiking in deep snow is difficult, if not unpleasant. And for kids, snow gets deep before it does for adults. Snowshoes, which fit over ordinary boots, turn walking *through* snow into walking *on top of* snow. In the Philadelphia region, you can snowshoe on most trails that are made for hiking, but don't go on trails with exposed rock expanses.

- Unlike downhill skiing, cross-country skiing can be enjoyed anywhere there's snow and straight lines; you don't need steep hills and you don't have to travel far—you needn't leave the city, in fact. Wide-open lawns and fields, woods trails, canal trails, and rail trails: all are amenable to skis. Kids can easily pick up the motion of skiing, which is a stylized walking/gliding, and they'll love flying over the snow.

The Pennsylvania State Park system issues a snow report for parks during winter, so you can keep up on where the snow is; see www.dcnr.state.pa.us/stateparks/winter/wintera.aspx.

Trip 58

Smedley Park

It's easy to get to this well-loved park, where families can walk in the woods along Crum Creek.

Address: 20 Papermill Road, Springfield, PA
Hours: Sunrise to sunset daily
Fee: Free
Contact: www.co.delaware.pa.us
Bathrooms: Near the playground
Water/Snacks: None
Maps: www.co.delaware.pa.us/summer/SmedleyTrails.pdf
Directions by Car: Take I-95 South to I-476 North to Exit 3. Turn right onto East Baltimore Pike, and then take the first left onto Papermill Road. Continue across the trolley tracks to the parking on the left. *GPS coordinates*: 39° 54.860′ N, 75° 21.593′ W.
Directions by Public Transit: Take the SEPTA 101 Trolley to the Papermill Road stop.

The popular 120-acre Smedley Park is conveniently located, whether you're traveling by car or public transportation. It's a small park with a big heart that takes advantage of its location along Crum Creek. For young children, it's good for a short walk in the woods.

Starting from the parking lot, cross the pretty arched pedestrian bridge over the creek to reach the woods trails. The dirt paths lead under I-476, as well as upstream with the creek, along a rocky hillside. If kids look carefully they will find "gems"—small, ruby-colored garnets studding the glittery, mica-laden rocks called Wissahickon schist. There is some climbing up and down; be prepared with sturdy shoes. Upstream of the bridge the creek is wide and rocky, good for splashing or wading in warm weather. As you go farther upstream, the terrain becomes steeper and rockier, with large outcroppings that have even more garnets.

Below the parking lot are a small, recently constructed playground and a shaded picnic area. The new Environmental Center, which focuses on gardening, is surrounded by plantings; the center itself is not designed for children but it is a nice place for young kids to look for butterflies among the plants and

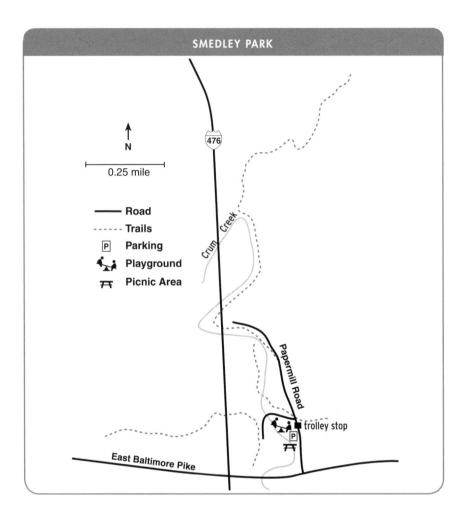

flowers. Fishing is permitted in the creek (warmwater fishing only, as it's not stocked). The best access is along the bank between the two bridges.

Remember: Dogs must be leashed.

PLAN B: Across Baltimore Pike, you can gain access to trails along Crum Creek at Scott Arboretum (Trip 60).

WHERE TO EAT NEARBY: Either head to Media or Swarthmore on Baltimore Pike, or stop in at the Springfield Mall, just east of Smedley.

Trip 59

Jenkins Arboretum & Gardens

Paved paths wind downhill through woodlands, past shrubs and native flowers to a big pond.

Address: 631 Berwyn Baptist Road, Devon, PA
Hours: Trails and grounds open 8 a.m. to sunset daily; education center open
    9 A.M. to 4 P.M. daily
Fee: Free
Contact: jenkinsarboretum.org, 610-647-8870
Bathrooms: Restrooms in education center
Water/Snacks: Water fountain in education center and behind it
Maps: jenkinsarboretum.org (click on Gardens)
Directions by Car: Take I-76 West to Exit 328A and merge onto US 202 South
    toward West Chester. Continue onto US 202 to the exit for PA 252 North/
    Valley Forge Road. Turn left at the end of the ramp. Continue straight
    through the traffic light, crossing Swedesford Road. Continue over the bridge
    and bear right onto Devon State Road. Turn right onto Berwyn Baptist Road.
    The main entrance and parking lot is up the hill on the left. *GPS coordinates*:
    40° 3.618′ N, 75° 26.094′ W.

With its beautiful hillside setting, stroller-friendly paved trails, and diversity of plants, Jenkins Arboretum is a quiet, pretty locale to enjoy the outdoors with very young children. Its 46 acres are a mix of wide-open vistas along a pond and curvy paths among native wildflowers, lush ferns, flowering shrubs, and mature woods.

Admission to the nonprofit arboretum is free (donations and memberships are welcome). Kids will love the whimsical water fountain, a sculpture that suggests a tree stump. It's behind the education center, a recently constructed environmentally friendly building. Greeters there are happy to help you get acquainted with the walking trails.

The grounds have 1.5 miles of trails, which are especially attractive in spring and early summer, when the azaleas and rhododendrons are blooming. The fall foliage is also splendid. Maps along the trails are at kids' height. Wander the wide, well-marked paths in any direction; you won't get lost and you can keep an eye on children running ahead of you. Don't miss the long-distance hilltop views north to Valley Forge and beyond. Sculptural benches are along

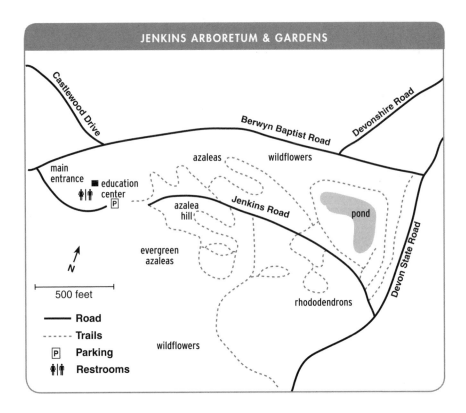

JENKINS ARBORETUM & GARDENS

Castlewood Drive

Berwyn Baptist Road

Devonshire Road

Devon State Road

azaleas

wildflowers

main entrance

■ education center

P

azalea hill

Jenkins Road

pond

N

evergreen azaleas

500 feet

rhododendrons

─── Road

----- Trails

P Parking

Restrooms

wildflowers

the paths; young kids will enjoy climbing on and off them. They'll also find the sliding tree-branch garden gate near the visitor center to be fascinating.

A wide grassy area above the pond invites running downhill to the water (the pond itself is fenced to protect the plantings around it). Instead of an interpretive sign here, a wind-up box plays recorded information.

Remember: Pets are not allowed. Stay on the paths and grassy areas. You can picnic around the education center but no food is permitted in the gardens.

PLAN B: Valley Forge National Historical Park (Trip 27) is nearby, with many miles of trails.

WHERE TO EAT NEARBY: South on Berwyn Baptist Road leads to Lancaster Avenue (US 30), a commercial thoroughfare.

Scott Arboretum and Crum Woods

Walk or bike on Swarthmore College's quiet campus, and then hike down the ravine to the woods along Crum Creek.

Address: 500 College Avenue, Swarthmore, PA
Hours: Grounds open sunrise to sunset daily; office open Monday through Friday, 8:30 A.M. to noon and 1 to 4:30 P.M.
Fee: Free
Contact: scottarboretum.org, 610-328-8025
Bathrooms: At Parrish Hall and Kohlberg Hall
Water/Snacks: Water fountains at Parrish Hall and Kohlberg Hall
Maps: At arboretum office; scottarboretum.org (click on Visitor Info)
Directions by Car: Take I-95 South to I-476 North to Exit 3 (Media/Swarthmore). Turn right onto Baltimore Pike. Stay in right lane; in less than 0.25 mile, turn right at the light onto PA 320 South/Chester Road. Turn right at the second light onto College Avenue. The arboretum parking lot is the second driveway on the left. *GPS coordinates:* 39° 54.381′ N, 75° 21.118′ W.
Directions by Public Transit: Take the SEPTA Regional Rail Media/Elwyn line to Swarthmore station. Walk uphill via Magill Walk; turn right in front of Parrish Hall at the top of the hill, past the library to the arboretum office. Or, take SEPTA bus 109 to Chester Road and College Avenue. Walk up College Avenue to the arboretum office.

The 300-acre Scott Arboretum extends throughout Swarthmore College's campus. Together with the adjacent Crum Woods, it makes a great destination for family walks.

Interspersed among the lawns and academic buildings are small themed gardens, groves of specimen trees, and themed plant collections. The Theresa Lang Garden of Fragrance, the Pollinator Garden, and the Terry Shane Teaching Garden are true to their names and are good for kids. At the Winter Garden, you'll find flowers that bloom in cold months.

Walkways are paved or grassy, suitable for strollers, and the campus is relatively flat or gently sloped. Bikes can be used on the campus. Adirondack chairs are scattered around the lawns—there's even a set made for giants, at the main building overlooking Magill Walk. You can picnic on the lawns under the trees. Sculptures, ranging from classical to contemporary, add to the fun of

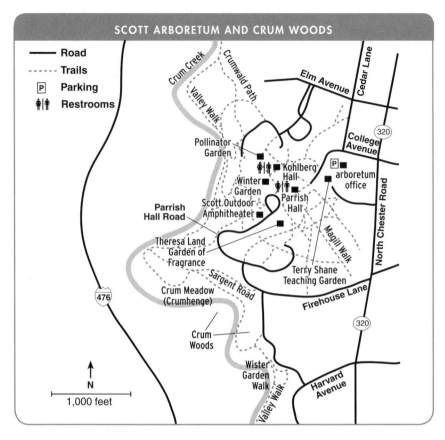

SCOTT ARBORETUM AND CRUM WOODS

- Road
- Trails
- P Parking
- ♀|♂ Restrooms

Crum Creek
Crumwald Path
Valley Walk
Elm Avenue
Cedar Lane
Pollinator Garden
College Avenue
320
Kohlberg Hall
P arboretum office
Winter Garden
Parrish Hall Road
Scott Outdoor Amphitheater
Parrish Hall
North Chester Road
Theresa Land Garden of Fragrance
Magill Walk
476
Sargent Road
Terry Shane Teaching Garden
Crum Meadow (Crumhenge)
Firehouse Lane
320
Crum Woods
Wister Garden Walk
Harvard Avenue
Valley Walk

N
1,000 feet

wandering the paths. The paths are not named, but families can put together a loop walk or bike ride around campus by keeping in mind that the main building is in the center at the top of the hill.

Crum Woods, a 220-acre natural area of forest and meadows, borders the landscaped areas of the campus. Trails lead down to the woods from behind the amphitheater. Crum Woods is a ravine surrounding Crum Creek, a small, rocky stream. This steep, rocky area is quite different from the campus (proper footwear is advisable). About 3.5 miles of trails cover the grounds, for pedestrian use only. Follow Valley Walk Trail along the creek to "Crumhenge," a 6-acre meadow where you'll come upon mysterious standing stones.

The creek can be reached from numerous points along Valley Walk Trail. Slow, shallow, and wide, it invites splashing and wading.

Remember: Dogs must be leashed.

PLAN B: For more-extensive bike and hike trails on paved and unpaved surfaces, go to Ridley Creek State Park (Trip 57).

WHERE TO EAT NEARBY: Follow Chester Road to Swarthmore's business district.

Trip 61

Marsh Creek State Park

A large lake is great for paddling and fishing, and is surrounded by rolling hills with easy hiking paths.

Address: 675 Park Road, Downingtown, PA
Hours: Park open sunrise to sunset daily (fishing/boating permitted 24 hours)
Fee: Ground free; fee charged for pool and boat rental
Contact: www.dcnr.state.pa.us/stateparks, 610-458-5119; boat rental: marshcreeklake.com, 610-458-5040; horseback riding: hopespringshorsefarm.com
Bathrooms: At boat launch parking lots and pool lot
Water/Snacks: Snack bar (seasonal) at boat rental
Maps: www.dcnr.state.pa.us/stateparks (click on Find a Park)
Directions by Car: Take I-76 West (Pennsylvania Turnpike) to Exit 312 (Downingtown) and merge onto PA 100 North. Drive 1.6 miles, then turn left onto Ticonderoga Boulevard. Continue 0.6 mile to Park Road and drive 2 miles to the park entrance and the east boat launch parking. *GPS coordinates:* 40° 3.975′ N, 75° 43.252′ W.

Tucked into populous north–central Chester County, Marsh Creek State Park is a beautiful forested gem that spreads over 1,727 acres, including a 535-acre lake that offers great family boating and fishing, and hiking and biking trails in the surrounding fields and woods.

The lake is superb for families to build their boating expertise. The wide lake can get quite breezy, which is ideal for learning to sail or windsurf, but you're always within sight of the shore. There are also several long, peaceful arms off the main lake, excellent for fishing or exploring by paddling. Young anglers can also fish from the dock or in shallows around the shoreline. Sailboats, canoes, kayaks, paddleboats, paddleboards, and electric motorboats are available for rent at the boat rental building, as are fishing rods.

Trails meander through the woods and fields surrounding the lake. About 6 miles are open to mountain bikes; horses are permitted on part of this section. Hope Springs Horse Farm, in the park on North Reeds Road, offers horseback riding lessons for all ages.

The remainder of the trails are pedestrian-only. All trails are natural footpaths. On the west side, they wind down to the East Branch of the Brandywine

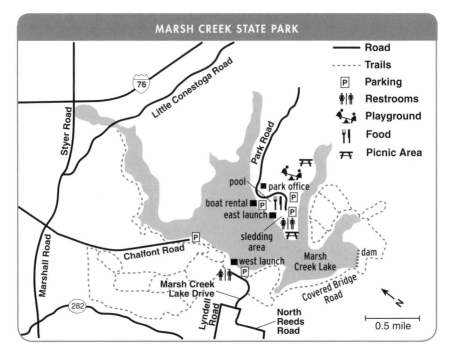

MARSH CREEK STATE PARK

Creek; other than this steep section, they're generally level or gently sloped. Kids will enjoy playing in the creek or along the lakeshore.

The forested lake attracts waterfowl and many other birds and wildlife. Turtles are not only here in profusion, basking on logs or artificial platforms, but they're remarkably tolerant of (quiet) boaters. Bald eagles are not uncommon.

No swimming is allowed in the lake, but a swimming pool is near the east boat launch, and a playground is located nearby. Picnic tables are scattered around the parking areas, or you can spread a blanket on the grass and take in the beautiful views.

In winter, the lake is open for skating or ice fishing. Winter hikes in the woods offer great views of the lake; just be prepared for wind chill close to the water.

Remember: Hunting is permitted in about 900 acres of the park. During hunting season, wear blaze orange on the trails. On summer weekends, the main parking lots get crowded. The east boat launch is an alternative parking area; for hiking or biking, use the lots on Chalfont Road or Milford Road.

PLAN B: In Downingtown, on Norwood Road, the Struble Trail (Trip 62) is a paved creekside trail for walking or biking.

WHERE TO EAT NEARBY: Shops and restaurants are in the village of Eagle on PA 100.

Trip 62

All Ages

Struble Trail and Uwchlan Trail

A very pretty, family-friendly multiuse trail leads along the East Branch of the Brandywine Creek.

Address: Norwood Road near PA 282, Downingtown, PA
Hours: 8 A.M. to sunset daily
Fee: Free
Contact: chesco.org/ccparks, 610-942-2450
Bathrooms: Portable toilets at parking areas
Water/Snacks: None
Maps: chesco.org/ccparks (click on Trails); uwchlan.com (click on Information, then Parks & Recreation)
Directions by Car: For the Norwood parking area: Take I-76 West (Schuylkill Expressway) to Exit 328A and merge onto US 202 South. After 11.1 miles, exit onto US 30 West toward Downingtown. Continue on US 30 for 7 miles to the exit for PA 282/Wallace Road. Turn left onto Norwood Road. The parking area is on the right. *GPS coordinates*: 40° 1.013′ N, 75° 42.210′ W.

The Struble Trail is a wide, paved multiuse trail along the East Branch of the Brandywine Creek beginning in Downingtown Borough. It's popular with families for biking and walking, yet nowhere near as crowded or fast-paced as some of the other trails in the region.

Young kids can enjoy lots of straightaway to get their biking legs in shape. Although relatively short (currently 2.6 miles, though when finished it will be 16 miles), the trail is a great choice for families. A former rail bed, the trail has a level, easy grade for its entire length and follows a lovely tree-shaded stretch of the wide, meandering creek between Dorlan Mill Road (south of Marsh Creek State Park) and Norwood Road. There are several well-gated road crossings.

A spur trail at Norwood connects to Kardon Park in Downingtown, and above the dam near the Norwood access is a popular swimming hole. Plans are in place to connect the trail to the north with Marsh Creek State Park (Trip 61) and Springton Manor Farm (Trip 70), and beyond, for a total of 16 miles.

The creek is stocked with trout; along the trail are great fishing access spots.

At about 1.75 miles north of the Norwood parking area, the trail connects with the Uwchlan Trail, in Uwchlan Township. This is another paved trail, narrower and a bit hillier than the Struble Trail. It crosses several roads, with

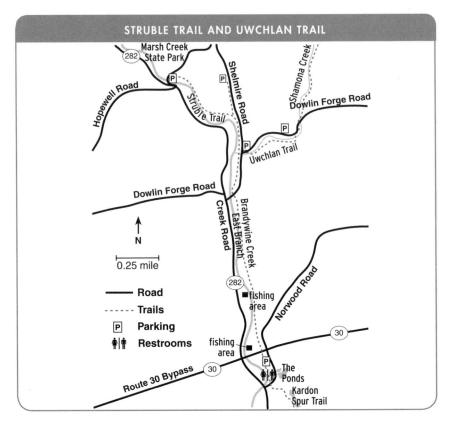

Marsh Creek State Park
282
Hopewell Road
Struble Trail
Shelmire Road
Shamona Creek
Dowlin Forge Road
Uwchlan Trail
Dowlin Forge Road
Creek Road
Brandywine Creek East Branch

N
0.25 mile

—— Road
------ Trails
P Parking
Restrooms

282
fishing area
Norwood Road
30
fishing area
30
Route 30 Bypass
The Ponds
Kardon Spur Trail

marked but ungated crossings. While perhaps too challenging for training wheels, it's excellent for older kids to bike or walk on. It follows the rocky Shamona Creek up a pretty, wooded valley; the stream narrows to a trickle just south of a country club near Milford Road. (This is a good turn-around point—although the trail continues through residential neighborhoods from there, it's not particularly scenic.) Along the Uwchlan Trail are several ruins and interpretive signs describing the history of iron making at Dowlin Forge, charcoaling and logging in the valley, and a gristmill.

Remember: Dogs should be leashed. Parking areas are in several spots beside the main Norwood access point; see map. A delayed-harvest (artificial lure only) trout fishing area is on the East Branch of the Brandywine between Shelmire and Dorlan Mill roads.

PLAN B: Springton Manor Farm (Trip 70), which administers the Struble Trail, has more trails, as well as a working farm open to visitors; Marsh Creek State Park (Trip 61) nearby has boating, a swimming pool, and hiking trails.

WHERE TO EAT NEARBY: Continue on PA 282 a short distance into Downingtown.

Trip 63

Harmony Hill Nature Area

Lush woods and towering rocks beautifully frame a family-friendly multiuse trail along the East Branch of the Brandywine Creek.

Address: 1183 Harmony Hill Road, Downingtown, PA
Hours: Dawn to dusk daily
Fee: Free
Contact: eastbradford.org, 610-436-5108
Bathrooms: None
Water/Snacks: None
Maps: eastbradford.org (click on Maps)
Directions by Car: Take I-76 West (Schuylkill Expressway) to Exit 328A and merge onto US 202 South. Go 11.5 miles to the exit for US 30 Downingtown. Continue for 5 miles to the US 30 Business/Lancaster Avenue exit. Turn left onto Lancaster Avenue. After 0.3 mile, turn left onto Quarry Road, then after 1 mile, turn right onto West Boot Road. After 1.3 miles, turn left onto Skelp Level Road and continue for approximately 1.7 miles to the intersection of Harmony Hill Road. Turn right onto Harmony Hill Road and continue approximately 0.6 mile to Gibson's Covered Bridge. The parking area will be on your right, just before the bridge. *GPS coordinates*: 39° 58.577′ N, 75° 40.952′ W.

The East Branch Brandywine Trail, a multiuse paved path good for walkers, bikers, and strollers, runs along its namesake creek for 2.6 miles beginning at the Sugar's Bridge Nature Area at Skelp Level Road (the M. John Johnson Nature Center). Easiest access to this trail is from the parking area at Harmony Hill Road, about 1 mile north. The trail is popular with families because it is flat, wide, and pretty, with no busy road crossings. (There is a gated crossing at Harmony Hill Road, which is lightly traveled.)

Just north of Harmony Hill Road, the trail connects to 6.5 miles of natural-surface bike/hike trails that climb into the rocky wooded ravine of Harmony Hill Nature Area. These hilly trails are much too challenging for younger bikers but not a problem for hiking—especially for older kids. (Remember to keep an eye out for the bikes.) The woods are remarkably rich and full of wildlife and the rocks that the trail traverses are lustrous. From rock outcrops along the way, and an overlook at the top of the ridge, there are good views

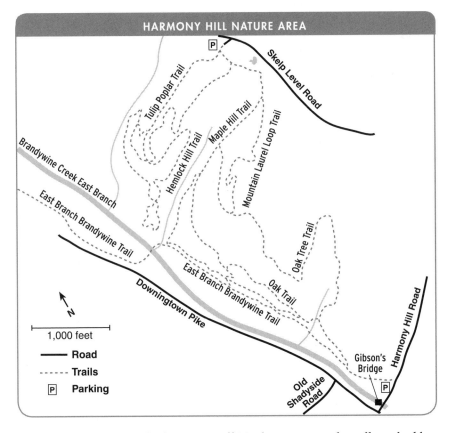

Tulip Poplar Trail

Skelp Level Road

Maple Hill Trail

Mountain Laurel Loop Trail

Hemlock Hill Trail

Brandywine Creek East Branch

East Branch Brandywine Trail

Oak Tree Trail

East Branch Brandywine Trail

Downingtown Pike

Oak Trail

Harmony Hill Road

Gibson's Bridge

Old Shadyside Road

N

1,000 feet

—— Road
- - - - - Trails
P   Parking

across the valley when the leaves are off. Trails are extremely well marked but it helps to consult the map at the kiosk in the parking lot to get an idea where they cross each other. A good hour-long loop hike follows the white-blazed trail uphill from the East Branch Brandywine Trail; this trail ends at a fork with the blue-blazed trail going in both directions; continue on the blue trail counterclockwise to loop back to the fork via the green-blazed trail.

You can fish from many access points along the creek. Boats can be put in for paddling from Gibson's Bridge at Harmony Hill Road (a downstream take-out is at Shaw's Bridge Park, where swimming in the creek is popular).

Remember: Dogs must be leashed. Alternate parking is at the M. John Johnson Nature Center on Skelp Level Road, where additional natural footpaths traverse the hills and connect to the paved trail.

PLAN B: Marsh Creek State Park (Trip 61) nearby has a large lake for paddling and fishing, and a swimming pool.

WHERE TO EAT NEARBY: Harmony Hill is between the commercial areas of Downingtown and West Chester on the US 322 bypass.

Trip 64

French Creek State Park

A wide variety of trails in lush forested hills surround quiet lakes, offering delightful family hiking, boating, fishing, mountain biking, or camping.

Address: 843 Park Road, Elverson, PA
Hours: Sunrise to sunset daily (camping and fishing permitted 24 hours)
Fee: Trails, free; fees charged for pool, boat rental, and camping (see website for details)
Contact: www.dcnr.state.pa.us/stateparks, 610-582-9680
Bathrooms: At park office, Scotts Run and Hopewell Lake boat launches, and many picnic areas
Water/Snacks: Water fountains at restrooms; snack concession at pool (in season)
Maps: www.dcnr.state.pa.us/stateparks (click on Find a Park)
Directions by Car: Take I-76 West (Pennsylvania Turnpike) to Exit 312 for PA 100 North. Turn left onto PA 401 and drive 6.5 miles. Turn right onto PA 345 and drive 3.4 miles to South Entrance Road, then 1.4 miles to Park Road and the park entrance. Follow signs to the day-use area parking lot.
GPS coordinates: 40° 11.902′ N, 75° 47.607′ W.

At more than 7,700 forested acres, with two lakes, miles of trails, a swimming pool, playgrounds, campsites, and many other amenities, French Creek State Park is a destination worth heading to no matter what your family wants to do outdoors. Because so many options await you, it is advisable to check a map beforehand and plan ahead. A good place to begin is at the day-use area by Hopewell Lake, where you can gain access to trails, boat rentals, and a swimming pool.

The deep, rich forests in the park are surrounded by several thousand acres of additional woods in parks and game lands, making it a haven for birds and wildlife of all kinds. The park naturalist leads guided walks suitable for families, and evening programming for campers.

More than 35 miles of well-maintained, color-blazed trails weave through the woods. Some of the trails are open to mountain bikes; others are open to horses. For families with young children, a good introduction to the park's trails is the

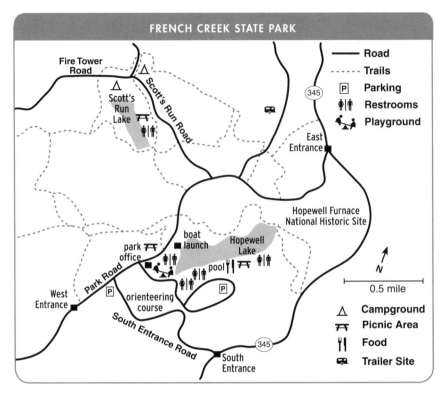

Fire Tower Road

Scott's Run Lake

Scott's Run Road

345

East Entrance

Road
Trails
P Parking
Restrooms
Playground

Hopewell Furnace National Historic Site

boat launch

park office

Hopewell Lake

pool

Park Road

West Entrance

orienteering course

South Entrance Road

345

South Entrance

N

0.5 mile

Campground
Picnic Area
Food
Trailer Site

level, hiking-only path that starts at the day-use area parking lot. It goes about 0.75 mile along the southern Hopewell Lake shore, providing close-up views of turtles, frogs, and dragonflies. For young kids, this may be enough. Just past the lake, the path intersects the yellow-blazed Horse-Shoe Trail. By continuing on the footpath into the woods for another 0.5 mile, you'll arrive at Hopewell Furnace National Historic Site (Trip 65). For a more challenging loop hike, turn left onto the Horse-Shoe Trail; it goes uphill back above the lake and returns to the day-use area via a brief walk on Boone Trail (note that both of these are open to horses, and Boone Trail is open to bikes).

In winter, most trails are suitable for snowshoeing, and ice fishing and skating are permitted on the lakes.

The park is a prime spot for learning the art of orienteering—finding your way by map and compass. Head to the self-guiding course west of Hopewell Lake. Be sure to get a map of the course at the park office, and bring your own compass.

Hopewell Lake and Scotts Run Lake offer easy, contained canoeing and kayaking with a mostly natural shoreline. Boats may be rented at Hopewell Lake in summer. Both lakes are stocked and are excellent for fishing; Scotts Run is a fishery for trout and other coldwater species. Visitors cannot swim in the lakes, but the large and popular pool on the south shore of the lake is open during summer months (fee charged).

Picnic areas are scattered around the park. Near the south entrance is a playground. The park is one of the few in the Philadelphia region with individual tent campsites; more than 200 are available (access from the road is off of Park Road beyond the day-use area). Cabins and yurts can also be rented.

Remember: Pets are permitted but must be controlled. There are mountain-biking trails but there is no access for road bikes.

PLAN B: Adjacent to French Creek, Hopewell Furnace National Historic Site (Trip 65) is a restored iron-making village that kids will enjoy touring, and there are numerous hiking trails. Natural Lands Trust's Crow's Nest Preserve, nearby, has many hiking-only trails.

WHERE TO EAT NEARBY: It's best to bring a picnic. A seasonal concession stand is available by the pool.

Trip 65

All Ages

Hopewell Furnace National Historic Site

Experience a vanished way of life at a restored iron-making village in a huge forested park.

Address: 2 Mark Bird Lane, Elverson, PA
Hours: Grounds and historical buildings open 9 A.M. to 5 P.M. daily from June through August, and Wednesday through Sunday, September through May; orchard open September and October, varying days; in May and September, buildings may be open additional days; call ahead
Fee: Free
Contact: nps.gov/hofu, 610-582-8773
Bathrooms: Outside the park office
Water/Snacks: Water fountain outside the park office; snack vending machine inside the office
Maps: nps.gov/hofu (click on Plan Your Visit)
Directions by Car: Take I-76 West (Pennsylvania Turnpike) to Exit 312. Take PA 100 North 9 miles to PA 23. Turn left onto PA 23 West and travel 7 miles to PA 345. Turn right onto PA 345 North and drive 4 miles to the park entrance and parking lots. *GPS coordinates*: 40° 12.417′ N, 75° 46.386′ W.

Southeastern Pennsylvania looks the way it does today in large part because of the iron forges of the eighteenth and nineteenth centuries. Iron making affected where people lived, where roads were laid out, where dams and towns were built. Hopewell Furnace, a restored iron-making plantation (village), re-creates the life of an iron-making community, including a charcoal furnace, a mammoth waterwheel, and a livestock farm. Set in a lovely 848-acre park, with many walking trails, the site is a great place for families to enjoy the outdoors and experience history at the same time.

Begin at the visitor center next to the main parking lot, where you can pick up a guide to the site, view exhibits, and watch a short film. A paved path leads downhill to the village below. You can take a self-guided tour of the site, and enter the restored buildings whenever the park is open. Throughout the year, visitors can attend special events such as sheepshearing; check the website for a schedule. In September and October, you can pick apples in the orchard.

Friendly farm animals are unofficial greeters at the restored Hopewell Furnace village.

The wide, gravel village paths are suitable for children of all ages (though not stroller-friendly). In addition, 12 miles of dirt trails suitable for school-age children lead through the site, connecting to trails in several adjacent parks and preserves that make up a huge forested area called the Hopewell Big Woods. These footpaths explore woods and follow small streams. You can walk a short section of the yellow-blazed, long-distance Horse-Shoe Trail by following the main village path south to PA 345, where the Horse-Shoe Trail follows Green Lane to Harmonyville Road. For longer woods hikes, take the Horse-Shoe Trail in the opposite direction, starting near the Charcoal Pits; it's about 0.25 mile to French Creek State Park, where you can connect to trails (some un-blazed) that follow the tree-lined shores of Hopewell Lake, or to the moderately difficult blue-blazed Boone Trail. Another option is to follow the green-blazed Lenape Trail along Hopewell Road, across PA 345, and to the Baptism Creek Trail, which passes by the historical Bethesda Church and connects to the Hopewell Trail in the quiet, forested Crow's Nest Preserve.

Remember: Pets are allowed in all outdoor areas of the park open to the public.

PLAN B: French Creek State Park (Trip 64) is adjacent to the site, offering hiking and biking trails, playgrounds, a lake for boating and fishing, and numerous campsites.

WHERE TO EAT NEARBY: Bring a picnic to enjoy in the picnic area next to the parking lot, or in the apple orchard.

In the Philadelphia region, experiencing history is as simple as taking a walk in the woods. It seems as if an old mill is along almost every stream, that a Revolutionary War skirmish occurred near every old stone bridge, and that every park was once a family estate.

Kids get excited about history that's part of a fun trip outdoors. It's easier to engage their minds when they're physically active and happy. History outdoors stimulates a child's imagination: They're hiking where soldiers cut wood for cooking fires; canoeing where mule-drawn barges carried coal; eating lunch on a stone wall from an iron forge.

Many trips in this book lead to places centered on a historic event, such as the Valley Forge National Historic Park (Trip 27) or Washington Crossing State Park (Trip 82), both of which preserve sites where key events occurred during the American Revolution. Here kids can hike or bike through the very same landscape where historic events occurred; they can learn about history from interpretive centers with exhibits, and from guides who can tell stories and answer questions. Other sites honor a historic figure, like the Daniel Boone Homestead (Trip 50), where kids can peer into Squire Boone's blacksmith shop and walk the woods where his son Daniel meandered.

The Philadelphia region became an early industrial powerhouse because of the abundance of swift-flowing streams that powered mills. Today, kids can get a feeling for those times at such places as Hopewell Furnace National Historic Site (Trip 65), where the two-story waterwheel that powered the mill still turns; Batsto Village (Trip 99),where the sawmill still cuts trees into lumber; or Newlin Grist Mill (Trip 54), where a mill still grinds corn into meal.

Historical agriculture is the focus at Howell Living History Farm (Trip 89), where kids can talk to real farmers about the centuries-old methods and tools they're using to till, plant, and harvest.

Experiencing history on such trips helps kids imagine the past on other trips, when they encounter its remains. Hiking and biking paths in the region's parks and preserves are replete with ruins of old structures such as mills, dams, forges, ice houses, and spring houses. Former canal towpaths and railway lines are now trails, with old locks and bridges. Many of these places include descriptive signs that tell the story of the past. All this history adds an extra dimension to the outdoors that will inspire kids to stop and look, read about, and imagine the history that happened here.

Trip 66

Schuylkill River Trail

Bike or walk along the Schuylkill River on a hard-surface, level, multiuse trail that connects city to countryside.

Address: Cromby trailhead, 829 Township Line Road, Phoenixville, PA
Hours: Variable, but generally sunrise to sunset daily
Fee: Free
Contact: schuylkillrivertrail.com
Bathrooms: None at Cromby trailhead; see map for location of other restrooms
Water/Snacks: None at Cromby trailhead
Maps: schuylkillrivertrail.com
Directions by Car: For the Cromby trailhead: Take I-76 West (Schuylkill Expressway) to Exit 328A for US 422 West. Take US 422 West to the Oaks exit. Turn left onto Egypt Road. After 3.1 miles, turn left onto Bridge Street/PA 29. After 1 mile, turn left onto Gay Street/PA 113. Stay straight to go onto Franklin Avenue. Take the second left onto Fillmore Street. After 0.7 mile, turn right onto Township Line Road. The trailhead parking lot is on the left.
   GPS coordinates: 40° 8.833′ N, 75° 31.750′ W.
Directions by Public Transit: The trail can be reached by SEPTA in Philadelphia at the Schuylkill Banks (30th Street station), and in Norristown via the Regional Rail Manayunk/Norristown line.

The 130-mile Schuylkill River Trail (SRT), which has been largely completed between Philadelphia and Phoenixville, and from Pottstown to Reading, as well as segments north, will eventually extend to Pottsville. The trail is hard-surface and level, excellent for family bike rides and walks (including walks with strollers).

Because the SRT is a long-distance trail, there are numerous options for planning a trip. Popular trailheads include the Schuylkill Banks and East Fairmount Park (Trip 8) and Manayunk trailheads in Philadelphia; Betzwood and Pawlings Road in Valley Forge (Trip 27); Mont Clare/Lock 60 (Trip 21) in Montgomery County; and the trailhead at Cromby, just north of Phoenixville in Chester County (completed in 2012).

From Cromby, the trail can be taken north 5.6 miles to Parker Ford, with great views not only of the winding river but also of a closed electrical generating station. From Phoenixville south, the trail can be taken 55 miles

The Schuylkill River Trail's Philadelphia segment features numerous sculptures, including a statue of Olympic rower Jack Kelly.

to the Schuylkill Banks. (As of this writing, the connector in Phoenixville to Cromby was under construction.)

Start any SRT trip by checking the SRT website, which has excellent, up-to-date maps and information about trail status, parking, trailhead amenities (such as bathrooms and restaurants), and trail conditions.

Biking or walking the trail is a great way to experience the Schuylkill River as it flows down from countryside to suburbia to city. The river is beautiful, tree-lined, wide, and stately. The towns and boroughs along its banks north of the city are rich with history. Along the trail, there are opportunities for kids to learn about navigational canals, the coal industry, and the American Revolution; to watch eagles, ospreys, and herons; and to enjoy the ever-changing scenery of a river view.

If you don't have a bike, you can borrow one for the day in Phoenixville under the BikeSchuylkill program that is designed to enable families to enjoy biking the trail. See the SRT website for details.

Remember: The SRT can get crowded, particularly on weekends. Some short sections of the SRT are currently on-road, but those roads are typically not heavily traveled.

PLAN B: At the SRT's trailhead in Schuylkill Canal Park/Lock 60 (Trip 21), there is access to the canal and river for paddling. The Upper Schuylkill Valley Park and Black Rock Sanctuary, south of Phoenixville on PA 113, have hiking trails.

WHERE TO EAT NEARBY: Family-friendly restaurants and cafés are in Phoenixville, near the Cromby trailhead.

Trip 67

All Ages

Hibernia County Park

Hike, paddle, fish, and camp at this hidden forest treasure surrounding a small lake.

Address: 1 Park Road, Coatesville, PA
Hours: 8 A.M. to sunset daily
Fee: Free
Contact: chesco.org/ccparks, 610-383-3812
Bathrooms: See park map
Water/Snacks: None
Maps: chesco.org/ccparks (click on Park Sites)
Directions by Car: Take I-76 West (Schuylkill Expressway) to Exit 328A and merge onto US 202 South toward West Chester. Take US 202 to the exit for US 30 West. After 11.6 miles, take the exit toward Reeceville Road/Coatesville. Turn left onto Fisherville Road, then immediately right onto Reeceville Road, which becomes Cedar Knoll Road. Follow it for 2 miles, then look for signs for the park. Park in the lot. *GPS coordinates*: 40° 1.801′ N, 75° 50.503′ W.

Hibernia County Park is a quiet refuge offering numerous opportunities for families to enjoy its woods, stream, and lake. Hibernia was historically an iron-making center; cottages, ruins, and other structures from the iron-making era remain.

The 990-acre park occupies the hills east and south of Chambers Lake, a reservoir created from a dam on the Birch Run. Surrounded by woods and farm fields, the serene 90-acre lake, which is open only to electric motors or unpowered boats, is a lovely spot to learn how to handle a boat.

South of the lake the West Branch of the Brandywine Creek runs through the park in a low, steep-sided valley, where there is easy hiking through lush woods. Rim Trail is a level, easy trail along the east creekbank via an old railroad bed that loops back after a steep but short climb up the ridge. Forge Trail explores the west side of the creek near the old dam. Birch Run Trail is fun; it climbs up the stream from the lower dam to the upper dam, revealing a view of the spillway. Other trails in the park explore the wooded hills overlooking the lake in and around the campgrounds and playing fields. The half-mile Lake Trail is wheelchair-accessible. Most trails are open to mountain bikes, horses, and cross-country skis.

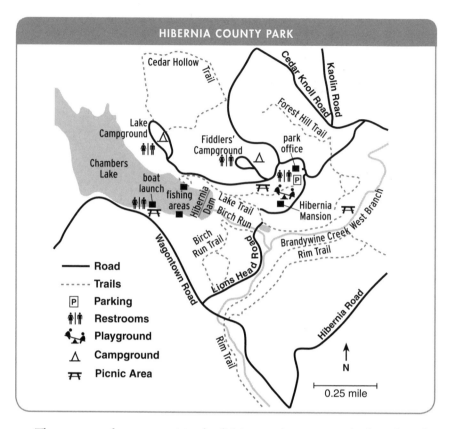

Cedar Hollow Trail

Cedar Knoll Road

Kaolin Road

Forest Hill Trail

Lake Campground

Fiddlers' Campground

park office

Chambers Lake

boat launch

fishing areas

Hibernia Dam

Lake Trail

Birch Run

Hibernia Mansion

Brandywine Creek West Branch

Birch Run Trail

Wagontown Road

Rim Trail

Lions Head Road

Hibernia Road

Rim Trail

— Road
----- Trails
P   Parking
Restrooms
Playground
△   Campground
Picnic Area

N

0.25 mile

There are ample opportunities for fishing on the trout-stocked creek or the lake, which is stocked with warm-water species. A fishing pier is at the lake's north end, or you can fish from the shore. In addition, Hibernia has a three-quarter-acre kids' fishing pond southwest of the mansion that's restricted to children and differently-abled individuals during trout season. Fishing rods can be borrowed at the park ranger station.

In addition to shady picnic groves, you can picnic along the lake, the pond, or the creek. Two playgrounds, one near the office for ages 5 to 12 and the other in the Old Dam area for all ages, feature state-of-the-art equipment.

Hibernia is an excellent destination for families seeking an introduction to camping. Two campgrounds have first-come, first-served sites (water but no showers). The Lake Campground is near the boat launch; Fiddlers' Campground is northwest of the mansion.

Remember: Dogs must be leashed. Swimming is not permitted in the lake.

PLAN B: Sadsbury Woods Preserve, west of the park, is a large nature preserve with many trails through Chester County's largest intact forest.

WHERE TO EAT NEARBY: It's best to bring a picnic.

Trip 68

Ages 5-8

Warwick County Park

This small, high-quality park features short nature walks or fishing along French Creek.

Address: 191 County Park Road, Pottstown, PA
Hours: 8 A.M. to sunset daily
Fee: Free
Contact: chesco.org/ccparks, 610-469-1916
Bathrooms: See park map
Water/Snacks: None
Maps: chesco.org/ccparks (click on Park Sites)
Directions by Car: Take I-76 West (Pennsylvania Turnpike) to Exit 312 and merge onto PA 100 North toward Pottstown. After 5.2 miles, turn left onto Horse-Shoe Trail, which becomes Nantmeal Road. Stay on Nantmeal Road and take the second right onto Iron Bridge Road. After 0.7 mile (the road briefly becomes Warwick Furnace Road), turn right onto County Park Road. Continue 1.2 miles to the park entrance on the right and park in the lot. *GPS coordinates:* 40° 10.111′ N, 75° 43.285′ W.

At Warwick County Park, natural areas fan out from a central open area with playgrounds and fields that extends below a ridge. It's easy to find your way around with kids for short but rewarding outings.

Attention to detail and high quality are the hallmarks of this park. The main trails all connect from the trailhead at the main entrance and make successive loops, so you can take hikes of short, medium, or longer duration. The trails are clearly blazed and well maintained. Iron Heritage Trail features interpretive signage designed to help kids imagine the woods when they were not the natural wildlife havens they are today, but instead sites for iron-making industry. Tree ID trail, a spur trail, teaches children how to identify common native trees by their leaves, bark, and fruit. A segment of the Horse-Shoe Trail, a long-distance trail that starts at Valley Forge, passes through the park on its way to the Appalachian Trail to the west. In addition to the main trails, an easy half-mile Nature Trail with educational signage, loops below the entrance drive, exploring meadows, vernal ponds, wetlands, and a creek.

An oddball feature of this park is the observation deck that can be reached by following the Horse-Shoe Trail uphill along the woods edge. The deck is

Warwick County Park spreads out along gentle rolling hills by upper French Creek.

a converted historical truss bridge that was moved from the French Creek crossing. Although the view from the bridge is less than magnificent, it's fun for kids to climb up and look out over the park.

Almost 2 miles of French Creek runs through the park. Trout-stocked, it is popular for fishing. Some parts of the creek in the park have been enhanced to create artificial-pool and riffle fish habitat. The park features a universally accessible fishing dock; follow the boardwalk from the lower end of the parking lot.

Two brand-new playgrounds—one for kids ages 2 to 5 and one for ages 5 to 12—are next to the parking lot.

Remember: Dogs must be leashed.

PLAN B: Green Valleys Association at Welkinweir (Trip 69) has extensive, pedestrian-only trails.

WHERE TO EAT NEARBY: Follow County Park Road north to PA 23. Saint Peters Village, off of PA 23, is a quaint commercial area.

Trip 69

Green Valleys Association at Welkinweir

Beautiful woodlands surrounding a country estate and arboretum offer outstanding walks and hikes.

Address: 1368 Prizer Road, Pottstown, PA
Hours: 9 A.M. to 5 P.M. Monday through Friday (to 4 P.M. in winter)
Fee: Free (donations accepted)
Contact: welkinweir.org, 610-469-4900
Bathrooms: Portable toilet near Education Building
Water/Snacks: None
Maps: At entrance kiosk (for hiking, be sure to get the Wild Areas Guide); greenvalleys.org/documents/welkinwier-hiking-brochure.pdf
Directions by Car: Take I-76 West (Pennsylvania Turnpike) to Exit 312 and merge onto PA 100 North toward Pottstown. Follow PA 100 past PA 401 at Ludwig's Corner, and continue 3.7 miles to Prizer Road. Turn left on Prizer Road. Welkinweir is 1 mile ahead on the left. Park in the lot. *GPS coordinates:* 40° 9.290′ N, 75° 41.031′ W.

At Welkinweir, a 197-acre historical country estate and arboretum that is the headquarters of the nonprofit watershed conservation organization the Green Valleys Association (GVA), beautiful hillside forests surround a large pond and landscaped grounds. The property features excellent short hiking trails, as well as easy paths through the interesting gardens.

Welkinweir spreads over two ridges and a valley in between. The near ridge, with the entrance, is landscaped. This is the site of the arboretum, the Estate House and Education Building, and a four-square Children's Garden that has flowers and plants with plenty of sensory appeal.

For kids a highlight of the 55-acre arboretum is the aptly named Great Pond, at the base of the hill below the eighteenth-century Estate House. All of the arboretum paths are wide, gently sloped, grassy or mowed surfaces. The path that leads down to the pond, through the Barn Ruins, passes under a weeping beech tree that's as big as a cottage, if not a house. Twisty, human-like trees guard the pond's banks. At the pond, look for herons, dragonflies, and frogs. Following the mowed path around the pond leads to a bridge over

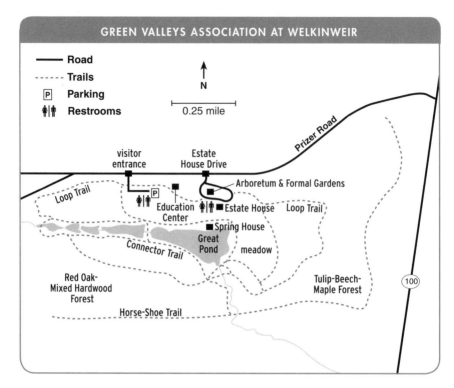

Road

Trails

P   Parking

🚹|🚺   Restrooms

N

0.25 mile

Prizer Road

visitor entrance

Estate House Drive

Loop Trail

Arboretum & Formal Gardens

Education Center

Estate House   Loop Trail

Spring House

Connector Trail

Great Pond

meadow

Red Oak-Mixed Hardwood Forest

Tulip-Beech-Maple Forest

100

Horse-Shoe Trail

a stepped waterfall; the view from the bridge back to the landscaped gardens and natural meadows is lovely.

Behind the pond is a second, forested ridge. Trails through the woods are more challenging than the arboretum paths, with steeper hills and narrow, natural footpaths, but they are easy to follow and rewarding. Here are towering trees and a dense understory full of birds and wildlife. In the valley, trails cross a small stream before climbing the ridge to return to the parking area.

GVA hosts nature education programs for families at Welkinweir and other locations. See the website for details.

Remember: Dogs must be leashed; discourage barking. No tree climbing is permitted. Picnic in the pavilion only. Trails are pedestrian-only except the Horse-Shoe Trail, which crosses the site and is open to equestrians.

PLAN B: Warwick County Park (Trip 68) has playgrounds and fishing as well as more hiking trails.

WHERE TO EAT NEARBY: Head back to PA 100 where shops and restaurants are in either direction.

Trip 70

All Ages

Springton Manor Farm

Explore a working farm and woods along the Brandywine Creek in this park that epitomizes Chester County's rural landscape.

Address: 860 Springton Road, Glenmoore, PA
Hours: Trails and grounds open 8 A.M. to sunset daily; butterfly house open June through September; farm tours available in summer (check website for hours and days)
Fee: Free
Contact: chesco.org/ccparks, 610-942-2450
Bathrooms: At park office, at farm parking area, and at farm during operating hours only
Water/Snacks: None
Maps: chesco.org/ccparks (click on Park Sites)
Directions by Car: Take I-76 West (Schuylkill Expressway) to Exit 328A and merge onto US 202 South. After 11.1 miles, exit onto US 30 West toward Downingtown. Continue on US 30 for 8.2 miles, to the exit for US 322 West, and follow it through Guthriesville. Take a soft right onto Springton Road at a traffic light. Cross Highspire Road. Continue 0.5 mile to the park entrance on the right. Follow Park Road to the parking lot ahead on the right.
GPS coordinates: 40° 4.200´ N, 75° 46.632´ W.

Springton Manor Farm, a Chester County Park, invites families to visit a working farm set in a forested park that offers hiking trails, a fishing pond, and a large butterfly house (in season).

Start by walking around the farm and meeting the goats, sheep, and cows; guided tours will give you access to more of the farm. Some of the paths are paved and stroller-friendly. Below the farm parking area is a fishing pond (catch-and-release) that's the perfect size for kids to learn on.

Penn Oak Trail, a 0.28-mile, paved, ADA-accessible interpretive nature trail, begins near the fishing pond. It winds past two huge oak trees that were growing here when William Penn arrived in Pennsylvania.

Indian Run Trail loops around the park for about 2.5 miles, along the creek in the woods and up and down the wildflower meadows and pastures on the hillsides. A hilltop observation deck provides views of the countryside. Other

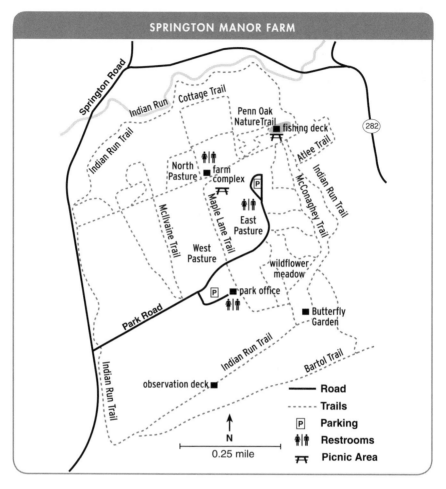

SPRINGTON MANOR FARM

Springton Road

Indian Run

Cottage Trail

Indian Run Trail

Penn Oak NatureTrail

fishing deck

282

Atlee Trail

North Pasture

farm complex

McConaghey Trail

Indian Run Trail

Maple Lane Trail

East Pasture

McIlvaine Trail

West Pasture

wildflower meadow

Park Road

park office

Butterfly Garden

Indian Run Trail

Indian Run Trail

Bartol Trail

observation deck

N

0.25 mile

—— Road

- - - - Trails

P Parking

Restrooms

Picnic Area

trails wind through the park and connect with one another to offer a variety of walks. Some trails are open to mountain bikes and horses.

The large butterfly house contains a huge variety of butterflies native to the area, along with their favorite food plants. In season, kids will love to walk among the fluttering insects; naturalists explain the life cycle of these beautiful creatures and how we can create gardens that help them thrive.

In winter, the butterfly house is closed, but the park's trails are great for snowshoeing or cross-country skiing if any snow is on the ground.

A picnic area is near the farm parking area.

Remember: Pets are not allowed within the farm complex. Check the website to make sure the farm and butterfly house are open if that's your plan.

PLAN B: Struble Trail (Trail 62), a multiuse paved trail, is great for family biking.

WHERE TO EAT NEARBY: It's best to bring snacks or a picnic.

Trip 71

All Ages

Myrick Conservation Center

Take in long views, picnic by a shaded pond, or explore a small woods stream along a variety of trails in a peaceful Chester County environmental education center.

Address: 1760 Unionville-Wawaset Road, West Chester, PA
Hours: Trails open dawn to dusk daily
Fee: Free
Contact: brandywinewatershed.org; redclayvalley.org, 610-793-1090
Bathrooms: None
Water/Snacks: None
Maps: At parking lot kiosk
Directions by Car: Take I-76 West (Schuylkill Expressway) to Exit 328A and merge onto US 202 South toward West Chester. After 16.3 miles, take the Paoli Pike exit and turn right onto Paoli Pike. Continue onto East Gay Street. After 0.8 mile, turn left onto South High Street, then turn right onto PA 842 West. Drive 3.6 miles, then turn right onto PA 842 West/South Bridge Road. Continue to follow PA 842 West. The entrance is ahead on the left.
GPS coordinates: 39° 54.774′ N, 75° 40.856′ W.

At Myrick Conservation Center, kids of all ages can explore a variety of trails that go through farm fields and woods along a stream and across rocky ridges. Trails are designed to lead kids through the diverse habitats of a typical Chester County landscape that is also a serene refuge for wildlife.

The Myrick Center is the headquarters for two watershed associations (Brandywine Valley and Red Clay Valley), which operate the site as an environmental education center for local schools. Converted from a historical farm, the center looks in some ways unchanged since the nineteenth century. The fields are still planted with row crops; the surrounding hills are largely undeveloped. The big, red bank barn, which has signs describing what the various sections were once used for, contains classrooms. The grounds extend on both sides of PA 842.

The west side, where the main office and parking area are located, is flatter and easier for young kids. The trails are well maintained and easy to follow, though not blazed. Follow the broad, unnamed, mowed-grass trail that branches off from the Farm Loop through wildflower meadows that are full of summer butterflies to the quiet, concealed Turtle Pond, hidden in the brush.

Butterflies flock to wildflowers amid the extensive meadows at Myrick Nature Center.

Here you can enjoy a picnic while watching the frogs that seem to outnumber the turtles. South of the fields is a large, open woods with wide dirt trails; signs not only label different kinds of trees but also give some information about how to identify each tree, and what that tree is used for.

On the east side, trails are a bit more rugged, suitable for older kids; they climb onto the top of a high ridge that provides beautiful long-distance views of the Chester County countryside.

Also on the east side is the Hill & Stream Interpretive Trail, which goes along and across a small stream. Pick up a brochure describing marked features of interest at the office. For school-age kids, this is a fun way to learn about different habitats and buildings as they walk along.

Remember: Dogs are not permitted on the grounds between 9 A.M. and 3 P.M. Monday through Friday, and some trails are closed to dogs.

PLAN B: Harmony Hill Nature Area (Trip 63) has paved bike and walking paths, as well as more rugged hiking trails in woods, and also provides access to the East Branch of the Brandywine Creek for paddling and fishing.

WHERE TO EAT NEARBY: It's best to bring a picnic.

Trip 72

All Ages

Stroud Preserve

*Amble through expansive wildflower meadows and farm fields in a serene
rural landscape.*

Address: 350 North Creek Road, West Chester, PA
Hours: Sunrise to sunset daily
Fee: Free
Contact: natlands.org, 610-344-3443
Bathrooms: None
Water/Snacks: None
Maps: natlands.org (click on List of Preserves, then Stroud)
Directions by Car: Take I-76 West (Schuylkill Expressway) to Exit 328A and
   merge onto US 202 South toward West Chester. Continue 16.3 miles to the
   Paoli Pike exit. Turn right onto Paoli Pike, then continue onto East Gay
   Street. Turn right onto North High Street then left onto West Biddle Street.
   Turn left onto North Everhart Avenue, then continue onto Hannum Avenue,
   which becomes PA 162 (Strasburg Road). Follow PA 162 for 1.8 miles to Creek
   Road on the left. Follow Creek Road 0.3 mile to the preserve entrance and
   parking lot on the right. *GPS coordinates*: 39° 57.175´ N, 75° 38.853´ W.

The 571-acre Stroud Preserve is an extraordinarily well-maintained natural
area, a mosaic of farm fields, wildflower meadows, and woods that provides
opportunities for walking, nature observation, and fishing. It's a place made
for spending quiet time together discovering the wonder of small things,
enveloped by the serene Chester County countryside.

A wide old stone bridge next to the parking area crosses a branch of the
Brandywine Creek. It's a good place for introductory fishing lessons. Follow
the trails along the creek to find more-secluded spots for angling.

The woods walks just past the bridge are flat and good for very young
children. Older kids will take to the challenge of trails that run up and down
the rolling hills. Many of the trails go around crop fields, so kids can follow
the fields' progress from tilled earth to hay rolls. Horses are permitted on
some trails; since this is horse country, an up-close-and-personal encounter is
not unlikely.

Extensive open meadow views reward learning how to use binoculars to
watch hawks soar high overhead or rare bobolinks bursting out of tall meadow

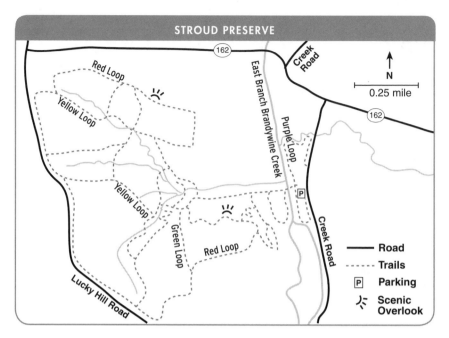

grasses, burbling their electronic-sounding song. Budding photographers will find a profusion of subjects, from close-ups of flowers and horses to long-distance landscapes with gorgeous light. Numerous benches provide ample opportunities for resting and snacking.

Trails are easy to navigate—well marked and cleanly trimmed—with maps available at the trailhead and at key points throughout the preserve. In a clever touch, the meadow trail markers also function as bird nesting boxes. In spring and summer the birds play peek-a-boo. In early summer, bobolinks nest in the upper meadows.

Natural Lands Trust, the nonprofit that manages the preserve, has a smartphone app called SCVNGR that engages kids in interactive, fun activities as they follow the trail. Download the app from the preserve's website.

In winter, if it snows, Stroud's trails are excellent for snowshoes or skis.

Remember: Pets are permitted only on the gravel trail and must be leashed. Stroud has plenty of trails that go along, though not across, streams and ponds, so it may not be the ideal place to take kids who crave a good splashing.

PLAN B: Myrick Conservation Center (Trip 71) is nearby; it offers similar trails and a pond where you can picnic. Natural Lands Trust plans to develop the 1,263-acre ChesLen Preserve, also nearby, into a nature center; it has extensive similar trails as well as access to the creek for paddling.

WHERE TO EAT NEARBY: Return to the borough of West Chester, where there are many restaurants.

Delaware

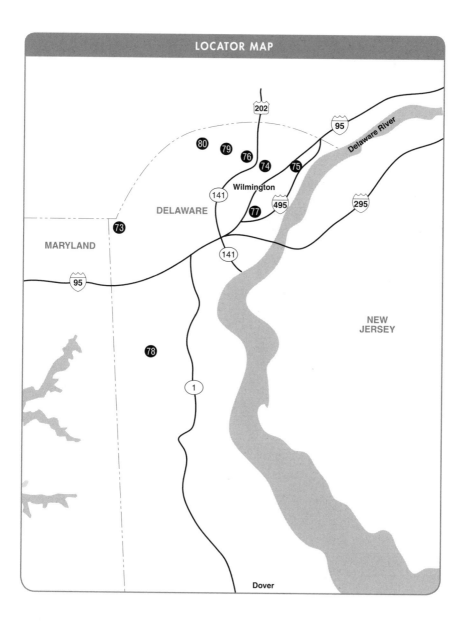

White Clay Creek State Park

Hike or bike along the creek or in forested hills with abundant wildlife in this huge, bi-state park.

Address: 880 New London Road, Newark, DE (or 404 Sharpless Road, Landenberg, PA)
Hours: Grounds open 8 A.M. to sunset daily; office open Monday through Friday, 9 A.M. to 3 P.M.
Fee: Nonresidents, $6 per vehicle; residents, $3 per vehicle (March through November); pedestrians and bikes, free
Contact: destateparks.com, 302-368-6900; www.dcnr.state.pa.us/stateparks, 610-274-2900; whiteclayfriends.org
Bathrooms: At nature center, Carpenter Recreation Area, and parking areas
Water/Snacks: None
Maps: destateparks.com/park/white-clay-creek; www.dcnr.state.pa.us/stateparks (click on Find a Park)
Directions by Car: To Carpenter Recreation Area, take I-95 South into Delaware. Take Exit 3 and merge onto DE 273 West. After 5 miles, turn right onto New London Road (DE 896). Continue for 2.5 miles to the parking area on the right. *GPS coordinates:* 39° 42.766´ N, 75° 46.569´ W.

White Clay Creek is such an outstanding natural feature that it couldn't be contained in just one park! It is two parks in one, as the park extends out of Delaware into Pennsylvania, where it becomes the White Clay Creek Preserve. The parks are seamlessly connected by trails, and this trip description treats them as one park, though the far larger portion is in Delaware.

The park comprises 4,555 acres of low, forested hills and meadows surrounding the White Clay Creek. Because of its ecological importance, the creek has been designated a Wild and Scenic waterway and is protected by the National Park Service. Birds, fish, amphibians, and other wildlife are abundant.

Thirty-seven miles of trails cover a wide variety of terrain, some open to bikes and others for hiking only. Some trails have sections that are hilly, suitable for kids with some hiking or biking experience, but numerous cutoff and connector trails make the trails easier.

Some level, hard-surface trails are open to both hikers and bikers. Edwin Leid Trail, a multiuse trail along shaded banks, showcases the creek's beauty.

Mason and Dixon began their survey at a point marked in White Clay Creek State Park.

The paved Pomeroy Rail Trail extends 2.7 miles south of Hopkins Road, following an old rail bed; lighted and stroller-friendly, it's open 24 hours a day. It crosses the creek via a trestle bridge and loops back via the Tri-Valley Trail.

The park is also of historical importance; Charles Mason and Jeremiah Dixon began their amazing survey of the boundary line separating Pennsylvania, Delaware, and Maryland here. Take Bryan's Field Trail (which begins at the Possum Hill parking area) to see a Mason-Dixon Historic Monument, at the point where the surveyors began their westward trek.

The creek, which is stocked, is popular for trout fishing; the Cattail and Millstone ponds (in the Carpenter Recreation Area) are also open to anglers. White Clay is beautiful in winter for snowshoeing on the trails.

Remember: Pennsylvania and Delaware have different rules and regulations regarding hunting. Note that in addition to the park office parking, other lots may be closer to the trailheads.

PLAN B: A variety of hiking and biking trails are in the 2,072-acre Pennsylvania side of the park; parking is along London Tract Road.

WHERE TO EAT NEARBY: It's best to pack a picnic. In the park's Carpenter Recreation Area is a playground and picnic area.

Trip 74

All Ages

Alapocas Run State Park

The Can-Do Playground, rock climbing, trails through a pawpaw grove—all in downtown Wilmington!

Address: 1914 West Park Drive, Wilmington, DE
Hours: Grounds open 8 A.M. to sunset; office open 8 A.M. to 4 P.M. daily from March through November, and Monday through Friday from December through February
Fee: Nonresidents, $6 per vehicle; residents, $3 per vehicle (March through November); pedestrians and bikes, free
Contact: destateparks.com, 302-577-1164
Bathrooms: In Blue Ball Barn and near the Can-Do Playground
Water/Snacks: None
Maps: destateparks.com/park/alapocas-run; delawaregreenways.org/media/ndgtrail.pdf
Directions by Car: Take I-95 South into Delaware to Exit 8 for US 202 North. Take the first exit for DE 141 South/DE 261 North. On the exit ramp, stay to the left for DE 141 South. At the light, turn left to go under US 202. At the next light, turn left onto West Park Drive. The entrance to the park is on the left, just before the traffic circle. Proceed to the parking lot. *GPS coordinates:* 39° 46.617′ N, 75° 32.735′ W.
Directions by Public Transit: Take SEPTA Regional Rail to Wilmington, then bus 2 toward Brandywine. Get off at Concord Pike and Independence Mall. The park is a 0.8-mile walk from there: Cross Concord Pike, then walk south to West Park Drive; cross DE 141 to Blue Ball Barn.

Alapocas Run is not your ordinary city park. It features a rock-climbing wall, a pawpaw grove, and the coolest playground around. The park is at the confluence of the Alapocas Run and the Brandywine Creek. Trails wind through the wooded areas along the stream.

The Can-Do Playground, near Parking Lot C, is designed to be usable by any child regardless of physical, sensory, or mental abilities. Kids of all abilities play together here, where they get to exercise both their bodies and their imaginations. It's a supersafe playground too, so parents can relax and enjoy watching the fun.

For more exercise, head to the rock-climbing wall, a remnant of an old "blue rock" (granite) quarry near the Brandywine Creek. Bring your own equipment,

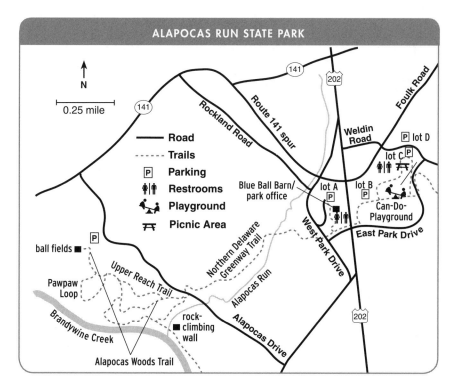

Map legend:
- —— Road
- ----- Trails
- P Parking
- Restrooms
- Playground
- Picnic Area

Blue Ball Barn/park office

ball fields ■

Pawpaw Loop

Brandywine Creek

Upper Reach Trail

Northern Delaware Greenway Trail

Alapocas Run

Alapocas Drive

Alapocas Woods Trail

rock-climbing wall ■

West Park Drive

East Park Drive

Can-Do-Playground

lot A, lot B, lot C, lot D

Weldin Road

Rockland Road

Route 141 spur

Foulk Road

141, 202

---

and make sure you know what you're doing. The park staff regularly offers instruction, and has a summer rock-climbing camp for kids.

Several short, easy trails wind through the park. Alapocas Woods Trail begins at the ball-field parking area; it winds through the woods and connects to the PawPaw Loop Trail which leads through a large patch of pawpaw trees, the only tropical tree native to the Philadelphia region. These trails are for hiking only. A 2-mile portion of the 10.4-mile paved/crushed stone Northern Delaware Greenway Trail, which is open to bikes as well as pedestrians, traverses the park along the Alapocas Run to the Brandywine.

The Blue Ball Barn, where the park office is located, is a converted stone barn that houses the Delaware Folk Art Collection. Interactive exhibits engage kids. The renovated barn itself was Delaware's first LEED (Leadership in Energy and Environmental Design)-certified public building, and you can see some of these features, such as the sunshades in the patio.

Remember: You must obtain a rock-climbing permit to use the wall. Dogs must be leashed.

PLAN B: Brandywine Creek State Park (Trip 76), with many trails for both hikes and bikes, is north. The Brandywine Zoo is in nearby Brandywine Park.

WHERE TO EAT NEARBY: Concord Pike/US 202 is a busy commercial street.

Trip 75

All Ages

Bellevue State Park

Follow level bike or walking paths around expansive open grounds and a large fishing pond in a pleasant former duPont estate.

Address: 800 Carr Road, Wilmington, DE
Hours: Grounds open 8 A.M. to sunset daily; park office open 8 A.M. to 4 P.M. daily, April through October, and Monday through Friday from November through March
Fee: Nonresidents, $6 per vehicle; residents, $3 per vehicle (March through November); pedestrians and bikes, free
Contact: destateparks.com, 302-761-6963
Bathrooms: At picnic area and in park office
Water/Snacks: Water fountain in park office (when open)
Maps: destateparks.com/park/bellevue; delawaregreenways.org/media/ndgtrail.pdf
Directions by Car: Take I-95 South into Delaware to Exit 9 and turn left onto DE 3 South (Marsh Road). Take the first left onto Carr Road. The park entrance is on the right. Proceed past the entrance booth to the office parking area. *GPS coordinates*: 39° 46.863′ N, 75° 30.123′ W.

Bellevue State Park retains the spacious feel—and quirky features—of the former William duPont estate along the Delaware River that the state converted into a park in 1976. It offers easy hiking, biking, and fishing in a pleasant setting.

Start at the park office to gain access to level paved trails, good for biking or easy walking. Bikes for kids and adults, including an adaptive bike for riders with disabilities, are available for rent at the park office.

A 1.6-mile section of the Northern Delaware Greenway Trail, a multiuse paved trail, leads through the park and connects to the paved trails that start at the park office. You can begin at Bellevue and continue a longer bike ride along the 9-mile trail, which connects the Delaware to the Brandywine. In Wilmington, it gives access to the Brandywine Zoo and the Blue Ball Barn (see Trip 74, Alapocas Run State Park).

Unpaved trails open to hikers and equestrians crisscross the park as well. While most of the park is open grassy areas or fields, the Bellevue Woods Nature Preserve at its northern end is a small woods with several small streams.

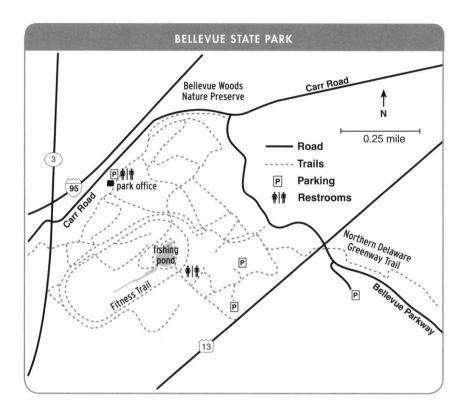

BELLEVUE STATE PARK

Bellevue Woods Nature Preserve

Carr Road

N

0.25 mile

— Road

---- Trails

P Parking

Restrooms

park office

fishing pond

Fitness Trail

Northern Delaware Greenway Trail

Bellevue Parkway

95

3

13

If it's fishing you're looking for, head to the large catch-and-release pond in the center of the park. It is surrounded by an oval, 1.125–mile, crushed-stone walking track (Fitness Trail), originally a training track for Mr. duPont's thoroughbred horses.

Many picnic tables are scattered through the park; a large area with many tables overlooks the pond. On the other side of the pond is a playground.

Remember: Dogs must be leashed.

PLAN B: Alapocas Run State Park (Trip 74) features the Can-Do Playground, along with paved and unpaved trails.

WHERE TO EAT NEARBY: A commercial strip is along Philadelphia Pike (take Carr Road to Bellevue Parkway through Corporate Center).

Trip 76

All Ages

Brandywine Creek State Park

It's all about the Brandywine here: Discover the creek and its forested hills.

Address: 41 Adams Dam Road, Wilmington, DE

Hours: Grounds open 8 A.M. to sunset; office open 8 A.M. to 4 P.M., Monday through Friday (open daily April through October)

Fee: Nonresidents, $6 per vehicle; residents, $3 per vehicle (March through November); pedestrians and bikes, free

Contact: destateparks.com, 302-577-3534

Bathrooms: In the park office, and at the Thompson Bridge and Rockland Road parking areas

Water/Snacks: None

Maps: destateparks.com/park/brandywine-creek

Directions by Car: Take I-95 South into Delaware to Exit 8B for US 202 North. Take the first exit for DE 141 South/DE 261 North. On the exit ramp, stay to the left for DE 141 South. Turn left onto Foulk Road, and then continue onto DE 141 South for 0.7 mile. Turn left onto Childrens Drive, then right onto Rockland Road. After 1.6 miles, turn right onto Adams Dam Road. The park entrance is on right. Proceed to the parking lot. *GPS coordinates:* 39° 47.993′ N, 75° 34.808′ W.

Brandywine Creek State Park is a pure nature park, extending along both sides of the Brandywine Creek and into its surrounding rocky, forested hills. You'll find biking and hiking trails through the deep, rich woods and along the creek and its tributary streams.

Check in at the nature center when you arrive; there you'll find a wealth of detailed trail descriptions, and enthusiastic staff available to answer questions.

The level, hard-surface Northern Delaware Greenway Trail, reached from the Thompson Bridge or Rockland Road parking areas, parallels the creek for 2.5 miles; it's an easy, stroller-friendly family walk or bike ride past sheer cliffs, along the winding creek. For slightly more-challenging beginner walks, follow the well-maintained loop trails—Hidden Pond and Indian Springs— that descend to the creek, starting at the park office and nature center. Bikes are not permitted on these trails. Wildlife is abundant in the woods and along the streams. Begin at the trails' shared starting point in the Tulip Tree Woods Nature Preserve, where huge old trees tower over the trails. Follow the trail

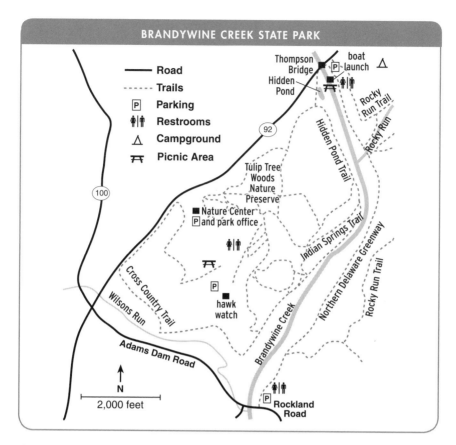

BRANDYWINE CREEK STATE PARK

Legend:
- —— Road
- - - - - Trails
- P Parking
- 🚻 Restrooms
- △ Campground
- 🛆 Picnic Area

Map labels: Thompson Bridge, boat launch, Hidden Pond, Rocky Run Trail, Rocky Run, Hidden Pond Trail, 92, Tulip Tree Woods Nature Preserve, Nature Center P and park office, Indian Springs Trail, Northern Delaware Greenway, Rocky Run Trail, Cross Country Trail, Wilsons Run, hawk watch, Brandywine Creek, Adams Dam Road, 100, N, 2,000 feet, Rockland Road

downhill to where the red-blazed Hidden Pond Trail branches off; it leads along the creek's banks, through a floodplain, then turns uphill to skirt the small Hidden Pond that lives up to its name (take a short spur trail that bridges a stream to glimpse the pond). It then loops back uphill to the office through woods and open meadows.

A public boat launch for canoes and kayaks is at Thompson Bridge. Several dams affect flow conditions downstream of the bridge. A good way for families to get acquainted with canoeing or kayaking the Brandywine is to participate in one of the regular guided paddles sponsored by the park (fee charged; equipment is provided).

Young anglers can fish in trout-stocked Wilsons Run, parallel to Adams Dam Road, and in the Brandywine downstream of Thompson Bridge.

Remember: Dogs must be leashed.

PLAN B: Nearby Alapocas Run State Park (Trip 74) features a playground and short trails.

WHERE TO EAT NEARBY: It's best to bring snacks or a picnic.

All Ages

DuPont Environmental Education Center

Along the riverfront in downtown Wilmington, you'll find hike and bike trails that climb high above a tidal marsh wildlife refuge.

Address: 1400 Delmarva Lane, Wilmington, DE
Hours: Trails open dawn to dusk daily; visitor center open Tuesday through Saturday, 11 A.M. to 5 P.M., and Sunday, noon to 4 P.M., from late March to early November; and Tuesday through Saturday, 10 A.M. to 3 P.M., and Sunday, noon to 4 P.M., from late November through early March
Fee: Free
Contact: duponteec.org, 302-656-1490
Bathrooms: In visitor center (when open) and outside of building (lower level)
Water/Snacks: Water fountain inside visitor center (when open)
Maps: Displayed at entrance
Directions by Car: Take I-95 South to the DE 4/Martin Luther King Boulevard exit. Follow the riverfront signs and turn left onto Martin Luther King Boulevard/Lancaster Avenue. Turn right onto Justison Street. Turn right onto Shipyard Drive, which merges with Delmarva Lane. Stay straight until you reach the education center driveway, and continue to the parking area. *GPS coordinates:* 39° 43.449′ N, 75° 33.721′ W.
Directions by Public Transit: Take the SEPTA Regional Rail Wilmington/Newark line to Wilmington station. Walk 0.2 mile to the intersection of 2nd Street and King Street and take bus 12 to Chase Center (last stop). Walk 0.3 mile to the education center.

The DuPont Environmental Education Center (DEEC) at the Russell Peterson Urban Wildlife Refuge is an expansive and beautiful marshland wildlife refuge, integrated into the heart of downtown Wilmington by a multiuse trail along the Christina River. Hiking and biking trails along stroller-friendly boardwalks wind high above the refuge on a pedestrian bridge and on the ground through the marsh, providing intimate encounters with resident amphibians, birds, mammals, fish, reptiles, and plants.

The 212-acre refuge was built from reclaimed industrial wasteland. The story of the reclamation is one of several interactive exhibits featured in the small but impressive visitor center. Within sight of the bridge is an osprey

Look for muskrat tracks in mud below tall marsh grass at DuPont Environmental Education Center.

nesting platform, where in summer the large birds of prey raise their young in a huge nest made of sticks. The beautiful "green" building was designed to have a minimal environmental footprint. It's worth a visit for the state-of-the-art technology that engages children with nature and the features of the site. Kids will enjoy looking through a bird-spotting telescope on the open-air balcony, perhaps eyeing sandpipers snagging tiny crabs from the mudflats, or osprey circling back to the nest, talons gripping fish for their young.

From the trails, kids will find it easy to spot the wildlife of the marsh. Ducks, turtles, frogs, herons, and fish are common, as are butterflies and dragonflies in summer. More-secretive marsh dwellers, such as red foxes and muskrats, are not as easily seen, but their tracks in the mud give them away; kids can play detective and try to figure out where the animals went and what they did.

The DEEC is focused on education and engagement with the public (especially kids), from the friendly staff eager to answer young visitors' questions, to daily walks with a naturalist. The Delaware Nature Society holds numerous programs for families at the DEEC throughout the year, in which naturalists introduce children to the marsh's birds, insects, and wildlife. (Fees may be charged.)

Remember: Dogs must be leashed.

PLAN B: Explore downtown Wilmington, including the nearby Delaware Children's Museum.

WHERE TO EAT NEARBY: Return to the Riverfront area (near the train station) to find restaurants.

Trip 78

Lums Pond State Park

A family favorite: You don't have to travel far to get to this park for quiet paddling, easy hiking, and plenty of camping.

Address: 1068 Howell School Road, Bear, DE
Hours: Grounds open 8 A.M. to sunset daily; office open 8 A.M. to 4 P.M. daily, April through October, and Monday through Friday from November through March
Fee: Nonresidents, $6 per vehicle; residents, $3 per vehicle (March through November); pedestrians and bikes, free
Contact: destateparks.com, 302-368-6989
Bathrooms: At park office, playground, and campgrounds
Water/Snacks: Water fountains at park office, playground, and campgrounds
Maps: destateparks.com/park/lums-pond
Directions by Car: Take I-95 South into Delaware to Exit 1A (Middletown). Take DE 896 south. After 6 miles, turn left onto Howell School Road. After 0.25 mile, turn right into the park entrance. Proceed to the parking lot.
GPS coordinates: 39° 34.245′ N, 75° 43.846′ W.

As close as it is to Wilmington and Philadelphia, Lums Pond State Park feels like it's in the remote backwoods. Families can enjoy boating, mountain biking, hiking, and camping.

The centerpiece of the park is 200-acre Lums Pond—the largest freshwater pond in Delaware—which is surrounded by a mixed pine and hardwoods forest. The pond invites paddlers to explore its quiet shorelines. The park rents canoes, kayaks, sailboats, rowboats, and pedal boats from Memorial Day through September (check the website or call ahead for exact rental schedule and rates). Or bring your own boat to the ramp on Red Lion Road.

The pond is also excellent for fishing; in addition to local freshwater species, it is stocked with striped bass.

The park is essentially level or gently sloped throughout its 1,790 acres, so the hiking trails are all easy. A short, universally accessible Sensory Loop Trail is near the park office. The pedestrian-only Swamp Forest Trail is the easiest; it goes around the entire pond, a total of 6.4 miles, but the hike can

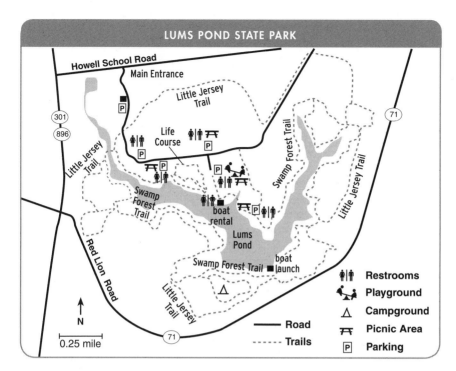

LUMS POND STATE PARK

Legend:
- ♦♦ Restrooms
- Playground
- △ Campground
- ⌲ Picnic Area
- P Parking
- —— Road
- ---- Trails

N
0.25 mile

be done in pieces. The trail is all level, leading through forests and wetlands on natural footpaths or boardwalks, so kids can spot frogs and turtles without getting their feet wet. The moist forests are full of wildflowers in spring; birds, amphibians, and other wildlife are abundant. The 8-mile Little Jersey Trail takes a wider loop around the pond and some open grassy areas; it is open to mountain bikes and horses. This trail is a good one to introduce kids to mountain biking, since it is wide and not exceptionally hilly. In winter the flat trails are excellent for cross-country skiing.

On the south side of the pond, with easy access to the boat launch and trails, are 68 tent campsites with showers; pets are permitted (there are also four equestrian campsites). Yurts are also available for rent.

A playground is near the boat rental in Area 2. Picnic areas are located all around the pond.

Remember: Dogs must be on a leash except in the off-leash area off of Buck Jersey Road in the northeast part of the park. Swimming in the pond is not permitted.

PLAN B: Northeast of Lums Pond is Fort Delaware State Park; this park, which is reachable only by ferry, is fun for kids to visit to enjoy the novelty of a Civil War island fort.

WHERE TO EAT NEARBY: It's best to pack a picnic.

Camping is a great family activity, whether you choose close-to-home overnights, weekend explorations, or weeklong adventures. Many state parks, and some county parks, allow overnight camping. Here are some tips as you're planning:

- *Practice makes perfect.* Consider a trial run. Pitch a tent in the backyard for your first overnight with kids, and let them help set up camp. Experiment with sleeping bags, mattress pads, and sleeping arrangements; even practice making a fire in a fire ring.
- *Do your homework.* Scout out trails and campsites.
- *Know your children's limitations.* Consider first "car camping" at a drive-in campground with amenities such as showers. When you're ready to venture farther, try walk-in or float-in campsites, which provide more quiet and a stronger connection with nature. Wharton State Forest in New Jersey, Trap Pond State Park in Delaware, and, a little farther away, Pennsylvania's Promised Land State Park have campsites a short walk from parking areas. Try backpacking or canoe/kayak camping as your children's abilities and interests expand.
- *Get the right gear.* Pack plenty of layers. Check the weather before you head into the woods. Bring rain gear, and extra socks and shoes. Pack clothes in waterproof bags, and bring a tarp or two. Bring a sleeping bag for each person, and tents sized for at least one more person than the number planning to sleep there. Remember the child-safe bug repellent.
- *Engage kids' minds.* The great outdoors offers an unparalleled educational opportunity—but try to avoid the "classroom" feeling. Spark your children's imaginations by talking to them about wildlife, trees, and the constellations. Teach them map and compass or GPS skills.
- *Take bikes.* Most parks have trails or drives suitable for biking, and kids appreciate the feeling of independence it gives them. (Bring helmets.)
- *Go with another family.* Kids love to be with their peers, and social time will enhance their experience.
- *Bring toys that travel well.* A Frisbee, a bat and ball, board games, or playing cards can add to the fun without disrupting the "away from it all" atmosphere. Books or quiet toys are good during rain or downtime. Leave anything that makes noise at home; even small beeps can disturb other campers.
- *Fuel up.* Bring plenty of nutritious food and kid-friendly snacks for the trail, the campsite, and trips in between. Encourage children to drink lots of water to prevent dehydration (but not right before bed).
- *Be ready when nature calls.* Show children how to be self-sufficient (always pack toilet paper!), follow Leave No Trace principles in disposing of waste (see page xxvii), and use proper hygiene (bring hand sanitizer).
- *Build memories.* Take plenty of pictures and have children keep journals. Both help capture memories and generate excitement for the next adventure.
- *Camp often.* The more familiar kids become with the outdoors, the more comfortable they'll be, and the more they'll look forward to the experience.

Trip 79

Winterthur

Discover the joy of the unexpected at the Enchanted Woods, a children's garden-within-a-garden.

Address: 5105 Kennett Pike, Winterthur, DE
Hours: 10 A.M. to 5 P.M., Tuesday through Sunday
Fee: Adults, $18; children ages 2-11, $5; children under 2, free; Winterthur and American Horticultural Society members, free
Contact: winterthur.org, 302-888-4600
Bathrooms: In visitor center, at museum and Enchanted Woods, and elsewhere (see map)
Water/Snacks: Water fountains and café in visitor center and museum
Maps: Provided upon admission; winterthur.org (click on Visit)
Directions by Car: Take I-95 South into Delaware to Exit 7B (Delaware Avenue/ DE 52). At the end of the exit ramp, turn right at the light to head northwest. As soon as possible, move into the left-most lane (because the road splits); continue on DE 52 North about 5.5 miles. The entrance to Winterthur is on the right. Continue to the visitor parking area. *GPS coordinates*: 39° 48.578′ N, 75° 36.205′ W.

Winterthur (pronounced "Winter-tour") may be a somewhat expensive destination, but is worth a special trip for its unique Enchanted Woods; kids will also enjoy other features of the formal gardens and museum. Its grounds are beautiful and walkable at all times of the year.

In a 1,000-acre preserve that was once the Henry Francis DuPont dairy farm, Winterthur is perhaps the most beautiful of the former DuPont country estates that serve today as public gardens in the Brandywine Valley. Winterthur is famous for its huge collection of decorative arts and its 60-acre naturalistic gardens. But for families, the high point is the Enchanted Woods, a fantasy-play garden. Kids, even older ones and those not convinced of the reality of faery folk, will delight in exploring the garden, finding surprises around every corner and down every hidden path. There's a kid-scale bird nest with moveable eggs, a genuinely serpentine path, an old-fashioned maypole, a hollow tree with furniture, even a Green Man who seems to emerge from the woods itself. Don't stand too close to the toadstools—and watch for trolls under the bridge!

At Winterthur's Enchanted Woods, surprises are underfoot wherever you step.

It is possible to walk from the visitor center to the Enchanted Woods, or take a free, stroller-accessible garden tram to get a narrated, guided tour.

In the Glade (near the museum), kids will enjoy the koi pond and its giant, colorful fish that lurk close to the surface. Inside the museum, the Touch-It Room allows children to experience Colonial life through daily objects that they can pick up and examine, and clothes they can try on.

Winterthur's expansive landscape is perfect for picnicking. You can picnic anywhere on the grounds, including the lawn next to the Enchanted Woods, and picnic tables are near the museum.

The gardens are laced with paved paths, all easy for walking or for those with strollers. Trees and plants are labeled with their names. Beyond the gardens, mowed paths wind through the meadows and natural trails lead through the woods. Here, kids can practice their newly acquired knowledge of trees, plants, and fairies.

Winterthur offers numerous programs for children of all ages (even babies), introducing them to birds, flowers, and gardening (fee charged for nonmembers). Kids can also participate in a summerlong vegetable-gardening program (members only).

Remember: Your admission tag is good for two days.

PLAN B: In Wilmington, Brandywine Creek State Park (Trip 76) is a large forested area with hiking and biking trails.

WHERE TO EAT NEARBY: Commercial areas are along DE 52 closer to Wilmington.

Trip 80

All Ages

Ashland Nature Center

Walk easy nature trails in woods and meadows along the Red Clay Creek.

Address: 3511 Barley Mill Road, Hockessin, DE
Hours: 8:30 A.M. to 4:30 P.M., Monday through Friday
Fee: Adults, $2; children, $1
Contact: delawarenaturesociety.org, 302-239-2334
Bathrooms: Near visitor center
Water/Snacks: None
Maps: Displayed, with paper copies available, at entrance kiosk
Directions by Car: Take I-95 South into Delaware to Exit 7B and merge onto
    DE 52 North. Continue on DE 52 to Campbell Road/State Road 82. Follow to
    Barley Mill Road, and make a left. Cross the covered bridge, and the nature
    center entrance is on the left; continue to the parking area. *GPS coordinates:*
    39° 47.887′ N, 75° 39.619′ W.

At Ashland Nature Center, it's easy for kids to learn about nature while enjoying
walks through the woods and meadows that line the wadeable Red Clay
Creek. Ashland is the headquarters for the Delaware Nature Society (DNS),
a nonprofit organization that works to preserve open space and educate the
community about nature and the environment.

Four self-guided interpretive trails wind through the 242-acre preserve
(owned by the Red Clay Reservation, a private land trust). Each trail features
a different habitat. You can pick up brochures at the entrance kiosk that are
keyed to numbered posts along the trails. Each trail takes about 45 minutes to
an hour to walk.

Take the easy Floodplain Trail from the visitor center down a gently
sloping hill through a young woods to get down to the creek, where kids can
look for small fish zipping around the shallows or crayfish hiding under rocks.
A spur from this trail takes you to an old mill dam and railroad bridge. On
your return, if you continue along the creek instead of going back uphill, you'll
get to see the restored 1850 covered bridge.

The three other trails have some slightly steeper sections, but all are
designed for children, and all loop from the visitor center. Nature's Bounty
Trail focuses on the ways different local cultures use common plants that

At Ashland Nature Center, you'll encounter huge sycamore trees in the Red Clay Creek floodplain.

you encounter along the trail (such as sassafras and willow trees) and the animals that live in the various habitats. Succession Trail descends to the Birch Run and back along the Red Clay Creek floodplain, leading through hillside meadows and both pine and deciduous woods; it shows how trees and shrubs take over cleared fields. Along the way, kids can learn how to tell the age of a tree. Treetop Trail explores a hillside woods, teaching visitors about native trees and plants; in wintertime, you can enjoy expansive views of the valley from hilltop meadows.

A seasonal butterfly house next to the headquarters building allows kids to get up close and personal with caterpillars and butterflies. A sledding hill is below Succession Trail, and the trails can be hiked with snowshoes in winter.

The DNS offers numerous programs at Ashland for families that encourage exploration of nature at the preserve, ranging from toddler programs on such topics as seeds, wings, or snakes, to a Young Naturalists Club for 9- to 12-year-olds, to a beginning family backpacking course.

Remember: Dogs must be leashed. A small picnic area is near the entrance.

PLAN B: Winterthur (Trip 79) is nearby, with walking trails and the Enchanted Woods.

WHERE TO EAT NEARBY: It's best to bring a picnic.

Section 7

New Jersey

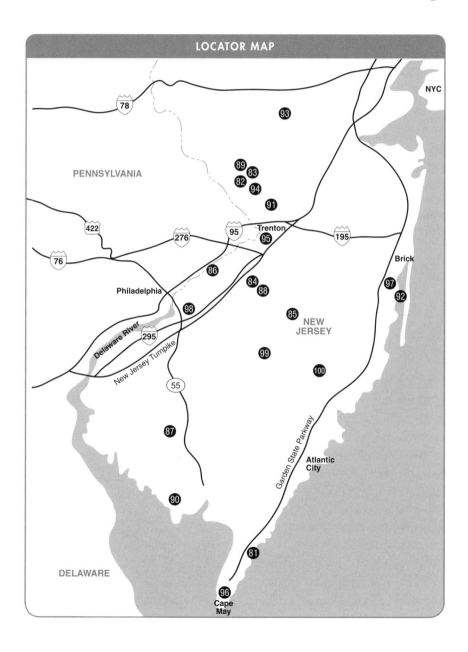

Trip 81

All Ages

The Wetlands Institute

Walk a trail in fiddler crab territory, paddle the tidal creeks, or climb a tower for an awesome view of the extensive salt marsh.

Address: 1075 Stone Harbor Boulevard, Stone Harbor, NJ
Hours: Hours vary by day and season, and maintenance or special events
　　occasionally necessitate closure to the public; call ahead to verify hours
Fee: Ages 13 and older, $8; ages 3-12, $6
Contact: wetlandsinstitute.org, 609-368-1211
Bathrooms: In the main building
Water/Snacks: Water fountain and vending machines in the main building
Maps: wetlandsinstitute.org (click on Visit Us)
Directions by Car: Take I-76 East (Schuylkill Expressway) to Walt Whitman
　　Bridge and cross into New Jersey. Continue on I-76 to NJ 42 South, which
　　becomes the Atlantic City Expressway, to Exit 7 South. Take the Garden State
　　Parkway South to Exit 10B on the left to merge onto Stone Harbor Boulevard.
　　After 2.5 miles, the Wetlands Institute entrance and parking area is on the
　　right. *GPS coordinates*: 39° 3.688′ N, 74° 46.343′ W.

The Wetlands Institute is situated on 6,000 acres of coastal wetlands near Stone Harbor and Cape May. This ecosystem, where the tides run in and out twice daily, covering and uncovering the marshes, is home to distinctive communities of plants and wildlife. The institute provides a variety of fun ways to explore this salt marsh habitat on land or by water.

Start at the visitor center, which has interactive displays about coastal wetlands. In summer, an "osprey cam" shows what's going on in a real osprey nest. Terrapin Station, devoted to the life history of the native diamondback terrapin, is the first of its kind in the world. Climb spiral stairs, painted with an under-the-sea mural, to the top of the 40-foot-high Observation Tower for a splendid panoramic view of the marsh and the shore. Then take a walk on the easy, 0.25-mile Salt Marsh Trail; it's made of crushed shells and is ADA- and stroller-accessible. You'll get close-up views of fiddler crabs darting (sideways) back and forth from their burrows. Informational signs along the trail explain the nature of the salt marsh. The trail leads to a vista from a 125-foot pier extending over a tidal creek, where the huge resident colony of laughing gulls

Look for laughing gulls and fiddler crabs along the tidal creeks on the Wetlands Institute's Salt Marsh trail.

may induce the same mood in the kids. (Note: The pier was destroyed during Hurricane Sandy. As of this writing, plans are in place to rebuild.)

Explore this area from a different perspective by kayaking around the shallow marshes; kids will be enthralled by being at the same level as the plants and wildlife, moving with the same currents. The institute's guide map, Jersey Island Blueway (on website or for sale at visitor center), is an introduction to the backbays, marshes, creeks, and channels of the South Jersey Shore. (Although the institute promotes paddling, there is no boat rental or public launch site there. Use the 81st Street municipal ramp in Stone Harbor.)

The institute offers programs throughout the year that feature guided walks in the marsh, on the beach, and in the dunes; bird and wildlife tours; naturalist-led paddles; and other hands-on activities. Summer Family Night programs for younger children feature live animals.

Remember: Dogs are not permitted in the buildings.

PLAN B: The Nature Center of Cape May (Trip 96) has an observation deck, and easy, stroller-friendly boardwalk hiking trails are at Cape May Point State Park.

WHERE TO EAT NEARBY: Continue on Stone Harbor Boulevard to the town, where you'll find many kid-friendly restaurants.

Trip 82

All Ages

Washington Crossing State Park

Exploring where Washington's army crossed the Delaware River in 1776 is a good way to exercise kids' historical imaginations.

Address: 355 Washington Crossing-Pennington Road, Titusville, NJ
Hours: Grounds open 8 A.M. to 4:30 P.M. daily; park office open 9 A.M. to 3 P.M. Monday through Friday; visitor center museum open 9 A.M. to 4 P.M. daily
Fee: Nonresidents, $7 per vehicle; residents, $5 per vehicle (Memorial Day weekend to Labor Day); bikes and pedestrians, free
Contact: www.state.nj.us/dep/parksandforests, 609-737-0623; a schedule of programs is available at washingtoncrossingaudubon.org
Bathrooms: In visitor center museum and at Green Grove, Knox Grove, the nature center, and at the end of the parking lot off River Road
Water/Snacks: Water fountains and vending machines at visitor center and nature center
Maps: www.state.nj.us/dep/parksandforests/parks (click on List of Parks)
Directions by Car: Take I-95 North into New Jersey to Exit 1 for NJ 29 North to Lambertville. Follow NJ 29 North to Washington Crossing. Just past the bridge to Pennsylvania, turn left into the parking area. *GPS coordinates:* 40° 18.550′ N, 74° 50.783′ W.

Washington Crossing State Park extends along the Delaware River where George Washington landed the Continental Army on Christmas night, 1776, before vanquishing the British at the Battles of Trenton and Princeton. The park combines history and nature, providing delightful family outings on the trail or on the water.

Because of its forested riverside location, the park is a bird and wildlife hotspot. The nature center, which is geared toward families, offers exciting hands-on exhibits, as well as a learning lab, a live-observation beehive, and wildlife specimens. A naturalist is available to answer questions. Educational programs organized by the Audubon Society teach kids about what they'll see outdoors, and about practical skills, such as how to use a compass.

Fifteen miles of trails are in the park, providing a variety of opportunities to explore the forests and streams. They are all natural footpaths, blazed in colors that correspond to the map. Some are open to mountain bikes and horses. In

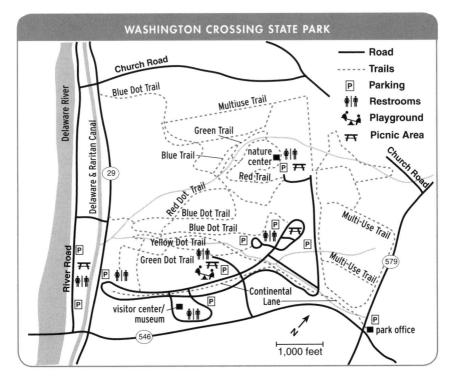

Road
Trails
P Parking
Restrooms
Playground
Picnic Area

Delaware River

Church Road

Blue Dot Trail

Delaware & Raritan Canal

Multiuse Trail

Green Trail

Blue Trail

29

nature center

Red Trail

Church Road

Red Dot Trail

Blue Dot Trail

Blue Dot Trail

Yellow Dot Trail

Green Dot Trail

Multi-Use Trail

Multi-Use Trail

579

River Road

P

Continental Lane

P

visitor center/ museum

546

N

park office

1,000 feet

winter, the interior trails are great for skiing or snowshoeing. Those in the northern portion of the park are hilly; although they may be too challenging for young children, the Red Trail loop from the nature center is easy to follow and includes a spur trail to a wildlife-viewing blind. For an easy 2-mile loop hike, start at the museum, following Continental Lane; return via the Yellow Dot Trail past an open-air theater, then through woods along a creek to the Red Dot Trail, which crosses the field back to Continental Lane. Along the Delaware & Raritan Canal, the level, hard-surface towpath, which is open to bikes, is a good option for strollers or young families (see Trip 95). The canal itself may be paddled upstream or downstream.

Several picnic areas are in the interior of the park, as well as along the river.

Remember: A reenactment of the river crossing is performed every Christmas Day. A festive dress rehearsal takes place the second Saturday in December, when food and craft vendors fill the park; this is a good day to visit.

PLAN B: Walk across the bridge to the Pennsylvania side of the Delaware River, which is a state historic site and museum and 500-acre recreational area.

WHERE TO EAT NEARBY: A small commercial area is near the corner of NJ 29 and County Road 546, or continue up NJ 29 to Lambertville.

Trip 83

Stony Brook-Millstone Watershed Association Reserve

Easy trails with interpretive signs make this a great expedition for families to discover woods, a pond, streams, and meadows.

Address: 31 Titus Mill Road, Pennington, NJ
Hours: Grounds open dawn to dusk daily
Fee: Free
Contact: thewatershed.org, 609-737-3735
Bathrooms: Portable toilets at main parking area and at Wargo Road
Water/Snacks: Water fountain outside nature center
Maps: thewatershed.org (click on Conservation, then Trails); njtrails.org
Directions by Car: Take I-95 North into New Jersey to Exit 4B. At the top of the exit ramp, turn left onto NJ 31 North. At the traffic circle, go straight onto Pennington Road, which becomes Main Street. At the traffic light in Pennington, turn right onto Delaware Avenue, which becomes Pennington-Rocky Hill Road. Past Bristol-Myers Squibb's main entrance, make the first left onto Titus Mill Road. There will be a Road Closed sign—go around it. Pass Wargo Road on the right, then turn right to enter the Stony Brook-Millstone Watershed Association at the long paved driveway. Parking is on the right. *GPS coordinates:* 40° 21.165′ N, 74° 46.295′ W.

The 930-acre Stony Brook-Millstone Watershed Association Reserve is the headquarters for central New Jersey's oldest environmental organization, which protects the 265-square-mile watershed drained by the Stony Brook and the Millstone River.

Ten miles of trails are on the reserve, all for foot travel only (including skis and snowshoes in winter). They explore woods, meadows, farm fields, wetlands, and a pond. These natural footpaths, some with elevated boardwalks in wet areas, are almost all essentially level, with the exception of boulders and slight hills in the Mount Rose section, the portion of the Watershed Trail north of the Moores Mill Road parking area.

For kids, a delightful first destination is Wargo Pond, a 4-acre pond with a dock that has both fencing and benches, a safe alternative for even young

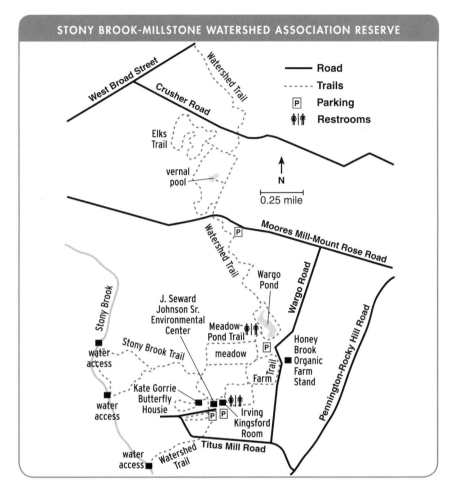

Map legend:
— Road
---- Trails
P Parking
Restrooms

West Broad Street
Watershed Trail
Crusher Road
Elks Trail
vernal pool
N
0.25 mile
Moores Mill-Mount Rose Road
P
Watershed Trail
Wargo Pond
Wargo Road
Stony Brook
J. Seward Johnson Sr. Environmental Center
Meadow-Pond Trail
water access
Stony Brook Trail
meadow
P
Honey Brook Organic Farm Stand
Farm Trail
Pennington-Rocky Hill Road
Kate Gorrie Butterfly Housie
water access
P P
Irving Kingsford Room
water access
Watershed Trail
Titus Mill Road

children to observe the birds, dragonflies, and turtles who make the pond their home. Informative signage describes the plants and wildlife that kids can expect to see there. The pond can be accessed from the Wargo Road parking area, as well as via trails from the nature center. Catch-and-release fishing is permitted from the dock and shoreline.

The Stony Brook itself, a shallow and—yes—stony brook, can be accessed by Stony Brook Trail (a 2-mile round-trip loop to the stream and back) and the southern end of Watershed Trail (a 1-mile round-trip to the stream and back). It's a friendly stream that kids will enjoy exploring.

The Watershed Association provides educational programming throughout the year, designed for children and families. At the time of writing, the nature center was closed for renovation and a new environmental center was under construction.

The Kate Gorrie Butterfly House, open from late April to October, enables kids to share space with native butterflies and caterpillars and watch them feeding on wildflowers.

You can picnic at tables near the parking areas or anywhere on the grounds; you'll find occasional benches along the trails.

Remember: No smoking; dogs must be leashed. No bikes on trails. The trails can get wet and the pond trails buggy, so be prepared with appropriate footwear and insect repellent. Pack out your trash. Hunting is regularly conducted in fall; trails may be closed.

PLAN B: Rosedale Park on Federal Road, across from the Mercer County Equestrian Center, has trails, a large playground, and good picnic facilities.

WHERE TO EAT NEARBY: Pennington has many small shops and eateries on Main Street and NJ 31.

Trip 84

Ages
5-8

Rancocas Nature Center

This small nature center features easy trails designed for young children.

Address: 794 Rancocas Road, Mount Holly, NJ
Hours: 9 A.M. to 5 P.M. Tuesday through Saturday, noon to 5 P.M. Sunday
Fee: Free
Contact: njaudubon.org, 609-261-2495
Bathrooms: At visitor center
Water/Snacks: Water fountain at visitor center
Maps: njaudubon.org (click on Centers, then Rancocas)
Directions by Car: Take I-95 North to Exit 26 for the Betsy Ross Bridge.
Cross into New Jersey, merging onto NJ 90 East. After 1.6 miles, it becomes
NJ 73 South. Continue 3.7 miles and merge onto I-295 toward Trenton. Take
Exit 45A toward Mount Holly. Go east on Rancocas Road for 1.5 miles to
the nature center entrance on the right. Continue up the gravel drive to the
parking lot on the right. *GPS coordinates*: 40° 0.199′ N, 74° 49.257′ W.

A natural area near the Rancocas Creek, Rancocas Nature Center is operated
independent of Rancocas State Park by the New Jersey Audubon Society. With
easy, well-maintained interpretive nature trails in a variety of habitats, this is
an ideal spot for young kids to explore the Pine Barrens close to Philadelphia.

Rancocas Nature Center is an environmental education center that focuses
on introducing children to nature. At the visitor center, in a nineteenth-century
farmhouse, a small natural history museum features live animals, a "please
touch" table, and wildlife exhibits. The staff is happy to provide guidance. Just
outside the building are both a Children's Garden, for very young kids, and a
Butterfly and Hummingbird Garden for all ages. The nature center offers a
variety of educational programs and field trips.

On the grounds, well-marked trails loop through the nature center's 58 acres
of mixed deciduous and evergreen woods, old fields, meandering streams, and
marshes. The trails are all easy and short, and are mostly level.

Take Orange Trail to get to the creek through the wetlands, which can be
muddy. Yellow Trail, close to the visitor center, goes by the small Dragonfly
Pond. Blue Trail leads through wetlands and a mixed hardwood and conifer
forest. From Blue Trail you can cross over a small, clear stream by a footbridge

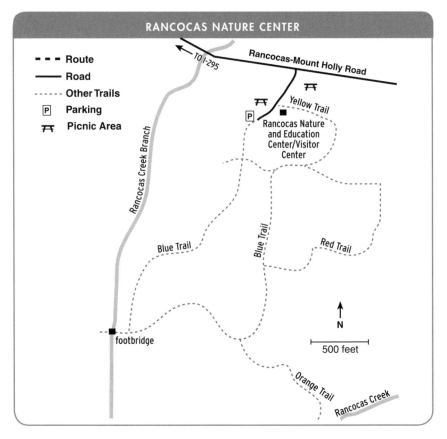

into the Rankokus Indian Reservation; it is not part of the nature center, but has a short nature trail open to the public (please stay on the trail).

Picnic tables are in two areas: near the entrance to the Children's Garden, and in the wooded area near the trailheads.

Remember: No dogs are permitted at the nature center. Hunting is regularly conducted in fall; trails may be closed.

PLAN B: Rancocas State Park is a 1,252-acre park with hiking and biking trails that connect to the trails of the nature center. No staffed facilities are on the site. For more information, see nj.gov/dep/parksandforests.

WHERE TO EAT NEARBY: Restaurants and shops are located in Mount Holly on High Street, Washington Street, and other streets.

At press time, New Jersey Audubon Society announced the closing of the Rancocas Nature Center in April 2013. Community groups hope to find a way to keep the center open. Rancocas State Park remains open. For updates, please check www.state.nj.us/dep/parksandforests/parks/rancocas.html.

Trip 85

All Ages 💲 🛖 🚶 🚴 ⚲ ⚓ ⛺

Brendan T. Byrne State Forest/ Pakim Pond

Walk through a quiet, flat pine forest to a pond surrounded by unusual carnivorous plants.

Address: Mile Marker 1, NJ Route 72 East, Woodland Township, NJ
Hours: Grounds open sunrise to sunset daily; office open 8:30 A.M. to 4 P.M. Saturday through Thursday, and 8:30 A.M. to 6 P.M. Friday
Fee: Grounds, free; fee charged for camping
Contact: njparksandforests.org/parks, 609-726-1191; njwildlifetrails.org/ PineBarrensTrails
Bathrooms: At park office (when open); seasonal restrooms at Pakim Pond lot
Water/Snacks: Water fountain by Pakim Pond
Maps: njhiking.com/nj-hiking-maps (click on Brendan-Bryne-Lebanon)
Directions by Car: Take I-676 East to US 30 East and cross the Ben Franklin Bridge into New Jersey. Merge onto NJ 38 East/Kaighns Avenue, and continue onto NJ 70 East for 26.3 miles, to the Four-Mile traffic circle. From the circle, take NJ 72 east. Continue 1 mile to the Brendan Byrne State Forest sign on the left, just beyond the fire tower. Turn left and take the forest road to the first paved road. Turn right; the park office is on the left. To get to Pakim Pond, follow the paved road approximately 2.5 miles to a stop sign. Turn left and follow the paved road to the parking area on the left. *GPS coordinates:* 39° 52.789′ N, 74° 32.025′ W.

Brendan T. Byrne State Forest, formerly Lebanon State Forest, extends over 36,647 acres in the Pine Barrens. More than 25 miles of sandy, flat trails wind through deep pine forests that harbor an amazing variety of birds, as well as amphibians and plants. In natural bogs you'll see the native cranberry, forebear of the commercial berry that is cultivated in large bogs visible from the road.

Pakim Pond is an easy introduction to the vast forest. A 1-mile trail to and around the pond starts near the pond parking area. The pond can also be reached by a walk on the 2.7-mile Cranberry Trail from the park office through the quiet pine forest; this level, hard-sand surface trail is suitable for older children. The beginning section of Cranberry Trail is paved and wheelchair-accessible. The flat trails are excellent for skiing or snowshoeing in snowy winters.

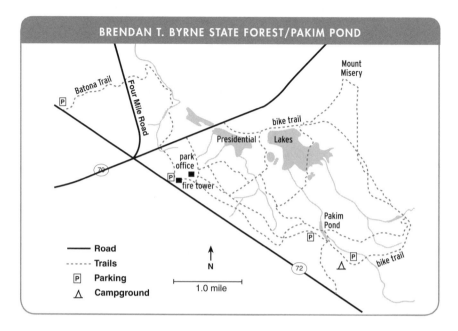

Road
Trails
P Parking
△ Campground

N

1.0 mile

The pond is a tea-brown color, typical of ponds and streams in the Pine Barrens, derived from cedar bark and iron in the soil. Around the pond you'll see some of the unusual plants of the region, such as the carnivorous sundew and pitcher plants; in spring the pond hosts breeding frogs and salamanders. A covered picnic area here has lovely views of the pond. If you bring your own kayak or canoe, you can paddle around the pond.

The pink-blazed, 50-mile Batona Trail passes through the forest at Pakim Pond. This long-distance Pine Barrens trail has several primitive campsites along its length. Other trails in the forest connect to the Batona Trail for longer loop hikes. A paved 10-mile loop is open to bikes and is suitable for kids of all abilities. For mountain bikes, Mount Misery Trail, reached via Cranberry Trail, is on sand tracks through the forest.

Eighty-two tent campsites (some pet-friendly) are available at the state forest campground east of Pakim Pond on Coopers Road. A playground is at the campground.

Remember: The best time to visit the Pine Barrens is spring, winter, or fall, when the insect population is lower than in summer. Always do a thorough tick check after your visit.

PLAN B: Whitesbog Village, in Brendan Byrne State Forest, features an old-time general store (open weekends), as well as self-guided tours of blueberry fields and cranberry bogs, and 18 miles of trails.

WHERE TO EAT NEARBY: It's best to bring a picnic.

Trip 86

Ages 5-8

Palmyra Cove Nature Park

Enjoy wide views of the Delaware River from a restored wild cove on the shoreline.

Address: 1335 NJ Route 73, Palmyra, NJ
Hours: 9 A.M. to 4 P.M. Monday through Friday; 10 A.M. to 4 P.M. weekends
Fee: Free (donations accepted)
Contact: palmyracove.org, 856-829-1900
Bathrooms: Restrooms at the Environmental Discovery Center
Water/Snacks: Water fountain at the Environmental Discovery Center
Maps: palmyracove.org (click on Events)
Directions by Car: Take I-95 North to Exit 27 (Bridge Street) to Aramingo Avenue. At the first traffic light, turn right onto Tacony Street and follow it to the Tacony-Palmyra Bridge. Cross into New Jersey and merge onto NJ 73 South; get into the extreme left lane just past the toll building for the Souder Street/Market Street exit. Turn left, go two blocks to Temple Boulevard, turn left, and immediately turn right into the parking lot, just before the toll plaza. Travel through the parking lot behind the toll building on the left, continue on the narrow local access road, and go under the bridge. The Educational Discovery Center will be in front of you to the right. The parking area is to the left of the building. *GPS coordinates:* 40° 0.103′ N, 75° 2.195′ W.

The 250-acre Palmyra Cove Nature Park was once a dredge spoil (the place where excess material from dredging was unloaded) and leaf dump. Now a thriving woodlands and wetlands featuring wide trails with beautiful riverside vistas, the park exemplifies the transformation of industrial brownfields into a natural destination in an urban setting.

The park's Environmental Discovery Center (EDC), which is geared toward children, houses interactive displays about the wide array of plants, birds, and other wildlife to be found in the park, and about the historical importance of Palmyra Cove and the neighboring Tacony-Palmyra Bridge. The EDC regularly schedules naturalist-led family hikes and educational programs. Call ahead for details.

The wide, level trails lead from the EDC through woodlands, wetlands, fields, ponds, a tidal cove, and along the river. In spring and fall, you'll see and hear the many birds that stop at these wild areas, which serve as important feeding areas during migration. Walk on Cove Trail along the tidal cove, next

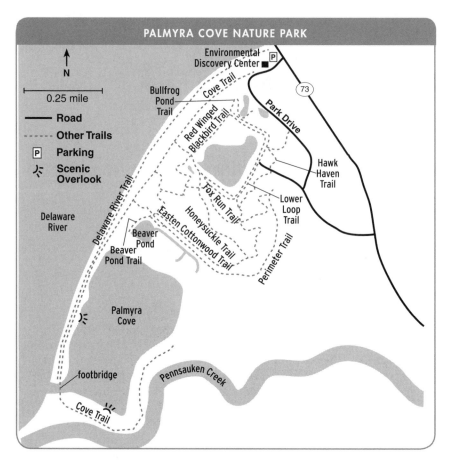

Environmental Discovery Center

73

N

0.25 mile

— Road

----- Other Trails

P Parking

Scenic Overlook

Bullfrog Pond Trail

Cove Trail

Red Winged Blackbird Trail

Park Drive

Hawk Haven Trail

Lower Loop Trail

Fox Run Trail

Delaware River Trail

Delaware River

Eastern Cottonwood Trail

Honeysuckle Trail

Beaver Pond

Beaver Pond Trail

Perimeter Trail

Palmyra Cove

footbridge

Pennsauken Creek

Cove Trail

to the Pennsauken Creek, with scenic overlooks of shorebirds that feed on the mudflats in migration season. The short Beaver Pond Trail (linked from the Cove Trail via the Perimeter Trail) goes along the edge of a former sand mine that is now Beaver Pond; the pond does host beavers and you can observe them swimming to and from their lodge.

At low tide, you can walk along the banks of the river along Delaware River Trail, where you'll be rewarded with views of the Philadelphia skyline and the bridge as it opens and closes to let big ships pass through. Peregrine falcons hang out on the bridge, feeding on birds that congregate along the shore. A "falcon cam" in the EDC provides a live, insider's view of their nest.

Remember: No dogs or bikes are permitted.

PLAN B: At Cooper River Park (Trip 98), there's much for the active family, including bike and hike trails and boating.

WHERE TO EAT NEARBY: In Collingswood, Haddon Avenue has family-friendly dining.

Trip 87

Parvin State Park

A lake with a sandy beach invites boating and swimming, and you can hike in the surrounding woods.

Address: 701 Almond Road, Pittsgrove, NJ
Hours: Sunrise to sunset daily; park office open 8 A.M. to 6 P.M. daily
Fee: $2 per person (age 4 and older), Memorial Day through Labor Day; otherwise, free
Contact: www.state.nj.us/dep/parksandforests, 856-358-8616
Bathrooms: At the visitor center (when open)
Water/Snacks: Water fountain at the visitor center (when open); snacks at the beach area in season
Maps: At park office; parvinstatepark.org/Park_Map.html
Directions by Car: Take I-76 East (Schuylkill Expressway) to the Walt Whitman Bridge and cross into New Jersey. Continue on I-76 East to NJ 42 South toward Glassboro/Vineland. After 25.3 miles, take Exit 35B to merge onto West Garden Road toward Brotmanville. Continue for 2.3 miles to Parvin Mill Road. Turn right onto Almond Road, and follow signs for the park entrance. Continue to the parking lot. *GPS coordinates:* 39° 30.648′ N, 75° 7.945′ W.

Parvin State Park's lakes in the woods have been a recreational destination for generations. Today, along with boating, swimming, and fishing in the waters, visitors enjoy hiking a network of easy trails in the woods. Because of its location on the edge of the Pine Barrens, Parvin straddles two kinds of forests—evergreen and deciduous—which gives it a distinctively diverse character.

Parvin was a base for the Civilian Conservation Corps (CCC) in the 1930s. The CCC built many beautiful reclaimed-brick structures that still grace the 1,100-acre park. The largest of these is the first building you see, the park office and bathhouse, which is in Parvin Grove, on the shores of Parvin Lake. Swimming is permitted at this location from Memorial Day through Labor Day; it is lifeguard-staffed.

Although the swimming area can be busy in season, paddling and fishing on the forested north side is serene. Parvin is the larger of the two park lakes; Thundergust Lake is narrow, and more interesting for angling than paddling. A canoe rental is located in Parvin Grove, and a boat launch is at Fisherman's

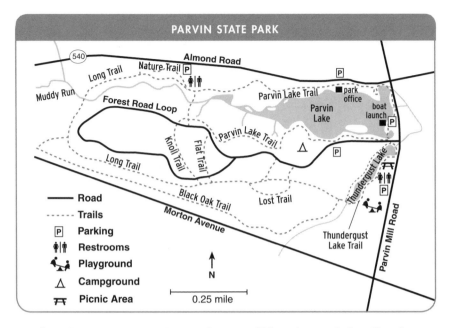

PARVIN STATE PARK

540 · Almond Road

Long Trail · Nature Trail · P

Muddy Run · Forest Road Loop

Parvin Lake Trail · ■ park office

Parvin Lake · boat launch · ■ P

P

Parvin Lake Trail · △ · P

Knoll Trail · Flat Trail

Long Trail

Thundergust Lake

Road
Trails
P Parking
Restrooms
Playground
△ Campground
Picnic Area

Black Oak Trail · Lost Trail

Morton Avenue

Thundergust Lake Trail

Parvin Mill Road

N

0.25 mile

Landing. Picnic areas are at Parvin Grove and Thundergust Lake, all with great views of the lakes.

A network of trails, easily reached from either of the picnic areas, traverses the woods and lakeshores. Along the way you'll explore not only hardwood forests but cedar swamps and pine woods typical of the Pine Barrens. A number of unusual plants and animals are found here, including the barred owl. Some trails are pedestrian-only; others are shared with bikes and equestrians (check the trail map for details). Relatively level or gently sloped, the trails are suitable for all ages, and can be made into long or short trips. The trails are well marked, though they do crisscross. A good introductory loop trail for all ages is the 3-mile Parvin Lake Trail starting at the park office; it goes around the lake through the woods, crossing streams and wet areas via walkways.

The paved loop trail around the park is especially good for family bike rides; the unpaved (dirt) trails open to bikes are level, and suitable for young or novice mountain bikers.

A campground with tent and trailer campsites (some pet-friendly), as well as cabins, is at Jaggers Point on Parvin Lake.

Remember: Pets are prohibited on the Parvin Lake beach and must be leashed in the campground. Pets are permitted on the trails as long as you clean up after them.

PLAN B: Glades Wildlife Refuge (Trip 90) has trails in a similar environment.

WHERE TO EAT NEARBY: It's best to bring a picnic.

Where can you introduce a child to a magical world of swimming and flying creatures, move without moving your legs, and cool off just by reaching out your hand? Out on the water in a human-powered boat. Young children will enjoy riding along; older ones will get a kick out of helping to handle a boat, or doing it themselves.

Some kids take naturally to the water, even seek it out. Others are fearful of this unfamiliar, unsolid environment. As with any outdoor activity, it's usually best to begin slow and small-scale, then build to more-challenging trips.

To start out, visit a quiet pond or lake, or a canal with a slow current. These kinds of places help a child feel safer. The Philadelphia region is full of opportunities to get out on the water surrounded by nature. Lakes good for novice boaters are at places such as Peace Valley Park (Trip 30), Marsh Creek State Park (Trip 61), Core Creek Park (Trip 33), Lums Pond State Park (Trip 78), and Parvin State Park (Trip 87), and there are the canals at Schuylkill Canal Park/Lock 60 (Trip 21) and D&R Canal State Park (Trip 95), all with commercial outfitters nearby. Many of these parks give beginner boating lessons.

Paddleboats may be a good first option for kids, especially nervous ones. These boats don't require any more skill than pedaling a bicycle does. Recreational kayaks are stable, easy to get into and out of, and easy to navigate, and they can be used by one person. Kids have only to learn one basic stroke to go forward; it's easy enough to pick up by watching. Consider tandem kayaks, with an adult in one seat and a child in the other. Canoes are just as stable as kayaks (if you don't stand up) and are easy to stuff with provisions, but are more difficult to learn to steer, and kids can't easily paddle a canoe by themselves. In contrast to paddle craft, sailboats require setup and handling skills, and lessons are a necessity, but they provide the thrill of riding on the wind. Another option for older kids is the stand-up paddleboard, a cross between a boat and a surfboard that's fun for short excursions.

Safety is paramount on the water (see Appendix A). Everyone should wear a PFD, or personal flotation device, and every boat should have a whistle. Make sure kids know to stay in the boat; even stable canoes and kayaks will tip when you lean too far. Be cautious where powerboats share the water. Bring sun protection and plenty of water to drink. A safe boater is a happy boater, and a happy young boater will find a lifetime's worth of waterways to explore.

Trip 88

All Ages

Historic Smithville Park

On the grounds of a nineteenth-century bicycle works, enjoy lake and woods trails while learning about local history.

Address: Meade Lane, Easthampton, NJ
Hours: Park grounds open 8 A.M. to dusk daily; mansion grounds open 8 A.M. to 5 P.M. daily
Fee: Free (donations accepted)
Contact: co.burlington.nj.us
Bathrooms: At the visitor center, by the Manor House, and at the Smith's Woods parking lot
Water/Snacks: Water fountain at Manor House and Smith's Woods parking lot
Maps: co.burlington.nj.us (click on Visit Us, then Parks, then Historic Smithville)
Directions by Car: Take I-76 East (Schuylkill Expressway) to the Walt Whitman Bridge, cross into New Jersey, and follow signs for I-295. Take I-295 to Exit 47A and take County Road 541 South. Take the jug handle to make a left onto Woodlane Road and continue to Smithville Road. Turn right onto Smithville Road, and follow through a blinking red light at Powell Road. The main park entrance is at Meade Lane on the right. Park in the lot. *GPS coordinates*: 39° 59.237′ N, 74° 45.023′ W.

A nineteenth-century "model industrial town," Historic Smithville today combines local industrial history with natural areas that are designed for children and families to explore its lake, woods, wetlands, and stream on foot or by bike.

The 312-acre county park is divided into a historical section and a natural area. The ruins of former industrial buildings, as well as the still-intact Manor House and the workers' more modest residences, together with a small museum, offer a fascinating glimpse into a vanished era. Of special interest are museum displays of the unusual nineteenth-century bicycle railway that enabled riders to pedal a monorail between Smithville and Mount Holly.

On the historical side of the park is the 22-acre Smithville Lake. Young children will particularly enjoy looking for fish and turtles from its 600-foot floating walkway. The 0.5-mile Ravine Nature Trail, an interpretive trail for pedestrians only, starts south of the visitor center, near the Park Avenue entrance. The trail's dense canopy includes huge old-growth trees, and there are views from a high bluff across the ravine.

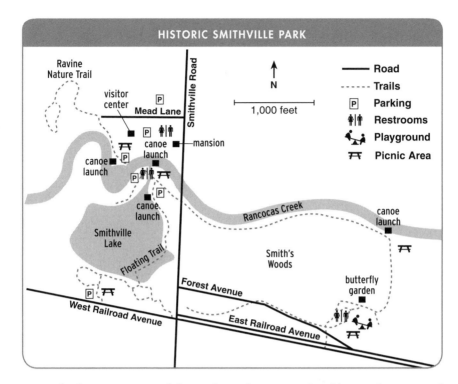

HISTORIC SMITHVILLE PARK

Ravine Nature Trail

visitor center

Mead Lane

Smithville Road

canoe launch

canoe launch

mansion

canoe launch

Smithville Lake

Floating Trail

Rancocas Creek

canoe launch

Smith's Woods

butterfly garden

Forest Avenue

West Railroad Avenue

East Railroad Avenue

N

1,000 feet

— Road
---- Trails
P Parking
Restrooms
Playground
Picnic Area

In the larger portion of the park, to the east, is Smith's Woods, a natural area developed especially for children. Well-maintained trails open to hikers and mountain bikes (and one for equestrians) explore the varied habitat of forest, meadow, and the Rancocas Creek. The longest trail is a 1.5-mile loop, and all the trails are suitable for kids. There is also a nice butterfly garden.

Both the lake and Rancocas Creek are open to canoes and kayaks. The small lake, which is open only to human-powered or electric motor boats, is good for novice paddlers and is an excellent spot for young anglers. The creek is more easily paddled upstream of Smithville, between Pemberton and Burlington County College, where it is relatively wide, slow-moving, and scenic, making for a good family paddling excursion. (For more information on the entire 14-mile Rancocas Creek Canoe Trail, see Burlington County's website.)

In Smith's Woods is a large and well-maintained picnic area and a sizable playground for young children.

Remember: Dogs must be leashed.

PLAN B: Go east on NJ 72 for hiking at Pakim Pond (Trip 85) or head west 5 miles on Rancocas Road to Rancocas Nature Center (Trip 84).

WHERE TO EAT NEARBY: Bring a picnic to enjoy at the picnic groves.

Trip 89

All Ages

Howell Living History Farm

Try out the tools, meet the animals, tramp the fields, and talk with the farmers as you take part in the all-consuming activities of nineteenth-century farm life.

Address: 70 Woodens Lane, Lambertville, NJ
Hours: 10 A.M. to 4 P.M. Saturdays, year-round (programs from 11 A.M. to 3 P.M.); 10 A.M. to 4 P.M. Tuesday through Friday, February through November; noon to 4 p.m. Sundays, April through November, for self-guided tours only
Fee: Free
Contact: howellfarm.org, 609-737-3299
Bathrooms: At the visitor center
Water/Snacks: Water fountain at visitor center; snacks available for purchase during Saturday programs
Maps: howellfarm.org
Directions by Car: Take I-95 North into New Jersey to Exit 1 and merge onto NJ 29 North toward Lambertville. Go 7.5 miles on NJ 29 to Valley Road. Turn right and drive 1.5 miles to Woodens Lane. Turn left; the Howell Farm entrance is 0.25 mile ahead on the right. Park in the lot. *GPS coordinates:* 40° 20.425′ N, 74° 54.277′ W.

At Howell Living History Farm, kids will experience firsthand the work and rewards of farming as it was practiced in the nineteenth century, with little mechanization. Whether or not they appreciate the specific historical aspects, they'll enjoy the immersion in the activity.

The 130-acre farm is owned by Mercer County, operated as a living museum and educational facility. A farm has been on this site since the 1730s. Much of the Pleasant Valley landscape around the farm looks unchanged in its rural character. After a visit to the farm, you can explore trails at nearby parks and preserves.

This is a working farm, where you'll find orchards, crop fields, barn animals, pastures, and gardens. The farmers produce crops and products using the methods employed during the period from 1890 to 1910, and raise livestock typical of that time. You can visit an eighteenth-century farmhouse, a nineteenth-century barn, a wagon house, a corn crib, an ice house, and other buildings, as well as outdoor locales such as an apple orchard, a beehive, an herb garden, and an outhouse. Although self-guided tours are available, it's

Equipment is available for hands-on inspection at the Howell Living History Farm.

more fun to visit on a guided tour; as you proceed through the demonstrations of 25 different farm operations, kids can interact with the farm workers.

Draft horses are used for plowing; kids will be thrilled to see these huge working animals up close, and they may even get a chance to try their hand at guiding the plow. Visiting the farm in spring is a special treat for kids because they get to see all the baby animals and birds.

The farm conducts weekly programs for children to learn about farming. In return, parents are put to work, collecting eggs, shucking corn, mixing feeds, or milking.

Picnic tables are near the visitor center.

Remember: This is a teaching farm; prepare the children for this before they arrive and advise them that it is not a playground. It is a good idea to wear rubber boots to walk around.

PLAN B: Hike nearby trails, such as the adjacent Dry Run Creek Trail of D&R Greenway (drgreenway.org), or take a hike or bike ride at Washington Crossing State Park (Trip 82).

WHERE TO EAT NEARBY: Continue north on NJ 29 to Lambertville, a lively river town with many shops and restaurants.

Glades Wildlife Refuge

Explore the ins and outs of an extensive tidal marsh along the Delaware Bayshore.

Address: Turkey Point Road, Downe, NJ
Hours: Dawn to dusk daily
Fee: Free
Contact: natlands.org, 856-447-3425
Bathrooms: None
Water/Snacks: None
Maps: natlands.org (click on List of Preserves, then Glades)
Directions by Car: Take I-676 East to the Ben Franklin Bridge and cross into
    New Jersey. Merge onto I-76 East, then NJ 42 South. Take Exit 13 onto NJ 55
    South toward Glassboro/Vineland. After 32.6 miles, take Exit 27 onto NJ 47
    South toward Millville. Merge onto North 2nd Street. Turn right onto County
    Road 555, then left onto Cedar Street. Take the second left onto South Race
    Street and continue on County Road 555 to County Road 553. Take the second
    right onto Maple Avenue. At Turkey Point Road, go straight into the refuge,
    where a small parking area is next to the kiosk. *GPS coordinates*: 39° 15.742′ N,
    75° 7.414′ W.

The 7,500-acre Glades Wildlife Refuge, a preserve owned by the Natural
Lands Trust, is an extensive landscape of tidal wetland along Delaware Bay. It
consists of saltmarshes, forests, and beaches, and hosts abundant wildlife,
including bald eagles and diamondback terrapins, migratory shorebirds
during spring and fall, and large flocks of snow geese in winter. This unusual and
beautiful environment invites kids of various ages to explore, with plenty of
room to roam and play.

A great way to discover the refuge is by paddling a canoe or kayak around
the shallow coves and winding inlets. You'll see all kinds of birds flying, fishing, and tending to their young; foxes, otters, and terrapins can be spotted too,
and crabs are plentiful on the mudflats. A public boat launch is at the end of
Turkey Point Road. The trust conducts guided paddles; call for information.
Be sure to check the tide tables before starting out so you are not paddling
against an incoming tide. On land, hiking trails lead to wildlife viewing areas.
Tat Starr Trail goes through a forest to the edge of a vast tidal marsh where kids

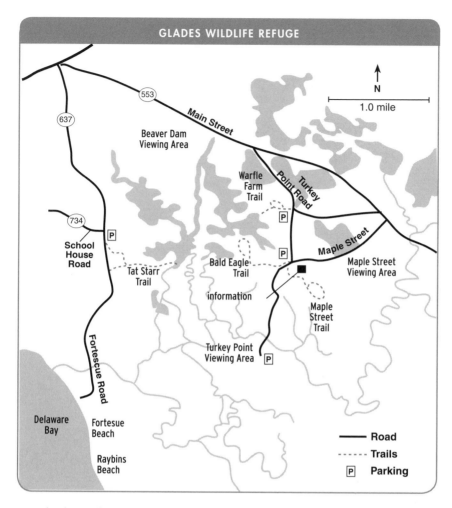

553

637

Main Street

Beaver Dam
Viewing Area

Warfle
Farm
Trail

Turkey Point Road

734

P

School
House
Road

Tat Starr
Trail

Bald Eagle
Trail

information

P

P

Maple Street

Maple Street
Viewing Area

Maple
Street
Trail

Fortescue Road

Turkey Point
Viewing Area

P

N

1.0 mile

Delaware
Bay

Fortesue
Beach

Raybins
Beach

——— Road

------ Trails

P   Parking

can climb an observation tower for a spectacular vista. Look for bald eagles, especially in winter, and other raptors, waterfowl, and shorebirds.

Fortescue Beach and Raybins Beach on the Delaware Bay are two of the best locations for observing the annual horseshoe crab migration, an incredible event in which huge, spiny crabs crawl by the thousands onto the beaches to lay their eggs. They in turn are followed by huge flocks of birds that feast on the eggs. Despite the apparent conflict, the crabs have survived for eons. Watching this is an unforgettable experience. Usually the peak spawning coincides with high lunar tides at the full and new moons in May and June. You can view the spectacle from the bridge. Check with refuge staff prior to your trip to confirm that the crabs have arrived.

Any time of year, kids will enjoy the wide, pristine sand beaches that give access to the gentle waves on the Delaware Bay. They can discover sandcastle worm "cities," run after fiddler crabs scurrying across the sand, watch barnacles open and close in tidal pools, or go for a swim.

Remember: Insects are prevalent here, especially during summer. Always do a thorough tick check.

PLAN B: Parvin State Park (Trip 87) has hiking and biking trails and several small lakes for paddling.

WHERE TO EAT NEARBY: It's best to bring snacks or a picnic to enjoy on the beach.

Trip 91

All Ages

Grounds For Sculpture

The whole family will delight in discovering hundreds of contemporary sculptures throughout a natural setting.

Address: 126 Sculptors Way, Hamilton, NJ
Hours: 10 A.M. to 6 P.M., Tuesday through Sunday (hours may be extended Fridays and Saturdays in December and during summer; check website)
Fee: Adults, $12; children ages 6 to 17, $8; members and children 5 and under, free
Contact: groundsforsculpture.org, 609-586-0616
Bathrooms: At the Museum Building, Domestic Arts Building, and Motor Exhibits Building
Water/Snacks: Water fountains at the restrooms; snacks and sandwiches at the Gazebo Café and the Peacock Café; fine dining at Rat's Restaurant
Maps: At entrance; groundsforsculpture.org (click on Visit)
Directions by Car: Take I-95 North, crossing into New Jersey, to I-295 South and take Exit 65B/Sloan Avenue West. Stay in the right lane after 0.2 mile, following signs for Grounds For Sculpture, and take the jug handle to cross over Sloan Avenue. Go through the traffic light onto Klockner Road. Take Klockner Road to the next traffic light and turn right onto East State Street Extension. After 0.8 mile, take the second left onto Sculptors Way, and continue 0.2 mile to the main entrance on the left. *GPS coordinates:* 40° 14.027′ N, 74° 43.288′ W.

Grounds For Sculpture is a spectacular, 42-acre landscaped park that invites discovery of art in a natural setting. Both paved and natural paths wind through an ever-changing mix of hundreds of large-scale contemporary works of art, many of them interactive, whimsical, and surprising.

Sculptures are tucked into wooded alcoves, along streambanks, and at scenic overlooks. Of particular delight to kids are the many life-size figures that re-create vignettes from Impressionist paintings. Colorful peacocks strut around the grounds.

Wandering the paths is a delight; the landscape is designed to stimulate the feeling that something new is around every corner. Within the park are a wide variety of natural "rooms" that act as outdoor galleries. There's a water garden, a gazebo, a footbridge, and an observation tower, as well as a wide meadow.

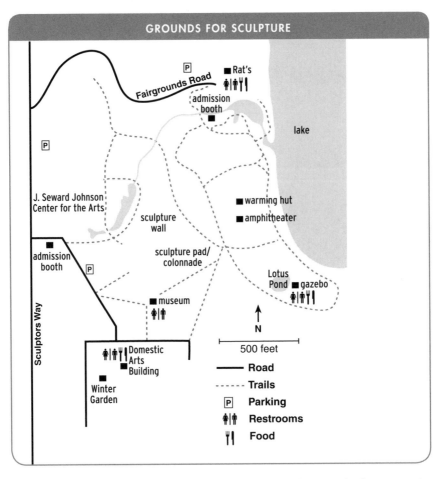

Fairgrounds Road

■ Rat's

admission booth

lake

J. Seward Johnson Center for the Arts

sculpture wall

■ warming hut

■ amphitheater

admission booth

sculpture pad/ colonnade

Sculptors Way

■ museum

Lotus Pond ■ gazebo

N

500 feet

Domestic Arts Building

Winter Garden

—— Road

----- Trails

P Parking

Restrooms

Food

The park is open year-round. In winter, kids will enjoy ducking into the warming hut for a respite from the cold, or visiting the changing exhibitions in the several indoor halls (many of which date from the 1920s, when the site was part of the New Jersey State Fairgrounds).

Grounds For Sculpture hosts numerous programs, workshops, and events, many of them kid-friendly, that encourage families to experience, learn about, and make art. Visit the website for more details.

Remember: No pets or outside food/beverages permitted. Children must be supervised at all times. While play is encouraged, note that the etiquette rules prohibit running. Only designated sculptures may be touched. Also note posted warnings about mature content.

PLAN B: Abbott Marshlands (Trip 94) in Bordentown offers great hiking trails.

WHERE TO EAT NEARBY: It's best to plan on eating on-site at one of the cafés.

Trip 92

All Ages

Island Beach State Park

Sandy beaches, tidal ponds, bay and ocean trails, guarded ocean swimming, and well-maintained facilities make this a favorite nature destination for active families.

Address: Central Avenue and 24th Avenue, Berkeley, NJ
Hours: Memorial Day to Labor Day: 8 A.M. to 8 P.M. Monday through Friday, 7 A.M. to 8 P.M. weekends and holidays; Labor Day to Memorial Day: 8 A.M. to dusk daily
Fee: Memorial Day to Labor Day: residents, $6 per car on weekdays, $10 per car on weekends; nonresidents, $12 per car on weekdays, $20 per car on weekends. All other times, $5 residents, $10 nonresidents
Contact: www.state.nj.us/dep/parksandforests, 732-793-0506
Bathrooms: In the pavilions; at the ocean beach swimming areas; at the interpretative centers
Water/Snacks: Concession stands at the ocean beach swimming areas in season
Maps: None
Directions by Car: Take I-676 East to the Ben Franklin Bridge and cross into New Jersey. Continue onto US 30. Merge onto NJ 38 East, then merge onto NJ 70. Drive for 18.5 miles; at the traffic circle, continue straight on NJ 70 East. At a second traffic circle, continue straight again to stay on NJ 70 for 18.4 miles. Take NJ 37 East/Little League World Champions Boulevard for 13.1 miles. Merge onto NJ 35 South via the ramp to Seaside Park/Island Beach. Follow for 0.7 mile and turn right onto Northwest Central Avenue. Follow for 5.8 miles and arrive at Island Beach State Park; several parking areas are in the park. *GPS coordinates*: 39° 54.341′ N, 74° 4.887′ W.

The 3,000-acre Island Beach State Park is one of the last undeveloped barrier beaches on the Atlantic coast, with more than 10 miles of pure white-sand beach. Here kids can experience the ocean, dunes, and shore in their natural state—sand and water, waves and wind.

The park has two natural areas, one at each end of the island, and a central recreation area with bathhouse and concession stand. Swimming is permitted at the 1 mile of beach at the recreation area; lifeguards are on duty in summer. Surf fishing is permitted here as well, and a wheelchair-accessible Fisherman's Boardwalk enables differently abled anglers to reach the water's edge. Surfing, sailboarding, and windsurfing are permitted south of the swimming beach.

*Paddling the Island Beach State Park bays, you'll
see the lesser-known side of the Jersey Shore.*

Canoeing and kayaking are allowed in the bay area; rentals are available at the concession area. Biking on 8 miles of designated bike lanes along the main road is good for older kids.

Facing the Atlantic Ocean on the east and Barnegat Bay on the west, the two natural areas offer 1,900 acres of sand dunes, tidal marshes, maritime forests, and freshwater wetlands. Island Beach is characterized by strong, and diverse, communities of plants and animals. Eight hiking trails enable exploration of these areas. These are all level, and all are less than a mile long, good for short family nature walks.

In the summer season, park staff lead guided walks, as well as canoe and kayak trips. Horseback riding is permitted on 6 miles of the beach, by permit, from October 1 through April 30.

Remember: The park has no picnic tables, but you can picnic on the beach. Strong surf and a bike path along a busy main road make this trip most suitable for school-age children. Dogs are allowed in the nonswimming areas.

PLAN B: Cattus Island Park (Trip 97) has playgrounds and easy trails for younger children.

WHERE TO EAT NEARBY: Several fast-food places are on the way to Island Beach.

Trip 93

Duke Farms

On foot or by bike, tour 1,000 acres of waterfalls, lakes, statues, winding roads, wildlife habitats, and farmland.

Address: 1112 Duke Parkway West, Hillsborough, NJ
Hours: 8:30 A.M. to 6 P.M., Thursday through Tuesday
Fee: Free (donations accepted)
Contact: dukefarms.org, 908-722-3700
Bathrooms: At the orientation center and throughout the park in solar-powered composting toilets
Water/Snacks: Water fountain and a café with child-friendly snacks at the orientation center
Maps: At orientation center; dukefarms.org (click on Visit)
Directions by Car: Take I-95 North and cross into New Jersey. Take Exit 7B and merge onto NJ 206 North. Take NJ 206 North approximately 22 miles to Overlook Way. Turn left. The Duke Farms entrance is on the left. Follow signs to the parking lot. *GPS coordinates:* 40° 32.793´ N, 74° 37.297´ W.

Duke Farms is a private park that is open to the public for the purpose of promoting environmental awareness and stewardship. Once the private estate of tobacco magnate J.B. Duke, today its farmland, woods, waterfalls, gardens, and lakes invite visitors of all ages and abilities to an extraordinary outdoor destination.

Almost 1,000 acres of Duke Farms is open to the public. More than 18 miles of pedestrian trails and 12 miles of bike paths, including 4 miles of paved, stroller-friendly, wheelchair-accessible paths, are on the property.

Begin at the orientation center in the Farm Barn, where you can learn about the park's history and mission through interactive exhibits. You'll find out how the facility generates its own power with a solar array, and uses constructed wetlands to purify wastewater. For a small fee, kids can borrow an Eco-Kit: a canvas shoulder bag with binoculars, a compass, note pad, and field guide to help identify plants and animals. Duke Farms offers something for all ages and abilities to enjoy. The walking trails vary from gravel, wood-chipped, or mown grass; bike trails are paved or gravel. Trails wind through the bucolic setting, offering plenty of opportunities to observe wildlife, or take in the scenery.

Extravagant floor-to-ceiling displays of plants crowd the conservatory at Duke Farms.

The solar-powered Great Waterfall at Vista Lake is programmed to flow for 10 minutes a day beginning at 12:30 p.m.

In addition to the trails, for those unable (or too tired) to walk, a motorized tram stops at selected areas. In winter, you can use your cross-country skis and snowshoes on the grounds.

Kids can use self-guided activity sheets (on the website or at the orientation center). Bring a GPS to explore the 11-station geocaching course. Duke Farms also conducts numerous family programs about nature and the environment throughout the year. Check the website or call ahead for details.

Remember: No pets are permitted on the grounds, and they may not be left in your vehicle. Duke Farms restricts activities to marked trails. Visitors are discouraged from any activity that can disturb nature. Carry out any trash.

PLAN B: Also at Duke, explore the marble sculpture garden in the ruins of the Hay Barn, the 1917 conservatory filled with native New Jersey plants.

WHERE TO EAT NEARBY: On NJ 206, you will find places to eat, but Duke Farms is the perfect spot for a picnic.

Trip 94

All Ages

Abbott Marshlands (Hamilton-Trenton-Bordentown Marsh)

Walk, bike, or paddle through a tidal marsh along the Delaware River.

Address: 18 West Park Street, Bordentown Township, NJ
Hours: 6 A.M. to 8 P.M. daily, April through October; 6 A.M. to 6 P.M. daily, November through March
Fee: Free
Contact: marsh-friends.org
Bathrooms: Seasonal portable toilets at the train station
Water/Snacks: None
Maps: marsh-friends.org/getting-there
Directions by Car: To Bordentown Beach access point: Take I-95 North and cross into New Jersey. Take Exit 7A to merge onto NJ 206 South toward Trenton. Follow signs for Bordentown historic district. Turn right onto Park Avenue and follow it to the end; the parking lot is just past the Bordentown (light rail) train station. After parking, walk past the station and make a left onto Prince Street. Walk past historical homes to the Thomas Paine Statue. Make a right onto Courtland Street, then a left on to Farnsworth Avenue. Walk down the hill, cross the railroad tracks, and follow the wooden walk and bridge next to the railroad tracks to the trails. The start of the trails is 0.2 mile from the train station. *GPS coordinates:* 40° 8.872′ N, 74° 42.949′ W.

The Abbott Marshlands comprise a remarkable natural area—a 1,250-acre freshwater tidal marsh that is a haven for wildlife, an enormously varied community of plants, and a green recreational oasis in a densely populated urban area. Linking Watson's Creek to Crosswicks Creek, where the latter empties into the Delaware River, it encompasses marshland, islands, bluffs, the D&R Canal, and the river. In addition to Bordentown Beach, additional access points to the marsh include Roebling Park-Spring Lake and Roebling Park-Watson's Woods, in Hamilton Township, and the D&R Canal Towpath Lock 1, which connects to a trail in Bordentown City.

Trails through the tidal Abbott Marshlands invite discovery of a rich ecosystem.

The trails near Bordentown Beach are easy and entertaining for kids, combining history with nature. A fun walk leads along a suspended bridge over the canal to the D&R Canal towpath trail, which affords magnificent views along the river. You'll also see the remains of Lock 1.

Interpretive signage explains the industrial history of the area. Along the tree-shaded towpath trail, kids will enjoy crossing over canal bridges and taking short paths to the banks.

Paddling the creek and inlets is an awesome way to get to know the marsh, but you have to go with the tidal flow. Ride in two hours before high tide, follow Crosswicks Creek or Watson's Creek, and turn around when the tide turns. You'll be rewarded with easy "always-downstream" paddling suitable for the whole family that provides an interesting perspective on the rich community of unusual marsh plants and wildlife. (Note: Exercise caution at the railroad trestle at the Crosswicks Creek entrance, and stay to the right with the incoming tide.) Check the website for tide tables. Boat launches are at Bordentown Beach and Watson Woods, and in Trenton.

The Friends for the Marsh and the Sierra Club conduct numerous programs, including guided walks and paddles, and family-oriented tours. Check the Friends website for details.

Remember: A new interpretive center is planned for Roebling Park, opening by summer 2013. The existing Mercer County nature center is open only for programs and events.

PLAN B: Hike or bike on the 70-mile D&R Canal towpath (Trip 95), which continues north of the marsh, past Trenton and up to Milford.

WHERE TO EAT NEARBY: In Bordentown, you'll find many options for food.

Trip 95

D&R Canal State Park

This linear park along the Delaware River is ideal for easy walking, biking, or paddling, with historical sites and beautiful views.

Address: Bull's Island, 2185 Daniel Bray Highway, Delaware Township, NJ
Hours: Park open sunrise to sunset daily; D&R Canal office open 8:30 A.M. to 4:30 P.M. weekdays
Fee: Free
Contact: www.state.nj.us/dep/parksandforests, 609-397-2949
Bathrooms: Outside the D&R Canal office
Water/Snacks: Water fountain by the D&R Canal office
Maps: www.state.nj.us/dep/parksandforests (click on D&R Canal State Park)
Directions by Car: Take I-95 North into New Jersey and take Exit 1 onto NJ 29 North toward Lambertville. Follow NJ 29 for 9.2 miles. Stay straight to go to NJ 179/Old York Road and turn left onto NJ 179/Bridge Street. Take the second right onto North Main Street/NJ 29. Follow NJ 29 for 4.4 miles and arrive at Daniel Bray Highway. The park will be on your left. Park in the lot. *GPS coordinates*: 40° 24.625′ N, 75° 02.095′ W.

The Delaware and Raritan (D&R) Canal parallels the Delaware River, connecting Frenchtown to Trenton. Thirty-four miles of pathways are along the canal. The level trails, converted from towpaths or rail beds, provide families with easy and safe walking or biking trips, with numerous options to stop at river towns or to cross into Pennsylvania to explore similar paths.

A fun and interesting access point to the canal is at Bull's Island Recreation Area. At this site (a peninsula formed by the intersection of the canal and the river), families can enjoy picnic tables, a playground, and views of the river. Walk along a nature trail that starts opposite the office and leads deeper and deeper into a lush floodplain woods to the point where the canal and river meet. Circle back and walk on the pedestrian suspension bridge that spans the river (see Trip 31).

Walk or bike along the canal via the path, which parallels NJ 29. The tree-shaded, hard-surface path (suitable for all bikes) gives occasional glimpses of the river through woods. The woods attract many songbirds, and you'll see ducks, kingfishers, and wading birds. Along the way are interpretive signs explaining the history of the canal and railroads. The historical Prallsville

Enjoy a refreshing shower at the Prallsville Mills lock "waterfall" after a hike on the D&R Canal.

Mills property is 3 miles south of Bull's Island; it consists of nineteenth-century mill buildings (some open for tours). A canal lock here creates an artificial waterfall, where splashing in the spray is a cool treat on a hot day. The Holcombe-Jimison Farmstead Museum north of Lambertville, open summer Sundays and all year on Wednesdays, has restored buildings open to visitors with demonstrations, including a blacksmith shop and print shop. The towpath continues past Lambertville, through Washington Crossing State Park (Trip 82) and into Bordentown (Trip 94).

With its leisurely flow, the canal can be easily paddled by kids, upstream or downstream. You can put in at Bull's Island and turn around when you feel like it. For more-experienced paddlers, a boat ramp at Bull's Island offers access to the river (boat ramp fees may apply).

The entire length of the canal may be fished, and access is easy from many points along the bank.

Remember: The campground at Bull's Island is closed indefinitely due to tree hazards.

PLAN B: Hike or bike the Delaware Canal on the Pennsylvania side of the river (Trip 31).

WHERE TO EAT NEARBY: In Stockton, a charming river town, you'll find several shops and restaurants.

Trip 96

Nature Center of Cape May

Explore a unique natural area, where the Delaware Bay meets the Atlantic Ocean.

Address: 1600 Delaware Avenue, Cape May, NJ
Hours: April 15 through October 31, Monday through Saturday, 9 A.M. to 5 P.M.;
Sunday, 11 A.M. to 4 P.M.; open other times for special events and programs.
Closed November 1 through April 14.
Fee: Free
Contact: njaudubon.org, 609-898-8848
Bathrooms: In the welcome center
Water/Snacks: Water fountain in the welcome center
Maps: Paper copies of local trails available in the welcome center
Directions by Car: Take I-676 East to the Ben Franklin Bridge and cross into
New Jersey. Merge onto I-76 East, then NJ 42 South, then the Atlantic City
Expressway East. After 36.6 miles, take Exit 7S and merge onto the Garden
State Parkway; take this to the end and continue over the Cape May Canal
Bridge into Cape May. Continue straight on Lafayette Street, pass over a small
bridge, and then make the first available left turn onto Sydney Avenue. Go
one block, and turn left onto Washington Avenue. Bear right and then turn
right on Texas Avenue. The road becomes Pittsburgh Avenue. Go to Delaware
Avenue and turn left. The nature center is two blocks down, on the right.
GPS coordinates: 38° 56.694′ N, 74° 53.981′ W.

Cape May is the end of the Jersey Shore, a peninsula where the Delaware
Bay meets the Atlantic Ocean. Here the bay shore and ocean shore converge,
with different plant and wildlife communities sharing adjacent spaces. It is an
important point on the migratory bird flyway, where, in spring and fall, hawks
and songbirds take a rest before (or after) making the long trip across the bay.
Dragonflies and butterflies also migrate through Cape May. The ocean and
bay are full of aquatic wildlife, as are the beaches, tide pools, marshes, woods,
and meadows.

A number of nature reserves and parks in the area, many with trails,
enable children to discover this fascinating environment. The Nature Center
of Cape May, run by the New Jersey Audubon Society, is a family destination
in itself, but also a jumping-off point for further exploration of the area's outdoor opportunities.

Ospreys nest on top of low poles at the bay shore in Cape May.

The Trucksess Welcome Center has a three-story observation tower that offers spectacular panoramic vistas of the Jersey Shore and its wetlands. (You can borrow binoculars for a better view.) Inquire about programs prior to your visit; numerous family-oriented trips, events, and outdoor hands-on workshops are scheduled throughout the year, with a focus on the diverse wildlife habitats. Activities include hiking, kayaking, paddleboarding, and fishing.

Outside are a children's garden and additional themed gardens that demonstrate plantings to attract wildlife (such as hummingbirds, butterflies, and songbirds). For a meal with an ever-changing view, have lunch or a snack at the picnic tables overlooking the harbor.

The Nature Conservancy's Cape May Meadows, on Sunset Boulevard (fee charged), has level walking trails around a diked tidal meadow behind the dunes. At Cape May Point State Park nearby, walk the beach or the trails in the woods, climb the lighthouse, or enjoy the hawk-watch platform views.

Remember: Bring binoculars for the best views of birds and insects. Seasonal beach tags may be required for ocean beach access outside the state park and Nature Conservancy sections.

PLAN B: The Cape May County Zoo, north of Cape May, is free and has more than 550 animals on 85 acres.

WHERE TO EAT NEARBY: Many restaurants are in the town of Cape May.

Trip 97

Ages 0-4

Cattus Island Park
(Cooper Environmental Center)

Footpaths lead to scenic open spaces overlooking the Barnegat Bay.

Address: 1170 Cattus Island Boulevard, Toms River, NJ
Hours: Park open dawn to dusk daily; Cooper Environmental Center open
8 A.M. to 4:30 P.M. daily
Fee: Free
Contact: occis.com, 732-270-6960
Bathrooms: At the Cooper Environmental Center and the park office
Water/Snacks: Water fountain at the Cooper Environmental Center
Maps: occis.com/cis/parks/cattusislandpark
Directions by Car: Take I-676 East over the Ben Franklin Bridge into New
Jersey. Continue on US 30, then merge onto NJ 38 East, and then NJ 70 East.
From NJ 70 East, take NJ 37 East/Little League World Champions Boulevard
for 10.8 miles, then turn right onto Bash Road. Turn left onto Fischer
Boulevard and follow it for 2.2 miles, and then turn right onto Cattus Island
Boulevard. Take the first left onto Cattus Island Road. Follow it for 1.5 miles
to the parking lot on the right. *GPS coordinates:* 39° 58.678′ N, 74° 8.273′ W.

The 530-acre Cattus Island Park along Barnegat Bay offers a variety of
opportunities to enjoy diverse island ecosystems in a serene atmosphere with
great views. The Cooper Environmental Center provides special attention and
guidance that makes this trip especially enjoyable for young children.

Well-maintained trails are designed to be enjoyed by beginning hikers, and
are ideal for young children. They are short, ranging from 0.27 to 2.2 miles,
for hikes up to two hours if you walk the full length of the trail and take your
time observing the wildlife. All the trails offer opportunities for discovery, like
watching ospreys hunt for fish to bring back to their nestlings or searching
out crabs on the tidal marsh. A 1,500-foot, wheelchair- and stroller-accessible
boardwalk trail leads to a bird blind overlooking the tidal marsh. Bike or walk
the 1-mile unpaved White Trail to the beach, where you can picnic or swim.

With the bay surrounding the park, it is a great place to try paddling or
fishing. A county boat ramp is available to launch canoes and kayaks. The park
conducts paddling tours that explore the island's coves and shores.

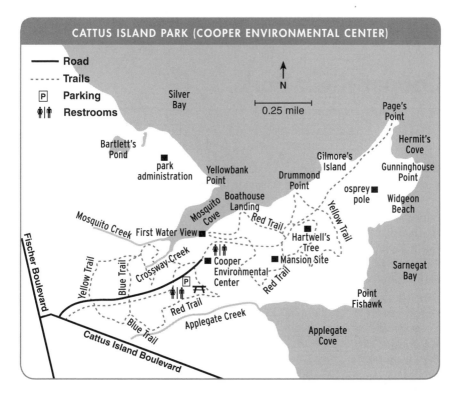

Road
Trails
P Parking
♦♦ Restrooms

Silver
Bay

N

0.25 mile

Page's
Point

Bartlett's
Pond

park
administration

Yellowbank
Point

Gilmore's
Island

Drummond
Point

Hermit's
Cove

Gunninghouse
Point

osprey■
pole

Boathouse
Landing

Mosquito
Cove

Red Trail

Widgeon
Beach

Mosquito Creek First Water View■

Fischer Boulevard

Yellow Trail

Blue Trail

Crossway Creek

Cooper
Environmental
Center

P

Hartwell's
Tree

Mansion Site

Red Trail

Yellow Trail

Sarnegat
Bay

Point
Fishawk

Red Trail

Blue Trail

Applegate Creek

Cattus Island Boulevard

Applegate
Cove

The Cooper Environmental Center is geared toward family discovery of nature; the attentive staff is happy to educate visitors. Young children will enjoy the displays of native reptiles and fish, and the hands-on exhibits. You can borrow adventure backpacks for kids, containing exploration tools such as nets to catch butterflies and other insects, containers to carry them, electronic bird identifiers, a magnifying glass, and booklets and brochures of the 300 plants and animals on the island. You can also borrow a GPS unit here (or bring your own) to follow the 21-location geocaching trail.

A playground and picnic tables are near the parking lot. In winter, the island is a special, quiet refuge; if it snows, the trails can be enjoyed by ski or snowshoe.

Remember: Dogs must be leashed.

PLAN B: Island Beach State Park (Trip 92) is 12 miles away. Fishing, crabbing, or angling enthusiasts may consider visiting Mantoloking Bridge County Park in Mantoloking, New Jersey.

WHERE TO EAT NEARBY: Fast-food restaurants are on NJ 37.

Trip 98

Cooper River Park

Water is the focus of this urban park on both shores of the Cooper River Lake:
Boat or fish in the lake, or walk along the shoreline.

Address: 130 North Park Drive, Pennsauken, NJ
Hours: Dawn to dusk daily
Fee: Free
Contact: camdencounty.com/parks, 856-216-2117
Bathrooms: At the stadium and boathouse; seasonal portable toilets throughout
the park
Water/Snacks: Water fountains by the ball fields, playground, stadium, and
boathouse
Maps: None
Directions by Car: Take I-676 East to the Ben Franklin Bridge and cross into
New Jersey. Merge onto NJ 30/NJ 70 East. Bear right after the overpass onto
NJ 70 East. Turn right at McClellan Avenue, then turn right onto North Park
Drive. Park in the lot. *GPS coordinates:* 39° 55.750´ N, 75° 5.059´ W.

Cooper River Park, a 340-acre urban park, offers many opportunities for family
activities along the Cooper River Lake, which is regionally renowned for its
rowing. You are sure to spot teams or individuals practicing the sport, seeming
to glide effortlessly over the calm water. Regular regattas are conducted from
March to November; see camdencountyboathouse.com for schedules.

While only rowing clubs can use the boathouse, you can bring your own
(nonmotorized) boat and launch it at the South Park Drive boat ramp. The
wooded shorelines make for a lovely family paddle or sail. The family-oriented
Cooper River Yacht Club, also on South Park Drive, offers sailing instruction
for kids 8 and up as well as adults, and has a community sailboat sharing
program (membership fee charged); see cooperriveryc.org.

The park has 4.4 miles of trails. Around the lake is a level paved trail that
is easy for beginning bikers. For more-interesting walking, take the pedestrian
trail to Veterans Island, which features views of the lakeshore. On the more
rugged streamside trails, kids will enjoy poking about the banks, or spotting
birds and small animals.

Kayaking in quiet waters is a fun way to explore the outdoors from a different vantage point.

Wildlife is surprisingly abundant at the park, especially near the wetlands and forested areas on the north side of the lake. Large flocks of egrets and herons roost here in late spring and summer, and songbirds stop to rest in the woods during early spring and fall migrations.

A large playground—advertised as the largest in the state—is off of North Park Drive. It's built to look as if it's rising out of water, with blue and green rubberized mats surrounding the equipment resembling ocean waves. Picnic pavilions are near the playground.

Remember: Dogs must be leashed except in the Pooch Park. This is an urban park and it can get crowded. (Note: As of the time of this writing, Camden County had announced a plan for major changes to the park, including additional riverside walking paths.)

PLAN B: Newton Lake Park in Collingswood, New Jersey, is a well-maintained park that may be a quieter alternative. It has 2 miles of paved roads along the perimeter of the lake that are good for biking, strollers, inline skaters, or wheelchairs.

WHERE TO EAT NEARBY: A restaurant is in the pavilion.

Trip 99

All Ages

Atsion Recreation Area and Batsto Village

Swim or paddle in a deep lake near the restored iron-making village of Batsto.

Address: 714 Route 206, Shamong, NJ
Hours: Atsion: park open from 9 A.M. to 8 P.M. daily, April 1 to October 31;
  swimming permitted from Memorial Day through Labor Day from 10 A.M.
  to 6 P.M.. Batsto: visitor center open 8 A.M. to 4 P.M. daily, year-round
Fee: Atsion: Memorial Day to Labor Day, residents: $5 per car on weekdays, $10
  per car on weekends; nonresidents: $10 per car on weekdays, $20 per car on
  weekends; all times, walk-in/bicycle, $2. Batsto: Weekends only, residents: $5
  per car; nonresidents, $7 per car. Camping is available at Atsion from April
  through October (fees apply)
Contact: www.state.nj.us/dep/parksandforests, 609-268-0444
Bathrooms: Restrooms with changing rooms and showers are at the main
  building at Atsion
Water/Snacks: Water fountain and concession stand at main building at Atsion
Maps: njhiking.com/nj-hiking-maps (click on Wharton State Forest)
Directions by Car: To Atsion: Take I-76 East (Schuylkill Expressway) to the
  Walt Whitman Bridge and cross into New Jersey. Continue on NJ 42 South
  to the Atlantic City Expressway. Take Exit 28 and turn left onto 12th Street.
  Continue onto Bellevue Avenue, then turn right to stay on Bellevue. Continue
  onto NJ 206 South. Atsion Lake is 7 miles ahead on the left. Park in the lot.
  GPS coordinates: 39° 44.767′ N, 74° 43.767′ W.

Atsion Recreation Area in Wharton State Forest is a pleasant lake that offers
young families opportunities for swimming, hiking, boating, and fishing.
It can also be used as a base for exploring other locations in the state forest to
enjoy the Pine Barrens.

Wharton is the largest single tract of land in the New Jersey state park
system. With its extensive forest, as well as ponds, streams, cedar swamps, and
bogs, it is a haven for wildlife. Many miles of trails wind through the forest,
including the 50-mile Batona Trail, and its rivers are excellent for paddling.

Atsion Lake is on the Mullica River, set in a quiet pine and oak woods.
The tea-brown waters of the Mullica, tinted by iron in the soil and by cedar
bark, give this deep lake an interesting color (and may dye swimwear!). The

The cedar lake at Atsion Recreation Area is tea brown in color, a characteristic typical of bodies of water in the Pine Barrens.

lake has a swimming beach with lifeguards. A bathhouse has showers and changing facilities, and canoe and kayak rentals are available. Two connected loop hiking trails—0.5 mile and 1 mile in length—begin at the parking lot and follow the south shore of the lake. Campsites with showers are on the north shore of the lake in the Atsion Family Campground. There are also a playground and a picnic area with grills.

In nearby Batsto Village, the site of a former bog-iron and glass-making industrial center, is now a restored village where visitors can discover the industrial and cultural history of the Pine Barrens. Children will enjoy the variety of buildings in the village, such as a blacksmith, piggery, sawmill, wheelwright, and general store. See batstovillage.org for details on visiting the site.

At Batsto you will also find the Mullica River Trail, a level, easy but long (7 miles) trail, which leads through the pine woods along sandy paths by the river. For young children, start with a short nature walk on the part of the trail that is closest to Batsto. Interpretive signs describe the unique Pine Barrens ecosystem.

Remember: Swimming is allowed only while lifeguards are on duty. No dogs are permitted in the swimming area. In summer, Atsion will be closed to visitors if it reaches maximum capacity, which is not uncommon. Call before setting out.

PLAN B: For a more challenging Wharton State Forest trip, paddle one of its rivers: the Mullica, Batsto, Wading, or Oswego (Trip 100).

WHERE TO EAT NEARBY: If not buying snacks at the concession stand, bring a picnic.

Trip 100

Ages 9-12

Oswego River

Paddle and swim in the prettiest river in the Pine Barrens.

Address: Lake Oswego Road, Chatsworth, NJ
Hours: Sunrise to sunset daily
Fee: Free; fee charged for camping
Contact: www.state.nj.us/dep/parksandforests, 609-268-0444
Bathrooms: Portable toilet at parking area
Water/Snacks: None
Maps: None
Directions by Car: Take I-676 east to the Ben Franklin Bridge and cross into New Jersey. Continue onto US 30 East, and then merge onto NJ 70 East. Follow NJ 70 East for 26.2 miles. At a traffic circle, take NJ 72 East. Continue 3.5 miles to County Road 563. Follow this through Chatsworth. Turn left onto Lake Oswego Road. Continue past the cranberry bogs to a large parking area on the right. *GPS coordinates:* 39° 44.085´ N, 74° 29.475´ W.

Is the Oswego River in Wharton State Forest the most beautiful of the beautiful Pine Barrens rivers? Few would say no. Clear, yet brown in color, it winds through deep pine forests full of birds. The banks are lined with trees, flowering shrubs, and wild cranberries.

A paddle on the river is a moderately challenging but extremely rewarding family trip, suitable for older children who have some experience kayaking or canoeing. A trip down the river will take four hours or longer, so it requires stamina. Bring plenty of water and food.

Start at tree-lined Lake Oswego, where a boat launch is right at the parking lot. A picnic area overlooks the water. You can take a swim in the wide tree-lined lake, or paddle around to get warmed up. Directly across from the launch is a dam at a dirt road; the river goes under the road in a culvert. Portage the boat across the road and down the other side to the river. Continue down the river, which winds in tight twists and turns. It is often shallow and may require carrying the boat for short distances in times of low water. The cool, clear river is shaded by pitch pines and white cedar trees; the banks are dense with flowering shrubs and low-running native cranberries. In sunny areas, look for carnivorous pitcher plants, which look like vases. Bald eagles and

*A paddle on the Oswego River is a trip into the heart
of the mysterious Pine Barrens wilderness.*

ospreys circle overhead; great blue herons stalk fish in the shallows, and several varieties of turtles bask on logs.

Sandy beaches are along the way, where you can stop and swim or snack. You can continue paddling for several hours, through a long open area at Martha Pond, and ending at the next portage, at Harrisville Pond (or Lake). End the day here with a swim or a picnic.

While no camping is permitted along the Oswego River, families can camp below Harrisville Lake, at Bodine Field, where 250 tentsites are in an unshaded, sandy area with primitive facilities (reachable by car with permits required).

Remember: Canoe and kayak rentals are available in the vicinity from several commercial outfitters ("liveries"). If you bring your own boats, they will also transport you or your boats to put-in and take-out points.

PLAN B: For young paddlers, it may be appropriate to arrange with an outfitter for a take-out prior to Harrisville Pond, shortening the trip. Nearby Atsion Lake (Trip 99) provides more-leisurely paddling, as well as swimming and camping with shower facilities.

WHERE TO EAT NEARBY: It's best to bring food with you.

SAFETY REGULATIONS AND PERMITS

Before your family goes fishing or puts a boat into the water, become familiar with the regulations of the state where the trip is located. Fishing may require a license (although kids typically do not need a license themselves), and depending on the type of fishing you're doing, there may be special permits required or restrictions on catch size. Boating is regulated for safety reasons, and while unpowered boats like kayaks, canoes, and sailboats are not nearly as regulated as powerboats, there are requirements you need to follow, including safety equipment that must be on board or worn. If you rent a boat, the outfitter will typically supply you with any required equipment. Boats may also be subject to registration requirements.

FISHING

In Pennsylvania, people 16 years and older must display a valid current fishing license to fish or angle from any waters within or bordering the state. An adult who assists a child by casting or retrieving a fishing line or fishing rod is not required to possess a valid fishing license, provided that the child remains within arms' reach of the assisting adult and is actively involved in the fishing activity. An adult may assist a child by baiting hooks, removing fish from the line, netting fish, preparing the fishing rod for use, and untangling the line without possessing a valid fishing license.

To fish in the tidal portion of the Delaware River or the Delaware Estuary, people 16 years and older (with certain exceptions) must register with the Pennsylvania Saltwater Angler Registry Program; register, for a fee, with the National Saltwater Angler Registry; or meet the saltwater angler registration requirements of another state.

At numerous places in the state, fishing is restricted to children 12 years old and younger. Always call ahead to confirm.

A Pennsylvania or New Jersey fishing license is valid on the Delaware River between New Jersey and Pennsylvania when fishing from a boat or from either shore.

For more information on these and other regulations, see fishandboat.com/regs_fish.htm.

People 16 years and older must have a valid fishing license to fish the fresh waters of New Jersey with handline, rod and line, or longbow and arrow. This includes privately owned lakes and other waters. New Jersey does not require a general saltwater fishing license but does require a limited number of saltwater licenses and permits for certain types of fishing. Additionally, most saltwater anglers need to register with the free New Jersey Saltwater Recreational Registry Program.

For more information on these and other regulations, see njfishandwildlife.com/fishing.htm.

People ages 16 to 64 years old need a license to fish, clam, or crab in Delaware's waters (including Delaware's jurisdictional portion of the Delaware River). The same license covers freshwater and salt water.

For more information on these and other regulations, see www.dnrec.delaware.gov/fw/Fisheries/Pages/NewFishingLicense.aspx.

BOATING

Below are summaries of certain regulations applicable to canoes, kayaks, and other paddling boats, as well as sailboats.

Unpowered boats used at Pennsylvania Fish & Boat Commission (PFBC) lakes or access areas, state parks, or state forests must be properly registered, display an official and valid PFBC use permit, or display an official and valid watercraft launch or mooring permit issued by the Department of Conservation and Natural Resources (DCNR). A launch permit issued by PFBC or DCNR is also required at many other public lakes or access areas (including the U.S. Army Corps of Engineers reservoir at Blue Marsh Lake).

PFBC issues launch permits valid for up to two years. The permits may be purchased online (www.theoutdoorshop.state.pa.us), from PFBC region offices, from authorized issuing agents, or from many state park offices. When purchasing a permit (valid for one or two years), you will be asked to provide the type of boat, make, year manufactured, and hull ID/serial number. For more details, see fishandboat.com/registration.htm.

The state-issued launch permits do not cover (and are not required for) boating access to county or municipal access areas. These areas may require local-issued permits. Check the relevant municipal or county website prior to setting out.

The National Park Service does not require fees or permits from the Betzwood boat ramp in Valley Forge National Historical Park (Trip 27).

There is no state requirement for obtaining a permit to launch an inner tube from a state access area, but tubes may not be launched at PFBC ramps.

There is no general permit requirement for unpowered boats (including canoes and kayaks) used in New Jersey. However, the state charges fees to use specified state park boat ramps from Memorial Day to Labor Day. Daily or annual "Five-Area" passes may be purchased at Bull's Island State Park or several other state park offices. See www.state.nj.us/dep/parksandforests/parks/feeschedule.htm#boats and www.state.nj.us/dep/parksandforests/parks/drcanal.html#boat. Municipalities may impose their own fees for usage of boat launch ramps. Check the relevant municipal or county website prior to setting out.

There are no launch permit requirements or fees for unpowered boats in Delaware.

LIFE JACKET REQUIREMENTS AND OTHER SAFETY REGULATIONS

Below are summaries of certain regulations applicable to canoes, kayaks, and other paddling boats.

All boats in Pennsylvania must have a U.S. Coast Guard (USCG)-approved wearable (Type I, II, III, or V) personal flotation device (PFD) on board for each person. The PFDs must be readily accessible. In canoes and kayaks, children 12 years of age or younger must wear a PFD in state waters while the boat is under way. For more details, see fishandboat.com/fishpub/summary/pfd.htm.

Note: Every person on a canoe or kayak must wear a PFD between November 1 and April 30.

Operators of canoes, kayaks, rowboats, and paddleboards are required to carry a device capable of sounding a prolonged blast for four to six seconds that can be heard by another boat operator in time to avoid a collision. An athletic coach's whistle is acceptable.

Any kayak, canoe, inflatable raft, or paddleboard on the water after dusk must have a hand-held or installed white light to be displayed in time to avoid a collision with another craft. When anchored or moored after dusk, an all-round white light must be displayed where it can best be seen for 360 degrees.

Paddleboards are considered boats as defined by the USCG if they are used outside the narrow limits of a swimming, surfing, or bathing area. As such, they are subject to regulations administered by the USCG and the PFBC, including PFD, sound-producing device, and navigation light requirements.

All boats in New Jersey must have a USCG-approved wearable (Type I, II, III, or V) PFD on board for each person. The PFDs must be readily accessible. In canoes and kayaks, children 12 years of age or younger must wear a PFD in state waters while the boat is under way.

Lights are required on all boats between sunset and sunrise and at times of decreased visibility. Boats 12 meters or less in length must carry a sound-signaling device (whistle or other device).

Between sunset and sunrise, visual distress signals suitable for night use, in the number required, shall be on board manually propelled boats. For more details see njsp.org/maritime/pdf/052212_boatsafetymanual.pdf.

All boats in Delaware must have a USCG-approved wearable (Type I, II, III, or V) PFD on board for each person. The PFDs must be readily accessible. In canoes and kayaks, children 12 years of age or younger must wear a PFD in state waters while the boat is under way.

A vessel of less than 12 meters in length must be equipped with a whistle or horn, or some other sounding device capable of making an efficient sound signal.

Between sunset and sunrise, an electric distress light must be on board manually propelled boats. For more details, see boat-ed.com/delaware.

OUTFITTERS

Families who want to go camping, hiking, bicycling, or boating and don't own equipment can rent or buy the basics for a fun outing. Equipment, gear, and clothing can be purchased for reasonable prices at many general retail stores. In addition, specialty stores have a wider variety and often rent larger pieces of equipment. Some recreational organizations (including the Appalachian Mountain Club) lend gear and equipment to members.

The outfitters listed below provide any of a range of services, including sale and rental of clothing, gear, and equipment for camping, paddling, hiking, and biking, and other outdoor activities. No attempt was made to list all outfitters or rental services, particularly for bikes, which are available in many areas.

Some outfitters also provide livery services (transporting people and boats to and from nearby points). Call for more details. No endorsement is made of any of these businesses. Also see fishandboat.com/livery.htm.

L.L. Bean
llbean.com
Numerous locations
Gear and equipment for sale

Eastern Mountain Sports
ems.com
Numerous locations
Gear and equipment for sale and rent

REI
rei.com
Numerous locations
Gear and equipment for sale

Cabela's
cabelas.com
100 Cabela Drive
Hamburg, PA 19526
610-929-7000

3D Outdoor Rentals
berkskayakbikerentals.com
Robesonia, PA 19551
610-488-1900

Brandywine Outfitters
canoepa.net
2096 Strasburg Road
Coatesville, PA 19320
610-486-6141

Hidden River Outfitters
hiddenriveroutfitters.com
57 East Schuylkill Avenue, #2
Pottstown, PA 19465

Northbrook Canoe
northbrookcanoe.com
1810 Beagle Road
West Chester, PA 19382
610-793-2279

Port Providence Rental
canoeandkayak.biz
264 Canal Street
Port Providence, PA 19460
610-935-2750

Bucks County River Country
rivercountry.net
2 Walters Lane
Point Pleasant, PA 18950
215-297-5000

Nature's Way Canoe and Kayak
naturecanoe.com
Routes 563 and 412
Quakertown, PA 18951
215-536-8964

Adams Canoe Rental
adamscanoerental.com
1005 Atsion Road
Atsion, NJ 08088
609-268-0189

Beaver Dam Boat Rentals
crabulousnj.com
514 Old Beaver Dam Road
and Route 553
Newport, NJ 08345
856-447-3633

Bel Haven Paddlesports
belhavenpaddlesports.com
1227 Route 542
Green Bank, NJ 08215
800-445-0953

Blue Ridge Mountain Sports
brms.com
301 N. Harrison Street
Princeton, NJ 08540
609-921-6078

Cedar Creek Canoe and Kayak Rentals
cedarcreekcanoenj.com
1052 Atlantic City Boulevard
Bayville, NJ 08721
732-269-1413

Delaware River Tubing
delawarerivertubing.com
2998 Daniel Bray Highway
(Route 29)
Frenchtown, NJ 08825
908-996-5386

Micks Pine Barrens Canoe
and Kayak Rental
mickscanoerental.com
3107 Route 563
Chatsworth, NJ 08019
800-281-1380

Paddle Creek
paddlecreekfrenchtown.com
26 Race Street
Frenchtown, NJ 08825
908-996-0000

Paddle Shack
paddleshack.com
5045 Mays Landing Road
Mays Landing, NJ 08330
609-909-5250

Princeton Canoe and Kayak
canoenj.com
1076 Canal Road
Griggstown, NJ 08540
908-359-5970

Princeton Canoe and Kayak
483 Alexander Street
Princeton, NJ 08540
609-452-2403

Wilderness Canoe Trips
wildernesscanoetrips.com
2111 Concord Pike
Wilmington, DE 19803
302-654-2227

INDEX

ABOUT THE AUTHOR

Susan Charkes is a longtime resident of the Philadelphia area, where she grew up. She is the author of *AMC's Best Day Hikes Near Philadelphia*, a hike leader with the Appalachian Mountain Club's Delaware Valley Chapter, and an avid kayaker and biker. She gives frequent public presentations about enjoying the outdoors.

As a child she hiked, sailed, biked, and camped in southeastern Pennsylvania, on the Jersey Shore, in the Poconos, on Chesapeake Bay, and in New England. She learned to swim at age 3 in Mohegan Lake, New York, and took her first weeklong backpacking trip on the Appalachian Trail at age 11. These outdoor adventures continued into adulthood. Her son, Nick, who now rides his bike to work every day, was introduced to hiking on family trips in Bucks County, Pennsylvania, and in many other places in the United States and Canada, and as a child learned to kayak off the coast of Maine.

Susan currently works as a freelance writer and editor. She also manages a nonprofit land trust. She is a poet and in her spare time enjoys chemical-free gardening and playing the saxophone.

Visit susancharkes.com for more details.

APPALACHIAN MOUNTAIN CLUB

Founded in 1876, AMC is the nation's oldest outdoor recreation and conservation organization. AMC promotes the protection, enjoyment, and understanding of the mountains, forests, waters, and trails of the Northeast outdoors.

People

We are more than 100,000 members, advocates, and supporters, including 12 local chapters, more than 16,000 volunteers, and over 450 full-time and seasonal staff. Our chapters reach from Maine to Washington, D.C.

Outdoor Adventure and Fun

We offer more than 8,000 trips each year, from local chapter activities to adventure travel worldwide, for every ability level and outdoor interest—from hiking and climbing to paddling, snowshoeing, and skiing.

Great Places to Stay

We host more than 150,000 guests each year at our AMC lodges, huts, camps, shelters, and campgrounds. Each AMC destination is a model for environmental education and stewardship.

Opportunities for Learning

We teach people skills to safely enjoy the outdoors and to care for the natural world around us through programs for children, teens, and adults, as well as outdoor leadership training.

Caring for Trails

We maintain more than 1,700 miles of trails throughout the Northeast, including nearly 350 miles of the Appalachian Trail in five states.

Protecting Wild Places

We advocate for land and riverway conservation, monitor air quality, research climate change, and work to protect alpine and forest ecosystems throughout the Northern Forest and Mid-Atlantic Highlands regions.

Engaging the Public

We seek to educate and inform our own members and an additional 2 million people annually through the media, AMC Books, our website, our White Mountain visitor centers, and AMC destinations.

Join Us!

Members meet other like-minded people and support our mission while enjoying great AMC programs, our award-winning *AMC Outdoors* magazine, and special discounts. Visit outdoors.org or call 800-372-1758 for more information.

APPALACHIAN MOUNTAIN CLUB
Recreation • Education • Conservation
outdoors.org

AMC IN THE DELAWARE VALLEY

AMC's Delaware Valley Chapter offers a wide variety of hiking, backpacking, climbing, paddling, bicycling, snowshoeing, and skiing trips each year, as well as social, family, and young member programs and instructional workshops. The chapter also maintains a 15-mile section of the Appalachian Trail between Wind Gap and Little Gap, as well as trails at Valley Forge National Historical Park. To view a list of AMC activities in Pennsylvania, Central and South New Jersey, Northern Delaware, and other parts of the Northeast, visit activities. outdoors.org.

AMC also runs the Mohican Outdoor Center in Blairstown, New Jersey, less than three hours from Philadelphia. Mohican Outdoor Center offers city dwellers a convenient base from which to explore the wilderness of the Delaware Water Gap. Go to outdoors.org/lodging/mohican for more information.

AMC BOOK UPDATES

AMC Books strives to keep our guidebooks as up-to-date as possible to help you plan safe and enjoyable adventures. If after publishing a book we learn that trails have been relocated or route or contact information has changed, we will post the updated information online. Before you hit the trail, check for updates at outdoors.org/bookupdates.

While enjoying a trip from this book, if you notice discrepancies with the trip description or map, or if you find any other errors, please let us know by submitting them to amcbookupdates@outdoors.org or in writing to Books Editor, c/o AMC, 5 Joy Street, Boston, MA 02108. We will verify all submissions and post key updates each month. AMC Books is dedicated to being a recognized leader in outdoor publishing. Thank you for your participation.

NEW!

kids.outdoors.org

Introducing Kids Outdoors Online Communities
for Boston, New York City, and Philadelphia.

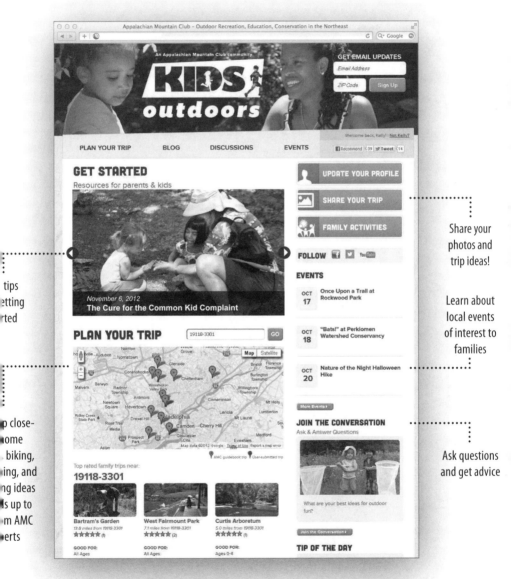

Share your
photos and
trip ideas!

Learn about
local events
of interest to
families

Ask questions
and get advice

tips
etting
rted

p close-
ome
biking,
ing, and
ng ideas
s up to
m AMC
erts

Join for local trip suggestions, maps, and tips for
getting the children in your life outdoors.

Appalachian Mountain Club

AMC's Best Day Hikes Near Philadelphia
Susan Charkes

Ideal for families, tourists, and local residents, this easy-to-use guide will help you embark on 50 of the best hikes in eastern Pennsylvania, New Jersey, and Delaware year round, from lesser-known excursions to area favorites, including several hikes on the Appalachian Trail.

$18.95 • 978-1-934028-33-9

Quiet Water New Jersey and Eastern Pennsylvania
Kathy Kenley

Explore the scenic flatwater lakes, ponds, and rivers of New Jersey and eastern Pennsylvania with this guide for families, anglers, and canoeists and kayakers of all abilities. This guide offers 80 trips, covering the best calm water paddling in the region.

$19.95 • 978-1-934028-34-6

Outdoors with Kids New York City
Cheryl and William de Jong-Lambert

Getting the whole family outside and active close to home is easy. This user-friendly guide features 100 outdoor experiences in and around New York City, where families can hike, bike, paddle, play, swim, or simply run around.

$18.95 • 978-1-934028-33-9

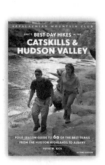

AMC's Best Day Hikes in the Catskills & Hudson Valley
Peter W. Kick

With more than 600 miles of trails within just a few hours of New York City, the Catskills and Hudson Valley region is a hiker's paradise. This guide leads beginner and experienced hikers alike along 60 of the area's most spectacular trails, from shorter nature walks to longer day hikes.

$18.95 • 978-1-934028-45-2